Walking Away

HUGH COLLINS was born and brought up in Glasgow and in 1977, after a lifetime of crime, was sentenced to life for murder. He was released in 1992 after serving sixteen years of the sentence. The first part of his life, covering the period up to his release from jail, was recounted in *Autobiography of a Murderer*. He is now married and lives and works in Edinburgh as a sculptor and writer.

Also by Hugh Collins

Autobiography of a Murderer

Walking Away

Hugh Collins

First published in Great Britain in 2000 by
Rebel Inc, an imprint of
Canongate Books Ltd, 14 High Street,
Edinburgh EH1 1TE

10 9 8 7 6 5 4 3 2 1

Rebel Inc series editor: Kevin Williamson
www.rebelinc.net

British Library Cataloguing-in-Publication Data
A catalogue record for this book is available on
request from the British Library

ISBN 1 84195 019 X

Typeset by Palimpsest Book Production Limited,
Polmont, Stirlingshire
Printed and bound by CPD, Wales

Walking Away I dedicate to my Father and my Mother, Wullie Collins and Betty Norrie.

> 'What matters most is
> how well you walk
> through the fire.'
>
> *Charles Bukowski*

ACKNOWLEDGEMENTS

I wouldn't be here without the good will of other people, and I sincerely hope this is made clear in the following pages. However, there are those I would like to thank for their support and encouragement in writing this book.

Caroline's parents. Douglas McNairn. Albert Faulds. Jackie, Charlie, Shug and Alex Collins. Doctor Jane Goldman and Gus McLean. Andrew Brown. Kevin Williamson and Angeline Ferguson. Irvine Welsh. James Kelman. Giles Gordon. Jamie Byng. Chris McLaren. Mike Marshall. Alan Muir. Tam Dean Burn. Linda McNee. Lorraine Dick Arnott. Anne Goring. Jock Scott. Davie Henderson and Nectarine Nine. Louise and Graham.

Chapter One

I'VE BEEN WAITING for this moment to happen for so long, I can't remember why it was so important in the first place. Sixteen years is just too long to hang onto an idea, any idea – particularly the idea of being freed from jail. The act of passing through a gate isn't what I have imagined freedom to be like.

I'm expected to hug trees, look at the sky in awe – truth is I've missed breakfast. I've had one slice of bread since yesterday morning: twenty six hours and thirty minutes without food is a long time to be hungry. I've tried to eat but nothing will stay down long enough to sustain me. Now the hunger that woke me up every morning during those sixteen years has been prolonged, and is threatening these next few moments with physical collapse. My forehead is damp with cold sticky sweat seeping from my scalp. Am I going to faint? Fuck. Please no. Please, no liberation dramatics in front of all these people.

– '*How do you feel?*' a voice asks.

There is a huge lens balanced on a tripod with metal legs propped up at the left of the access road. The eye is coldly watching my first few steps forward. Someone thrusts a microphone in my face, asking that same question.

– '*How do you feel?*'

World in Action are filming my being released but do my feelings have any relevance to such questions? Everything I have ever known in my life has been taken away from me.

Everything I have used to protect myself in a violent world has become defunct, I have been disarmed, dumped in this new space called outside, a place I know so little about, and expected to survive there.

– '*How do you feel?*'

Betty, my mother, is pulling my head down onto her shoulder, short stiff spiky silvery hair pricking the skin, lacquer stinging my eyes, perfume teasing my barren senses.

– 'Oh son. Oh son,' she whispers.

Caroline, my girlfriend, is behind her, quietly waiting for her turn to pull my head. Her brown eyes are smiling. I can smell the warmth flowing from her body.

– 'How dae ye feel?' someone else asks.

That fucking question again. How about – 'I'm missing my pals back in the jail.' The balding head now asking the question is my mother's common law husband, Jim Smith. He's smiling. He'd been smiling that first time too, the day she'd brought him to see me in the Special Unit. She'd been forced to bring me out into the open when they'd moved in together. Alec, my half brother's presence was one thing, but me? My situation posed problems in itself. Dolling herself up, disappearing every other night. What is Jim to think? Then there were those other little matters to consider, all those by the ways – 'Oh by the way, he's a murderer.'

How do you introduce your boyfriend to your oldest boy – the one who is a murderer?

My father had no difficulty at all with introductions – 'Tell them aboot stabbin screws son. That's ma boy ye know!'

Jim Smith had smiled that day – and is still smiling, fourteen years later.

Those first words – 'YER MUTHER'S A WUNDERFUL WUMIN!'

He'd barked them at me.

He's taken to calling me son in more recent times. Why

I'm not yet sure – there's little difference between us in age. My metamorphosis didn't involve a new daddy.

I pull back from my mother's half nelson – 'Ma Da noa here?' I ask.

Whooops! Where did that come from? She'll be furious that I have asked that. Fuck she heard it. Now I'll have to pretend I don't care, put the big act on for her that I had just wanted to make sure that he wasn't here – 'Naw? Good! Fuck him Ma!'

Was she there when he'd been released from his ten year sentence? They'd still have been husband and wife. She'd told me that she'd divorced him just recently. Why did she wait so long? She'd lie if asked. Their versions of events never add up. They too have that problem with the brain's gravity force – telling stories so often to themselves they become entangled, lodged in belief.

They too would begin by remembering and end in imagination, although it's likely his would have descended into sentiment brought about by jail, by isolation. Hope, I feel, would definitely have influenced his endings, degrading them with those fantasies of having a future with his boy, his wife, a life together, but then those disappointments, distorting, twisting them into warped conclusions – his wife with another man, a man fucking the woman he loved.

Me? I abandoned those thoughts the moment I was sentenced to life. I became, lived and breathed jail. I discarded the jail blues to become even more violent, even more immune to punishment, even more dangerous within prison. Change was beyond my comprehension. Change? What was that? I'd been a full blooded gang member from the sixties – The Shamrock.

A lifer? So what? Fuck you, was my attitude.

– 'Och, he'll be too busy wi the pals' she states.

I'm being led to a waiting car. The camera lens follows us down the access road onto the main road: the traffic flashes past in an endless screaming blur. I had planned to walk down that road in my imagination: have appropriate music in the background, a last look back at the prison, the hard clenched jawbone – 'You haven't broken me!' I know that this only happens in films but it kept me going for a while in there, thinking about this very day, the day of liberation, and that tree hugging.

A lifer walked down that same road last week and died instantly: hit twenty feet in the air by a bus, straight into the path of a Transit van coming in the opposite direction. A lifer beside him fainted at the sight of brains hanging from a garden fence, just by the bus stop. He later had to have stitches in a deep gash in his head having hit the edge of the pavement during his faint. My imagination hadn't taken traffic into account . . . I let myself be guided into the car . . .

WWWWWOOOOOOOOOOFFFFFFFFF!!!

My eyeballs bulge from their sockets as flesh on my face is dragged to the back of the skull: bared teeth and gums are frozen in a grimace by this sudden exposure to killer speed; there's leather under my fingernails.

– 'How dae ye feel son?' he's asking.

Jim and Betty keep talking at the same time, simultaneously cutting in on each other without listening – 'How dae ye . . .' Whoomph! 'Slow doon a bi . . .' Whoomph! 'Did ye tha . . .' Whoomph! 'Fuckin bam . . .' Whoomph! 'Wid ye slow doo . . .' Whoomph! The 369 Gallery looms up just ahead – thank fuck. My head snaps forward, hitting the front passenger seat as the car screeches to a halt outside the gallery. The dull thud catches my mother's attention – 'See you! Wit did a fuckin tell ye . . .'

Caroline's looking at me, smiling – 'You all right Hugh?'

My head is familiar with unexpected thuds but nods an assurance just the same – 'Am bran new Caroline.'

Andrew Brown, friend and director, explodes onto the street to greet us in a pink suit.

Jim's jaw drops – 'Jesus fuck [illegible].'

Andrew grabs me – 'Hugh! So good to see you! This is absolutely wonderful!'

He hugs my mother too – 'Betty! How are you?'

– 'Hi Andrew! Oh noa bad an yersel?' she smiles.

– 'Oh well, could be better. Isn't this wonderful!'

Jim has that smile on – 'Aye Andrew. Jim, pleased tae meet ye.'

Andrew has arranged breakfast – 'Yes, it's just at the top of Blair Street.'

The Bank Hotel has a rich interior, with this warm feeling of being centuries old, with row upon row of dusty half filled bottles behind the huge polished mahogany bar. It's a place where stories have been told over neat whiskies – tales passed down through time, told by those living . . . and those still haunting the old town of Edinburgh.

– 'How are you feeling Hugh?'

David and Kay Carmichael loom into view. Kay's tilted head looks like a dead prune with hair: her face, wizened and wrinkled with the wisdom of age, reminds me of an old oriental philosopher, but she is a retired social worker, cum author, cum feminist, cum politician, cum visitor, a Special Unit *friend.*

Kay's looking at me oddly, inquisitively, probingly – 'Hugh. How many prisons have you been in? Now, it's very important you remember.' I hated her patronising tones then and still do today, fourteen years later. My first hours of freedom, but she wants to know how many prisons I've been in. Will remembering prove a point? I'm not a fucking experiment. I pretend to think, but that beautiful brown mahogany bar seems more interesting, almost warm compared to that dirty yellow coloured cell I left back there, in that previous life called prison.

She's waiting for a response. I mean, do they ask monkeys how many times they've been caged, wired up, tortured? My vacant staring continues silently, aggravating, ignoring the question. The times I've been out of prison. Wouldn't that seem a more logical question? Fewer locations, less time to consider. That mahogany bar, it has such an inviting reddish colourful surface. Kay! You still here? What was that again? –'Now, it's very important you remember. You may be institutionalised' she persists. Now there's a revelation. After twenty six years of jails – you *may* be institutionalised. Now why haven't I thought of that? Kay, please go away, leave me alone. Haven't I been punished enough? Your good intentions are scarring my fucking brain forever, with more of your sociology. She had imposed friendship upon me, actually imposed her presence upon me in the unit. As a No Hoper I needed friends, friends who were not criminals, to show that I was changing, that I could indeed be rehabilitated, that it was possible for violent men to channel that excessive energy.

Those were the days of experimentation, of art-therapy, and oddly enough, a public who cared about rehabilitation as well as victims' restitution. These days though, they pander to the frustrations of the mob. Rehabilitation involves accountability and hard work. The authorities, however, are concerned solely with 'good behaviour' in prison, bribing the prison population, keeping the lid on the drug abuse, turning a blind eye – but someone has to take the flak for that daily tabloid outrage – who else?

Margaret Thatcher's tough on crime policy? Don't make me laugh. The truth of that great myth is that the Conservatives negotiated with violent prisoners. Kill each other but don't damage the structure, don't touch prison warders. When you cross that line they negotiate, lure you into control with better conditions, televisions, toys, even sex if you cross far enough into enemy territory with knives. They know that language so well. I wouldn't be here today otherwise. Yes, I threatened my way out of jail. That is the truth. Would you fuck with a 'sociopath' who had stabbed three warders, three punters from the trees looking for a uniform to wear? Any Labour government would have chained me in manacles to a wall. No, Mrs Thatcher's Secretary of State kindly negotiated a peace deal. I signed the paper, stating that I would not be violent in any circumstance in expressing my viewpoint, instead they would provide a mediator, one who would assist in my re-settlement with my fellow human beings, a welfare worker, a man who would ask – 'Killed anyone? No? Great! See you next month!' My man, he had a slight nervous stammer, an accent born and bred in the Borders. Rarely did I understand what he was saying. The nodding usually meant no one had been found dead in violent circumstances. Those endless tea and biscuits helped enhance what was to become a relationship, a partnership – a licence, for the rest of my life. Institutionalised? I don't know what fucking day it is. I don't know where I am. There lies ahead a great deal of nodding, tea and biscuits. Maybe, his head will fall off first, I'll be recalled to complete the life sentence for nodding with violent intent. Now who nodded first? – 'Wis self defence yer honour. He nodded first, honest!' This poor, nervous man has been appointed as my supervisor, a support act, my new advisor – *after* sixteen years of insanity, of violence, of hatred, of prison? I'd better go easy with the tantrums, get loads of biscuits, and hope for the best. I feel fond of him because he's a genuinely nice man, but I don't know what's inside me, have no idea of what's going to happen out here – that huge chip on my shoulder is burning.

I'm pure jail. I'm a potential time bomb, but I'm going to try. I have no desire to fail. No lifer has that desire, but a few sometimes fail. One fuck up though, and it's over, and it's forevermore. The backlash hits lifers still in waiting, processing involving years, regardless of families' hopes – it's political.

WWWHHHHOOOOOOFFFFFFF! – 'Awright big bruvva?'

Alec, my six foot half brother, crushes my ribs in an embrace. His fourteen stone grip lets go and I crash to the floor – 'How ye daen ya'n auld cunt ye?'

Poor Alec. Betty tried so hard to make sure he didn't turn out like me: driving him into an educational grinder with school, homework, school, more homework and then the great rubber stamp of intellectual approval – university.

Alec never played with other kids, never broke into shops, never even shagged a bird until he was an adult. No, he read books, read them day and night, read them for his mother, for her friends, for the Kay Carmichaels. Now, he can't express his emotions without aggression, always correcting people in that stupid smug way that makes you want to punch him – 'Humphh! Any daft bastard knows that!'

He's been 'performing' for people all his life: performing, to prove something to other people, that he is highly intelligent, that there's genius but it has all been designed to validate something else, something about *her* – 'O Alec lu-uuvs books! Alec's like his granda! Alec's granda luved tae read! Am the same funny enough' she would say. My mother rammed this down my throat for so long I wanted to kill him.

Alec's father had been thrown out before they'd got round to marriage, but this didn't deter the boy from trying to find his father twenty three years later.

I couldn't believe it when he told me – 'Wi-it? Are ye aff yer fuckin heid? Alec don't fuck yerself up wi aw their problems.' The father had laughed when his son asked to meet all his new half brothers and sisters. I knew he would but eh – nice touch Betty. She did succeed though. I mean, he's not like his brother, disturbed, institutionalised, fucked up, an arsehole – a murderer.

Betty's eyes are boring into the side of my head. I can feel her staring, wondering no doubt about how I feel. Does she see my old man? Where *was* she that day when he got out? I remember all the taxis stopping at the front close of my granny's house in Tharsis Street. My Da's handsome face stepping out from all those other men in their immaculately cut black coats, and scarred faces. He'd finished the ten years that day. Where was she then, on his liberation day? Why wasn't she there for him? He'd just finished a ten year sentence in jail. Did they still love each other? Did he hate her? I was too young to understand. I was a mere child, seven years old. I didn't know them really, but I looked for my mammy that day, I looked for them both, together, but that took a lifetime of violence, and a murder before it happened.

Someone suggested I write a book. A book about what exactly? Murder? Or prison? Maybe I should write a book. I mean, I've killed but don't know why. I know how it all happened, the physical facts from A to Z – but I don't know why I killed. Why not just say – he's dead, so what? Why bother finding out why? Will reason make sense of it? 'I felt like it' – Isn't this as good a reason as any other for killing?

Politicians too have their reasons – bombing countries, shooting terrorist suspects on sight, the slow motion murder of economic sanctions. Do reasons make it all all right? War, conflict, troubles, collateral damage. No matter how rational the arguments on national interests may seem, how sanitised the images on television may appear, the fact is that they are no different from any other act of murder.

An eye for an eye is merely revenge, an act of violence. Violence *is* action, it can't be categorised as acceptable or unacceptable, it is one singular motion.

When does killing become criminal? Is it clothing? Does it

become a murder only if and when someone wears a black coat? Do uniforms make it different? Human beings are complex and dangerous – all of them, not just certain types.

William Mooney, the man I killed. His brother too was murdered, killed by one of my relatives in a separate incident, and yet there are similarities: we all – the victims too – had a weapon. Is there a link? Has lightning struck twice? Is there a war going on in the streets with young men, and young women, called gang members? Or is this a different type of violence? They too can have reasons, economic or whatever.

Where does the reason become criminal?

Politicians. How do they face people? They kill thousands of people in one go. Drop a bomb, fire a missile. I think the term they use to describe mass murder is 'Acting with vigour'. In other words 'Fuck with us – We'll bomb you!'

Would High Court judges accept this as a defence? – 'We wur jist actin vigorously yer honour.' Somehow, I don't think so.

Acting vigorously? C'mon now, blow a few thousand away. Now that's what you call vigorous. I mean, who makes these decisions? The whole country, or just one man? A book? What would I write? Prison was good for me? These type of books have an element of sentimentality throughout them, the writer somehow becomes the victim, who needless to say is either rehabilitated, has become a born again Christian . . . or is innocent. The truth is that most prisoners are off their heads on release. They depart the premises, but few leave it. Below the relief and elation of being home lie hidden layers of rage, disappointments, frustrations, and real paranoia. I mean, they couldn't possibly feel anything else could they? Ever lived in prison? Believe me, it is an asylum. But no, these writers. Writers? Well, they are searching for reasons. They're possibly trying to hide from something they can't face, something they have done in a moment, a flash of temper, a violent deed.

Who knows. I'm no expert. I'm looking, feeling these first few hours, but a book? It's pure indulgence, it has to be.

Betty's boring gaze is bringing me out in patchy red blotches all over my face: I can't see them in the mirror behind the bar but can feel them burning. What the fuck's she staring at? – 'Ye awright en Ma?' I ask.

Andrew breaks the hold – 'Caroline. Why don't you two go off together, have a walk in the gardens? It's such a lovely day!'

Caroline and I don't need much persuasion – 'Yes, we could go for a walk somewhere nice, and maybe have a picnic. Hugh?' I have to get away from all these eyes. They keep staring at me, waiting for something, a statement maybe, a speech about how it is so wonderful to be out – now, almost five hours – 'Aye Caroline. That wid be great.' Oops. Betty's look doesn't pass unnoticed: the raised eyebrow. I've seen it before, a thousand times: the look that says 'Eh, a wee minute, wit aboot us . . . yer family?'

– 'Issat awright Ma?' I ask.

Caroline finds our coats, heading for the door – 'We'll noa be long' I say.

JESUSSSSSSSSFUCKINNNNNNKRRRRRRRRIST!

– 'Honest Caroline! She drives me crazy wi aw that fuckin kerry oan!'

Caroline pulls me up the grass verge to the top of a hill – 'You're her son Hugh. She's like any mother, just wants to be with you on your first day home. Look, do you know where we are?' she asks.

I'm puffed out from the steep climb. I'm fairly fit but have been walking on solid flat surfaces these past years: there are no hills in any institutions, there's only cell space and narrow corridors – 'Naw Caroline, where ur wi?'

To the east lies the city centre but over to the west – 'Fuck! S'that the jail? There's Saughton doon there! Caroline! Honest!

That's the hall a wis in! See it? An there at that wee windae . . . that was ma cell. A used to look up here every night, honest!'

We lie there together all afternoon, just holding hands, and staring up at the beautiful blue skies. I've longed for a moment like this – 'Thanks Caroline. They bastards doon there, if they only knew a wis up here watchin thum.'

Caroline is anxious to get back on time. The Liberation Party. I had almost forgotten all about it – 'They'll all be waiting Hugh' she says.

I don't give a fuck who is waiting. I'll never be on time for anything ever again: I've had sixteen years of waiting, waiting in corridors, in halls, at doors, waiting for some guy with a key – time someone else waited.

– 'Ca, honestly. This is sumthin av always wanted tae dae. Sleepin under the stars, an seein the dawn. Ramantic eh? Right, okay, we'd better get movin, but, thanks fur daen this.'

Chapter Two

THE 369 GALLERY is a huge dark building, it resembles an institution of sorts with those barred windows, the steel framed door at the front, but I'm at liberty to come and go as I please in this place. Here I can indulge myself in that pleasure of not waiting, of not going in, not going out, or being jarred by slamming heavy steel doors. I count as we climb up the stairwell with its white emulsioned walls – a huge pastel adorns one of the walls. It's one of Caroline's. I remember seeing her work when I first began an outside pre-release programme at the gallery towards the end of the sentence around 1991. I remember that first day out from jail: one painting in particular had caught my eye – a man, a figure breaking out of black bars, he appeared to have a weapon in his hand. The figure looked battered, broken, but defiant.

Her painting is modern, figurative yet abstract, and has fascinated me ever since that day.

– 'Well Hugh, how are you feeling?' a voice calls out.

Ken Murray's looking up from the second landing. Ken had been the driving force of the Special Unit at Barlinnie. I haven't seen him in years – 'Ken?'

I'm immediately filled with panic. What will he think of me? There have been a few fuck ups since the Unit. Will he lecture me about past incidents? He is a decent man, politically minded, caring, but too serious. What am I doing? I'm free now . . . I don't have to account to anyone. I don't have to keep apologising to people all the time for my past, my failures.

– 'How ye doin Ken?'

My face and hands feel dirty: I've scrubbed four times today but still feel grimy sweat all over. My internal organs are seizing up, cold sweat's running down my back, skin stretches against twitching muscles in an attempt to smile.

Ken's pumping my arm up and down: squinting from the corner of his eye, it's like an insect's, an eye with no lashes – observing me from a distance, taking me in, watching my every move, searching for signs of a drug habit no doubt.

– 'Eh Ken, this is Caroline. Ehm, eh Ken . . . Caroline, this is Ken. Ken wis in charge in the unit. Eh, wit? Naw ehm, naw ey wis the ehm, spokesman fur the, ehm, widye call it, the ehm, the COMMUNITY. The Special Unit . . . durin the seventies, eh Ken?'

– 'Hullo Caroline. Do you know who you're getting involved with?' he asks.

– 'Hi Ken. Yes, I do' she smiles, ignoring the dig.

I hear the hum of voices as we ascend the second floor. Who's all there? Sounds like a lot of people. The voices become more distinct as we get nearer – female, and male voices, glasses clinking, laughter, snatches of dialogue – 'Yes, how do you . . . This is . . . Have you met?'

I hear someone shushing everyone as we enter into the exhibition space – 'Here he . . . They're comi . . .'

– 'SSSSHHHHHH! THEYREHEEEEEEEEEAAAAAAAA-AAAAAARRRRRRRRRRRRRR!'

The din is deafening. People cheering and shouting. Caroline's clutching my hand as we face the packed room of people: packed full of glassy shining eyes, smiling toothy mouths, smears of red lipstick. I can taste perfume in my own nicotined mouth, smell people's bodies in my nostrils, feel their fabrics brushing past me. My arm is pumped like a one armed bandit – 'Hullo. How are you? Hullo. How are you? Hullo. How are you?'

Where's my Ma? Alec's head towers above everyone. Then I do see her, sitting in a chair with hands clasped on her lap and her head bowed. Jim's lounging against the wall: he's smiling, with a glass in his hand. Kay and Ken are standing directly behind my Ma – all staring at me. Ken's eyes are narrowed. Kay's fixed grin could mean any number of things. Alec's smirk though, that conveys my position – she's not pleased.

– 'Where the fuck huv you been? A don't give a fuck wit ye wur daen. Jimmy's been and left' she snaps – 'The poor guy coodny wait any longer. See you . . . ye make me fuckin sick so ye dae . . . yer jist like yer fuckin faither!'

Jimmy Boyle has been and gone. The very name cut into me like a knife: the hair on my neck is standing in a hackle, rage surges through to my face in a flush of blood. I can barely breathe – Jimmy fucking Boyle.

I try to explain – 'Wi wur up at th . . .'

– 'A don't give a fuck!' she spits back.

Jim defuses the situation: that bland smile – 'Where huv ye been son? Want a canna beer? How dae ye feel by the way?' he grins.

Andrew's been giving a speech on behalf of the gallery, but I haven't caught anything he's said. He's pulling me onto the floor, people are shouting – 'A speech! Spe-eech! Spe-eech! C'mon then! C'mon Hugh! C'MONNNNNNNNNNNN!'

Fucksake man. Where's the door? I'll have to get out of here. Where the fuck is that fucking door? Jesus Christ – 'Eh. Ad jist like tae, ehm say thanks. Thanks fur cumin the night. Ad like tae thank aw the people that supported me, eh it wisnae easy but eh maistly ma Maw. Ad like tae eh, thank ma Maw. A widny be here withoot aw the support she gave me, an ma family tae, eh, eh well anyway ehm . . . thanks!'

Please, please, where's the fucking DOOR? Any FUCKING door? I slam straight into a guy in my desperation to escape – 'Shug. How ye daen pal?' he asks.

– 'James Rea! Fuck me! When did ye get oot? You been here aw the time?'

James is dying of cancer with weeks to live. The last time I saw him we were in a cell, sitting at the door; some guy bursts in and stabs him five times, and here he is, standing there, smiling – 'How ye daen son?' he repeats – 'Heavy goin eh?'

We'd chased the dragon a few times, and done a few joints together, in Shotts Prison. He'd come from hospital, just to see me getting out – 'A thought ye might need a wee sumthin Shugs. A know wit this is like, there ye go man.'

I see the small package hidden amongst the bundle of bank notes being pushed into my hand – 'Thanks James. Yer a diamond. Ma fuckin heid's dun in wi aw this kerry oan. C'mon, wull dae a quick line . . .'

I shudder as the powder glides down my nasal passage and spreads throughout every tingling fibre of my body, the first line in twenty four hours – 'AWW! FUCK! THANKS! C'mon meet Caroline!' The powder brings immediate relief, confidence, a protective shield from the hands pumping hullos, the party crowd of strangers, but, there's a few familiar faces, lined faces who have been *there*, faces saying very little to people, but there's one who is saying a great deal, a voice from the past, and it's Glaswegian. Caroline's talking to him, a guy obviously showing everyone his biceps. Those broad back muscles and shoulders seem vaguely familiar, the voice too – 'Aye! The London Bridge! Check they guns hen! Here feel that! IRON! Ye could dae a washin oan eez stomach muscles. Look! A washin board hen! The Fridge at yer service! The Govan Bridge!' he's roaring.

Big Midge! I can't believe this. Midge too had been in jail with me, served a lifer. He had taken the blame on a murder charge to protect a close pal. I dig him in the ribs – 'How'ye doin ya big bampot ye?'

The Govan Bridge lifts me in a bear hug, laughing at the

top of his voice – 'HAUWW!! The auld yin! HAW! HAW! HAW! How ye daen Shug? HAW! Caught nippin yer burd there eh? HAW! HAW! Only kiddin auld yin! Check they biceps auld yin! Look! Could fry yer breakfast oan them eh! Here, didye think a wis gonny miss aw these wumin?' he's laughing – 'The London Bridge missus! At yer service!'

Kay's pulling at my sleeve, peering and whispering into my eyes – 'Ken's leaving now Hugh. I think you should say goodbye. He's not happy with the gangster types.' Gangster types? What's she talking about? Who does she mean? Midge? or James? Fuck her. I don't have to take this any more – 'Listen Kay. A don't know any gangster types. A think the gangster's been an gone twenty minutes ago . . . ask Betty.'

Caroline pulls me away – 'Hugh, come and meet my friends, Andy and Lorraine' she smiles – 'This is Hugh.'

I throw my hand forward – 'Eh? Witsat? Sorry Caroline. Who? How dae ye do Andy? Hi Lorraine, pleased tae meet ye hen' I stammer – 'Pleased tae meet ye.'

Andrew's calling – 'Hugh, phone for you!' He whispers – 'I think it's someone in jail.'

– 'Hullo?' I ask.

– 'How ye doin daftie?' a voice asks.

– 'Barry! Fucksake man! Here listen! Big Midge an James Rea ur here!'

Barry's finishing a life sentence for murder, a gang fight in Glasgow. A breach of the peace that just got out of hand. We were next door for about eight years in Saughton Prison. I'd met him on the stairs coming back from work one day. He'd been stabbed in the stomach by a short termer, a young guy, determined to make a 'reputation' for himself. I'd helped him across to the surgery with a screw – while the guy who had stabbed him had conveniently thrown the blade under my bed. I had tried to talk him out of taking revenge. He had a son, a wife, a family – 'Barry, blank it. The screws ur jist waitin fur it tae happen. Don't be kidded by them turnin a blind eye. Ye'll add oan years tae yer sentence. They'll dae it behind the scenes. The cons? Fuck them. Aw they're interestit in is sum entertainment, a battle tae break the boredom. Ye'v a wee boay oot there, a good faimily. Get yersel ootey this fuckin pitch. Stabbin um? Wit's that gonny prove? He'll walk right intae it anyway.'

Barry listened to the advice, but having been a boxer, he knocked fuck out of the guy a few weeks later. Well, at least he didn't kill him. Now, there's progress for you. No but seriously, here was a young guy who had made one mistake, more of an accident than an intent to kill. Now his back had been put to the wall by some crazy, and in an environment like jail, you can't walk away.

We had become friends as a result of the incident. It was good to hear him again, and feel the warmth of that jail familiarity, something I desperately needed tonight with all these strange faces saying – 'Hullo. How are you?'

I'm conscious of his position; telephone cards in a prison are a lifeline to families and are never used for idle chit chat – 'Barry, this is murder, tryin tae talk. Don't waste yer units. Phone me back the morra night, right! Wit's happenin anyway? When dae ye get oot?'

Barry laughs – 'Am in TFF, Shug. Trainin fur Freedom. S'fuckin brutal so it is. They daft screws won't get aff people's backs. Av got aboot five month tae go, an that's it, finito! Thank fuck! A hate this fuckin pitch' he hisses – 'How'r'ye handlin bein oot? Thuv warned me tae stay away fae you but al be up tae see ye, wull jist huv tae be a bit mer careful. A get a coupla hours oot every night. Al come doon tae that gallery. Any burds er? Anyway, how ye handlin it ya'n auld bam ye?'

The lies just pour out as usual – 'Brilliant Barry! Wit? Naw, it's an art gallery. Aye, a stay in a studio wi Caroline. Wit?

Aye, she's ma burd! Noa slow eh? Na, she's bran new big yin, a really good burd. Barry, haud oan a wee minute . . .'

I turn around to find my family leaving, hurrying through the door to the exit – 'Barry! Listen! Kin ye phone back? Aye, be here the whole day! Right see ye later big yin.'

I run down the three flights of stairs, into the street – they're gone. I see the car's red tail light flickering a left turn up into Blair Street – 'FUCK!'

I can't face going back upstairs. People will have seen them leaving – I just can't face the questions. I'll hide in the toilet to pull myself together first. I prefer the toilet, the soft lights, and the quietness alone. A toilet, preferable to the people grating against my shattered nerves.

The powder flooding through to those ragged nerve ends, soldering together my worn out nervous system, fusing those billion neurons into that welcoming smile they want to see. It's warm, soft, cushioning me from the hullos, and arm-pumping drunks.

The toilet mirror has the reflection of my whole body. I stand staring, an inch from the surface: my pinned pupils stare back until everything around them disappears. I hear music now from upstairs – thank God. They'll be dancing, forgotten why they're at the party in the first place, forgotten about my liberation day.

I keep staring, swaying slightly but staring, observing the image staring back.

Am I real? Where am I? This mirror could be anywhere, wish it was jail.

My family. Why did they have to leave like that?

Caroline, Andrew and their friends have remained behind but most have left. Marvin Gaye's playing full blast – 'Oh I heard it through the grapevine.' A guy wants to dance with me . . . so what. Why did they leave like that? Oh Oh . . . my man's taken a hard on, he's trying to shove his tongue down my throat – 'Here you! Fuckin poofs man! Where's Caroline, fucksake man?'

I find her in our studio, reading poetry with Lorraine – 'Hi Hugh. S'your Mum all right?' she asks.

I look down from the window as people leave – 'Aye, they hud tae leave . . .'

Lorraine's met them she says – 'She seems nice. Is Jim your father? What? Oh I see.

Oh sorry, I thought he . . .'

Why did they leave? – 'Naw it's okay Lorraine. He's bran new, he looks efter ur . . .' I try to explain – 'But thur noa merried, es noa ma Da.'

Why the big dramatic exit? Not even a goodbye?

Lorraine's inviting us for lunch tomorrow – 'Oh you'll be fine. Andy's a laugh, he liked you.'

She's leaving – 'So we'll see you tomorrow then. Andy's bought fish. Yes, about one o clock? Okay then . . . Night Hugh'

I prop myself up on the mattress. I lie back with my eyes closed but can hear them at the outside door. I like being behind my eyes, and listening to things. I did that a lot in jail – 'Oh I heard it through the grapevi . . .'

The party's beginning to die down; I hear people leaving, some are crashing out – or shagging somewhere – others disappearing, off to another party.

That new past is about to enter into almost day two of freedom.

I sit on the edge of the bed, rocking gently back and forth, head between my knees, my arms clasped around them to stop me rolling over – 'Yesss a heard it through the grapevi . . . iii . . . nnnnnne.'

Powder makes this so painless, it's absolute nothingness, numbed – 'Wers Caroline?' I wonder.

Caroline McNairn. Who is she, really? A Borders lassie,

originally from Selkirk. I like being with her, talking to her. She listens, and talks with me, not *at* me. The hilltop, it was amazing but how did she know? She'd laughed at all my efforts to climb up the fucking thing – laughed at all that stuff about flat surfaces in the jail. She's definitely not scared of me. I'd know immediately if she had any apprehensions about me. She likes me – understands me. I hope I don't have to prove anything to her? I'm tired of proving things to people . . . tired of people.

Caroline – 'YER A WUNDERFUL WUMIN!'

Betty and Alec – Why? Why did they have to leave like that? Why do they make me feel like this all the time? I'm trying my best with all this. What have I done to them? I mean who did the fucking time? Where was she when it was all happening, on the streets? Where was she when I was lying in the fucking gutter? When I lay soaked in my own fucking blood? When I didn't have a home? When I was a child? Tell me Ma. Where were you?

I'll tell you. You were with your bigshot boyfriends, my new uncles, all your hardcase boyfriends. The Wullie Collinses and all the other hard cases.

Jimmy Owens . . . was he a gangster? He was the first one I can remember. That night he gave me the toy yacht – they always gave me toys. That's right. I'd been playing in a basin of water. I could see them on the couch, he was on top of her. Those fucking horrible noises. I thought he was hurting her – my Mammy.

– 'Go away. Go n play wi yer boat' he kept saying.

Caroline's arm's around me. 'Hugh, why are you crying? Oh c'mon now, that's it, just lie back, that's it, you're safe now.'

I feel tired but I have to talk, I have to try, try to tell her, tell her everything about the past, tell her the truth about it all, whatever that is – 'Caroline, a honestly don't know wit's happened tae me. Av killed a guy, an a don't know why. Av dun a lotta really vicious things in ma life. A jist don't know why. Why a became like that. Betty luvs it. She luved cumin up tae the unit, the media attention, meetin aw they celebrities. Dun up like a fuckin prostitute. Witsat?' I ask.

Caroline asks if she visited me in other prisons – 'R'ye jokin? Caroline, honestly, she wisnae even at ma trial when a got the lifer. Efter ad stabbed the screws up in Perth. That's when she made ur furst appearance, the big drama! She's been tellin people that am dangerous ever since – that am disturbed.' I explain – 'Nae fuckin wunder eh? Caroline, am far fae stupit. A know a huvny been too clever, but hur tellin people am disturbed? People that a hud introduced hur tae, people that ad built up relationships wi, people a had trusted durin that period in the Special Unit? Tellin them that am aff ma fuckin heid? Disturbed?'

I shake my head – 'Aye, eh. Thur's somethin else, but a canny talk aboot it right noo. Ye probably won't believe me anyway, you're a wumin, you'll jist think am paranoid, maybe a am paranoid, but it's about hur – hur an Jimmy Boyle.'

We sit up all night talking about my past – 'A want ye tae know every'hing cos am noa a fuckin murderer, noa a real murderer, hidin up closes waitin fur a victum, a wumin ura wean. A know that av killed a guy but . . . it's hard tae explain. Jimmy Boyle an aw that mob in the unit blamed deprivation but there wur loadsa people that didnae become a criminal. A mean ye cannae jist say – "Oh, a had a hole in ma troosers, an ended up in the Special Unit!" Dae ye see wit a mean? Wit? Huv a changed? Ca, a don't know wit change means. A new identity isnae change, real change. Am the same person but a suppose yer changin every moment ey yer life.'

Caroline hides her horror as I reveal more and more about my past. She'd thought I'd just been in a fight, which had unfortunately led to someone's death. She is appalled by the violence, but listens, doesn't pass judgement. I vomit it all up, day after day, to her, and to anyone else willing to listen. I've no other conversation, but violence, it is everything I have known – 'Caroline, listen, a didny plan aw this, it jist happened.'

She's never met anyone like me before. I've never met anyone like her either. She is middle-class, an artist, and art historian. I'm a tamed thug, but I have decided, I want to marry her already.

Caroline had walked out of her previous marriage, but I don't think she was prepared for *me* – 'Aye! Wu'll jist get merried! Andrew kin be the best man! An Shirley kin be the bridesmaid! Here, al need tae get a new suit!'

Just like that, and never considering for a second her feelings about me, or marrying a murderer.

In jail, everything is immediate. Things are never thought through, it's just wham, get it going, fuck the long term. I'd had enough red tape. My only concern was getting a new suit – and me. What *I* wanted. Me! Me! Me! I've done sixteen years. The world owes me something. What that is I don't know, but – 'Smith's've good linen suits eh?'

A new suit. Sixteen years of fashion deprivation explodes onto the street. I couldn't break away from the suits, the black cashmere coats. 'Gangster' stamped all over me. I wouldn't even go to the local shop without shaving, showering and getting all tarted up. I'd feel people staring at me, and there's me too, thinking I looked the business. I had begun to suspect something wasn't right, you know, that feeling you get. Then in a bar one night, a whisper behind narrowed eyes – 'Izat cunt a copper?'

A copper? I looked like a fucking copper? Caroline's relieved to see the suits go but those trips to the shops take a bit longer, the showers, shaving, dressing up . . .

I mean, to get two pies?

Caroline's asleep, tired of the horror stories. I'm at that part of night when everything is silent. Time stops around now. I gaze through the window, at the dawn light. You *feel* the planet turning to the sun. Earth looks peaceful from space, the fantastic blue hue, the huge three dimensional globe, travelling, spinning, orbiting the sun. Further out into nowhere, everything becomes absolutely still as you look back, look back at time. Space is so vast, we recede into nothingness, into a distant speck of light, a light already extinguished by distance, by time . . . the past.

Have I been and gone? Am I just dreaming?

To live and die here is such a privilege, but what happens now? Where do I go from here? The world has changed so much these past twenty years. How do I fit in? Can I fit in . . . ever?

Coming out of prison is more traumatic than going in.

I mean, going in is the easy part, you know what to expect, everything is familiar, but out here?

I've been listening to the same spiel for sixteen years – You must fit back into society. You must lead a normal life. You must associate only with normal people. You must be normal . . . you must . . . you must . . . you must.

What the fuck *is* normal?

What do I fit *into*?

No one ever tells you what it is like out here, no one ever tells you what to expect, no one ever prepares you for freedom.

You listen on visits, watch news on television, listen to people, but all the information going in and out of prison revolves around crime. The *knowledge* in jail is all crime. It can't possibly be anything else so what is the purpose?

I came out expecting a perfect world, expecting perfect people but nothing in prison prepared me for life out here.

The moment I had waited for has been and gone. The idea

I had clung to for so long has evaporated like the steam on the window pane. I stare out . . . blaring traffic horns, frustrated engines and shouting signal a new day.

Wish I'd hugged a tree . . .

Chapter Three

– 'HUGH? CAROLINE? ARE you awake?'

Andrew's knocking at the door – 'Mornin Andrew. She's still sleepin. Breakfast? Nae bother.' I say – 'Al jist be five minutes.'

He's been fucking all night – 'God, what a day! Have you recovered? *Who* was that woman, Kay or something?' he asks. 'What a cheek! She gave me a row about my speech being inappropriate. Was she a prison visitor? Oh, I see, the Special Unit? No wonder prisoners become violent! Did you see them, all standing in the corner? Why did they leave so suddenly? Your family didn't seem very happy.'

Andrew and Caroline, I discover, had paid for the breakfast and the party – 'Yes. That bloody woman. They paid for their own breakfast. Oh, I know that your mum can be difficult, don't apologise. I'm just going on. Oh, Caroline, good morning. Hugh and I just doing the post mortem. What about you, enjoy the party? I was just saying there to Hugh . . . that bloody woman Carmichael! What a bloody cheek!'

Caroline just smiles – 'Oh well. How are you feeling? Did you sleep?' she asks.

I'm unsure to be honest – 'Naw, a jist sat lookin oot the windae. Al probably sleep the night. A feel a bit weird tae be honest. A wid be headin fur work in the jail right noo. Time is it? Aye, ad be oan the stane doon in Muirhoos. Here, dae ye fancy daen that the day, staunin at the bus stop an lettin the half eight bus go past?' I ask.

I can't talk without relating to prison. My body is free but my head is still locked up in there. Freedom is a bit like running on the spot – 'Oh, we did that too, in the jail.'

Caroline agrees to stand at the bus stop – 'Yes, bring it all to an end in a sense.'

Andrew's enthusiastic too – 'You can do whatever you want now Hugh!'

He's right. The boundaries of prison don't exist out here, that having to wait to be let through a door, having to continually ask permission to do something, to go somewhere, even to piss, are no longer part of living. They don't apply out here – 'That's right! So a kin! A kin dae anythin oot here.'

But breaking the habits of that lifetime? – 'Andrew dae ye mind if a use the telephone? Al huv tae phone ma Maw, an that. Al pay fur the call, it's tae Glesga.'

They both look at each other – 'Hugh! Do whatever you want! This is your home now so do whatever you want. You don't have to ask all the time.'

I find the most mundane tasks so embarrassingly difficult – 'Caroline, how dae these things work, these eh, we used phone cards in the jail.' This becomes my repertoire in almost every situation – 'Eh, how dae ye dae this . . .'

At forty two, I find it a humiliating process having to relearn everything, having to ask about basic facilities, like a telephone – 'Eh how does this work? Eh, how dae ye dae this . . . Eh, how dae ye dae that . . .'

I feel like a complete fucking bampot, an inadequate, not able to do anything without having to ask other people – 'Ehm, how dae ye . . .' I can't even go into a shop without someone with me, in case someone laughs at me, in case there's a freak out, someone battered.

Caroline dials the number – 'It's ringing Hugh' she says.

I take the receiver – 'Is that you Ma? It's me, Hughie. Did ye's get hame okay?' I ask. Her words rip through me – 'Nae thanks tae you' she quips – 'Listen, Hughie. Kay an aw these people have been good friends tae you. The least ye could've done . . . Wit? A don't gie a fuck wit ye wur daen wi Carol. Eh? Caroline, then, whitever the fuck ur name is.'

Why can't she just talk to me?

I sometimes wonder if this is really just a tactic, a method of preventing any dialogue between us – 'Listen. Huv you been tae the broo yet? Naw? Well, get yerself signed oan, an never mind aw the crap' she snaps.

The Job Centre. I knew she would start on this. Sixteen years in jail, and all she can come up with is the fucking dole.

But she's only getting warmed up – 'N'by the way, who are these people wi the fuckin cameras? *World in Action*? Jesus Christ!' she humphs dismissively.

I try to explain but before I can – 'Challengin Michael Howard? Who the fuck dae you think you are?' she shouts – 'N'wit aboot the stone carvin?' she demands.

I feel my chest tightening; I know what's coming next – 'Yer wit? Sore? A don't gie a fuck! Get doon tae that place an finish the fuckin sculptures' she says – 'A jist don't understaun you ye know.'

No! No! Please! Don't say it! Don't fucking say it – 'There's Jimmy, he's still daen es stone carvin but you?'

I slam the phone down – 'Bastard! Bastard! FUCKINNNN BASTARD!'

I pace up and down the studio. I shouldn't have phoned. I shouldn't have phoned. I fucking knew it. The fucking cow! Oh if it was Alec? *Calm down. Calm down. You're out now.* What? *You're out now.* That's right! I'm out! I don't have to depend on her or any of them. They have no control over me anymore. I don't have to phone every day. I don't have to listen to them. Fuck the lot of them! I'm free now – free!

Caroline tries her best to placate me but contact with my family always brings out the worst in me. They can't communicate a basic hullo without all this hostility. I find it so difficult to realise my own life, always worrying about what they are telling other people. They've projected such a disturbing picture to people, telling them lies, that I am irresponsible, almost willing me to fail. I am continually trying to justify myself to people as if everything I do is wrong. I'm fucking tired of it, tired of these people. I've survived sixteen years, survived sixteen years of my family, and all these people. The Ken Murrays, Kay Carmichaels and Jimmy Boyles. Who are they? What gives them a right to question what I do? I can blow my fucking brains out if I feel like it. What I do with my life is my own business. I'm fucking sick of them, sick of being controlled. Caroline sees the state they get me into – 'Hugh. Try not to feel upset. Go and have a shower, remember we're going to have lunch with Andy and Lorraine' she says – 'I'd said we would be there.'

My stomach seizes up with fear – 'Oh fuck, ad furgoat aboot that. Dae we need tae go Caroline?' I ask, terrified at the thought of having to sit at a table with people – 'Kin a jist gie it a miss? Say am noa well ur sumthin?'

Caroline laughs – 'Oh come on. They don't bite you know. Andy's a laugh so there is nothing to worry about. He's down to earth. You'll like him.'

Andy *is* a laugh, totally fucking mad. We can't stop laughing all through the meal, the one liners and funny stories have us in hysterics. His patter's brilliant!

Lorraine and Andy Arnott, they really are a good looking couple, both educated in art and Scottish history. Andy has recently been granted funding to open a printmaking workshop in Pilton – 'Aye, we're having a launch party in a coupla days. Caroline an you are invited so come along. Maureen Scott, and all that crowd fae Muirhouse will be there. Did ye finish the stone carving for them, the Mother and Child?' he asks.

The Mother and Child. Shit. I'll have to go back down there

to finish it – 'Naw Andy, al get it done shortly. This *World in Action* mob ur nearly finished filmin, so al get the stane finished then. A took a lotta shite fae they cunts doon there ye know. Aye, they treated me like an arsehole at times. Och jist daft remarks, but a liked Maureen Scott. She wis good tae me, trusted me.' I say – 'Aye, Maureen's a good wumin.'

Andy smiles knowingly – 'Muirhoos eh? There's a wee bitta rivalry there. Pilton and Muirhoos, thur like two different worlds, an yet they're really the wan community, it's mad' he says – 'Glesga's the same eh? Different areas, gangs an at. Is that why yer daen this documentary, for *World in Action?*' he asks.

I nod – '*World in Action*? Well, it wis tae try an help tae keep the Special Unit opened. The Scottish Office are tryin tae shut it doon' I explain – 'Michael Howard an aw this stupit shite that prison works. V'ye heard um? 'Prisin wirks.' S'a pure fuckin arsehole so ey is. Oops, Lorraine sorry there. A didnae mean tae . . .'

Andy laughs – 'Sorry? Och Hugh, Lorraine's fae Muirhoos. Think we've never heard any sweery words before? Think the programme'll help keep it opened, the unit? Ca, mer fish?' he asks.

I take a second helping too, feeling more and more at ease, no cutlery to worry about or, what hand to hold what in – 'Well, thur's problems Andy. Well, Jimmy Boyle's told the guys in there that am publishin ma "dirty diaries" so av been barred. The film crew as well.' I explain – 'TC Campbell phoned me an told me the score. TC? Aye, he wis wanney the guys dun fur the ice cream wars, but ey is innocent. Naw, honest. Ye get cons sayin that a lot, but naw, they guys really are innocent. Tommy Campbell an Joe Steele. They wur set up.'

Andy's fascinated as I continue – 'Everybody in the jail knows that. Scottish Office an the screws. Whola Glesga knows they guys ur innocent' I state – 'A don't know how they handle it. Screws, wan in particular burst the big yin's spleen, battered um while ey wis oan a hunger strike. Witsat? Naw Andy, the screws never get done for battur'n cons.'

Andy's stunned – 'Is it really that bad Hugh?' he asks.

I assure him it is – 'Wit aboot Jimmy Boyle? Thought he wis helpin people?' he asks. So did I – 'Jimmy? Claims that es helpin people but eh. Aye. Andy, honest, a wis jist tryin tae help keep the place opened but it's finished noo a think. That cunt puttin the mix in wi the guys up there.'

Andy's curious about the diaries – 'R'ye plannin a book Hugh?' he asks – 'Wit? Aye, sure, I'd be delighted tae read them. Aye, I'll drop by the gallery and have a look at them.' He hands me a book – 'Ye heard ey *Trainspottin*? It's by a guy fae Edinburgh, Irvine Welsh.'

A few days later we go to the launch. I have on a suit and a white overcoat – the Dick Tracy look. I just can't help myself, I need some fashion therapy.

Greater Pilton Print Resource. Andy's waiting at the door when we arrive – 'Hi Hugh, come on in, get a glass of wine.' I'm amazed. This guy's pulled together a workshop for local people when he could be living as an artist. He's taken his experience back into the community – 'Fuck me Andy! This is fuckin amazin man!'

He's wearing a suit too, but from a second hand shop – 'Like the coat Hugh?' he grins.

– 'Ye wanta machine gun an a hat?' the grin broadening into a smile – 'Ye look lik a guy fae Glesga!' he continues.

I know what he means – 'Och, a canny help masel Andy.' I laugh – 'Al Capone.'

I've never met anyone like this guy. He's not like most of the guys I know, headcases, pals though. But Andy? There is something unassuming, a quietness. Dare I say it – a beauty – about him.

I feel he is someone I could relate to, someone I could identify with, a young guy from a working class background, and yet involved with art.

I spot a friendly face, Maureen Scott – 'How ye daen Maureen? Aye, bran new. Al be doon tae finish the stane next week' I promise – 'Am stayin in the gallery. Well, they offered me this hoos in Niddrie. Naw, av nuthin against the people there. Maureen, a widnae last two minutes oot there. C'mon noo. Junkies an dealers aw o'er the place? Aye, nae bother pal, see ye later.' I say wandering off – 'Next week maybe.'

Maureen's a good decent hard working woman, striving to do something for people in her community. She'd taken me on when the prison were trying to finish off my attempt to find a stone carving project as a pre-release placement – 'Am warnin you boy! Any kerry oan an ye'll answer tae me, right?' she'd said that first day – 'Nae nonsense!'

I turn to pick up my drink; there's a guy, about six feet; he's leaning forward – kissing Caroline – 'The fuck ur you on?' I snarl, grabbing at the throat – 'S'ma fuckin burd ya cunt ye.'

Caroline's pulling me away – 'Hugh! Hugh! Stop it! It's Graham! Louise's husband!' she's shouting – 'Louise?' I ask – 'Louise who? Who the fuck is Louise?' Oh Jesus. Louise is Lorraine's sister. I don't know where to look. Graham's six feet is ready to take me apart – 'Look, eh. A apologise. A didnae know people kissed each other. A mean, aw fur fucksake.' I feel embarrassed. I've made a complete arse of myself in front of all these people. Andy rescues me – 'Hugh, calm doon man, c'mon o'er, meet Louise' he laughs.

Louise is looking at me, sternly. I turn back to Andy – 'Ye fuckin kiddin? She's ready tae knock me oot. Aw fuck. Andy please, tell thum am sorry' I beg – 'Please.' Caroline's laughing too, but agrees we should head back to the gallery – 'Hugh. What are we going to do with you eh? Everyone kisses outside, it's a greeting. Glasgow? I suppose they head butt each other?'

My head's down – 'Och, ye know wit a mean. Ye shake hauns wi people. Ye don't go kissin some guy's burd, ye'd get the face ripped aff ye fur that lark. Anywiy am sorry a embarrassed ye there. Still ma pal?' I ask, cuddling her as we leave.

Andrew's in hysterics when we eventually get back to the gallery – 'What? Graham's six feet Hugh?' he exclaims.

I don't know where to look – 'Aye, well, eh.' Mumble, mumble, mumble.

I hit the studio for the remainder of the day, but a party has been arranged for later on that night. Caroline looks in, to make sure that I'm all right – 'Hugh, Lorraine is coming by later. Andrew's having a party in his studio. Pardon? Oh, it's just some of his gay friends. Oh don't be silly, you'll be fine. Anyway you don't have to go, no, it's for his lover's birthday, it will be mostly a gay crowd. Andy's bringing your diaries back. No, he didn't say anything about them, just said he'd bring them round later.'

Andy appears with my diaries – 'Here Hugh, huv a wee smoke.' This is more like it. I roll a joint on the mattress – 'So, wit didye think ey the diaries Andy?' I ask.

What had been in my mind about these diaries? Am I still suffering from that Special Unit phenomenon, of everything being brilliant?

Andly floors me – 'Well, they're crap tae be honest. Well, not . . .' he says – 'How can I explain? It's not your voice Hugh. Write the way you talk. I mean you say things like "Oh I just popped out one night and slashed this chap for being rude to me". Noo d'ye see?' he asks – 'Write the way ye talk. V'ye read that book I gave ye? Try tae read it. He writes the way we talk. Wit? Aw fur fucksake Hugh' he laughs – 'Tra-iins? R'you serious?

Cunts watchin trains? Naw, it's aboot drugs an *Trainspottin*'s the title!'

I do fully grasp what he's saying, but how will readers understand, if my diaries aren't written in Standard English? How will readers know that I've changed? I try to explain this to him – 'Andy, a dae know wit ye mean but a huv tae show that av changed, that av educatit masel in the unit tae prove it wurked. Boyle's dun that.' Andy smiles – 'C'mon Hugh, how long were ye in? Forget Boyle, look, you'll have tae put aw this shite behind ye. Av had a difficult childhood but there's nae point tae this Special Unit stuff. We've aw had problems, there's nuthin special aboot yours.'

No one has ever spoken to me like this before – 'Sure Andy, sure' I mumble.

He's brought a computer – 'Dae ye know how tae work these things?' he asks. I look at the machine – 'Wit? Is this fur me? Andy, fur fucksake man. Aye, aye, a kin wurk it, two fingers. Ye'll huv tae eh, how ye put it oan an things like that. A kin type but the rest, eh' I declare – 'Eh? The noo? Aye fine, here there's a pencil. You write it doon, an al listen. Eh, al watch, naw, wait a minute. Aye, that's it! You say wit tae dae an al write it doon. Wit's that? Naw wit didye say there, furst? Press wit? Oh right. Aye a see noo. Right press that wan an then a press this wan. S'that right noo ur wit? Witsat? Right then, you write it doon an al dae us another joint' I suggest.

I fan the skins for another joint – 'Witsat? Aye, aye, a kin understaun yer writin. Wit's that bit there? Naw, a kin read yer writin if ye print it. Aye that's it noo, fuck me man. Am shteaminnnnn' I purr – 'Jesus, kinna hash is at?'

Caroline looks in – 'How are you two getting on?' she asks.

– 'Oh bran new, eh Andy? Look, Andy's gave us a computer! Aye, fur fucksake, a hud wan in the jail Caroline!' I climb up the pillows into a sitting position – 'Wit? Naw, am bran new. The wit? The party? Oh here, that's right, the party, ye comin Andy?'

Andy's going round and round on a swivel seat – 'Aye, might be a laugh' he replies. I grab a bath towel – 'Right, al get a quick shower, straighten masel oot a bit. Noa be long. Caroline dae a cuppa tea fur Andy.'

The remainder of the powder has been burning a hole in my pocket all day. I spread a line on the hand basin. I keep looking over my shoulder but there's no spy hole. I am alone. There's no one watching, and yet somehow that feeling is always there. Am I being watched?

I'll have to get off this stuff but fuck knows how. I might try to. Fuck it. Worry about it tomorrow. I snort the line, a shudder shoots through my body – 'Ohh ya fucker ye.' Ye-essss. A wee line and a shower, fantastic. I hang onto the steel frame, my spine bent like a bow, the blood spreads into the lumbar. Ye-esss. I look up to make sure this is not a jail dream. I am out. I'm in a shower, outside. Those bastards in there. I wish they could see me. Wonder what time it is? They'll all be getting ready for the lock-up, chasing a joint for bed. Jesus, I couldn't face that again. I couldn't go back to all that. Did I do sixteen years? I can't remember anything. I'm out but . . . Fuck! There's the door! Someone's at the door – 'Hugh? Hugh? It's me, Caroline. Will you be long? People want to use the toilet' she calls.

The toilet? I look around. Fuck! The ladies' fucking toilet! I'm in the fucking ladies' . . . I call out, calmly – 'Be oot in a minute Ca!'

The party's already started, it's all young men. The Young Conservative Party having a party. Andrew introduces us all – 'This is Hugh, Caroline and Andy!' Sleekit eyes are on me. I feel my dick being probed by young eyes. I can hear the innuendo of the questions. How long? Sixteen years without sex? Must be gay. I plonk down beside a pair of pin stripe trousers hiding below the table. Did he brush against my leg? I'm determined not to move. A coiffed fringe is leering in my face. The dreaded question has arisen – 'And what do you do then?' Andrew's devilish sneer. I smile across the the table – 'A dae murders.' You could have heard the proverbial penny, but they're fascinated, fascinated by violence, fascinated by prison, by homosexuality, jail rape – 'But you must have seen *something* in prison?' a voice suggests.

The party trails on into the night. Vodka, powder, hash, and wine. My obsessive drive is being fuelled by this poisonous concoction – 'Pass the wine . . .' Caroline and Andy? They're long gone, but me? This body has been purified, burned, shaped by physical training, fasting, basic food, hatred, fear, craving, and an intense desire for pleasure.

The heads of future cabinet ministers are hitting the table but the true hard liners are still going strong with me in shared indulgence – 'Pass the vodka . . .' We literally hog the table in our insatiable drives. I'm tonight's fantasy. Should I feel different that the audience is all male? Truth is, flattery is flattery, nothing more. The source is merely staring eyes and hanging jaws, they could be women, but then again, women are not so aggressively transparent, well, not all of them.

Some people are having sex in a dark corner of the room; black shadows create this bizarre fuck scene across the length of the room, the whimpering sounds as the guy is penetrated. I'm tempted to watch but I have stories to tell – 'Aye, there wis this guy in there, a complete bovril, the Horse's Heid. Screws wur even fuckin um. Ey wis the jail hurl. You'd see him puttin oan a limp, that wis him lettin every cunt know that es arse wis sore!'

They're loving it, squirming around, giggling – 'Oh Hugh, you must've had a lover? I mean, sixteen years?' that voice suggests again.

I'm loving it too, all the attention – 'Nah, men don't dae

anythin fur me. Av luved men in there, pals. Wit's that? Aye, av fucked wumin in the arse. The difference? We-ell, a big paira baws hingin doon, hairy legs an a three day growth. Naw, men don't turn me on. Sorry, but am jist noa a poo . . . gay. Thur nae drink left? Vodka's fine, pass me a gless. Aye, the jail eh?'

My insatiable drive is finally overcome by exertion and the horrors of a stark daylight flooding the studio – 'Fuck. Zat the time? Al see ye's later okay?' Cries of opposition go up – 'Oh Don't go . . . Oh well. See you soon. If you need tucked in, har! har! har!'

After forty eight hours my eyes finally close with exhaustion, but prison still occupies my subconscious world, terrorising me in my sleep. Caroline's arms are around me as I come screeching out of a nightmare – 'NAWW! PLEASE!' I lash out on the way up from hell – 'Hugh! Hugh! You're all right, you're all right, it's just a bad dream. You're safe, it's all right' she says, soothingly – 'You're safe.'

Fuckin nightmares. They never fucking stop, not even out here. It's always the same, being chased by people with knives, something terrible, terrifying, right behind me. I feel fear paralysing me, dragging down on me, and just as the thing is on me my eyes open – and I can't breathe, can't shout for help.

Caroline's awake – 'Mor-ninngg. Coffee Hugh? Goodness me, you look awful. What time did you come to bed? Oh they were loving it when we left. What? You're joking aren't you? Andrew is terrible. Oh well, that'll teach you eh? What would you like to do today then? There's an opening tonight at the National Gallery.'

Caroline introduces me to a whole new world of people, places, and events. Andrew lives through events. I'm dazzled by the glamour of this world but demons lurk below the surface. I don't fit in somehow. I become aware of what it means to be a murderer in a world where violence is reviled. I feel the pressure of glances, of comments, and whispers – *murderer, murderer, murderer.*

No one ever actually says anything outright but it's there all the time. Women are fine but men? Some men can't wait to tell me that they too have done some drastic deed, something terrible. I don't know why, but there's always one – 'Oh, I've held a gun . . . it was loaded too!' Wow. Big deal. Why the fuck are you telling me? I try to be polite – 'Oh, that's fascinatin.'

There are a lot of people too who are not interested in my past and simply take me at face value. People who have no need to fantasise through my past. People who want to help without all the usual fuss, about what they've done for me. It's people's good will towards me that makes me think differently, lets me move forward – otherwise it's all been a waste of time.

I want to change but if people don't let me then what was the point of releasing me in the first place? What if it all went horribly wrong? What if I killed again? The prison authorities would just say – 'He was all right in the prison.'

Duncan Thomson, Director of the National Portrait Gallery. Timothy Clifford, Director of the National Galleries of Scotland. These people could have simply told me to piss off. I am a murderer after all, but they didn't. They let me into their galleries, they let me meet people, let me be part of this world, but I have my moments.

– 'How ye daen hen? Ye look luvly in yer wee dress there!'

Caroline yanks me round a corner – 'God! That's Lady Antonia Dalrymple!'

Andrew's laughing. He's a bit of an outlaw in this part of the art world – 'Oh Caroline let him loose, we might have some fun.'

The woman in front of me thinks I'm her husband –

'Dahling! Isn't this wonderful! The Establishment being its most established. They'll all be fucking each other soo . . . Oh! Goodness! Oh fuck! I thought you were . . .' Never before had I heard 'fuck' sounding so deliciously sexy. I give her a nice sleazy filthy smile – 'Is that right . . . dahling?'

And so it goes, but it's not all a bed of roses. No, no. The honeymoon bubble begins to burst after the first few weeks of my release. I mean, wouldn't it be fantastic if you just came out and picked up the pieces, started that 'new life' you've been dreaming about for sixteen years? Well, with a giro worth sixty quid that's hardly likely now, is it, and the house in Niddrie? C'mon, that new beginning only happens in the movies and certain types of life-after-life books. Those old romantic stories with the 'It was a cold blustery night in Glasgow.' The truth is that being 'freed' is a fucking nightmare.

Chapter Four

OUR STUDIO IS directly above a night-club, The Pelican. The music blaring through the floor is bringing the previous night back with a vengeance. I'm still in our bed on the floor, it's actually vibrating, or is it just my head? When I open my eyes, everything seems blurred; the pain in my head is blinding. Jesus Christ . . . My hands are swollen and stinging with tiny cuts with slivers of glass embedded. They're blue-ish looking; long strips of Sellotape are cutting into my wrists – 'Wit the fuck is this?' I ask myself. Aw Jesus. Those bouncers last night. I try not to remember. Have I done anything?

The dried brain is trying desperately to blot things out, but the previous night's events are flashing through my mind in distorted images. Caroline blocking the door. She's on top of me, banging my head off the floor, physically struggling to hold me down. I can hear my voice, screaming at her – 'AL FUCKIN TAN THEY CUNTS!'

Jesus Christ. Have I had another nightmare? I can see knives flashing, they're tied to my hands.

Have I cut her face? The bars on the window throw a shadow across the floor, it must be early morning by the sounds of the street traffic. Broken glass lies just below the frame, shards of glass are scattered across the floor; broken furniture, strewn around everywhere, even the fridge is over on its side, table and chairs, completely wrecked, it's a shambles.

No, this is no nightmare.

Those stupid fucking bouncers. They just can't leave it

alone, always trying to act like heavies. Every time we go out, it's the same fucking thing. I like to go out for a quiet drink like everyone else, but without fail there is some bampot out to prove that he is a gangster.

Ach fuck. What's the point. I've blown it. I roll over. Where's Caroline? She must be with Andrew? I didn't hear her getting up. I'll bet they're talking about last night. No wonder. What am I going to say to them? They've done everything for me too. Fuck! I'll have to get out of here. I can't face them after this carry on. I've nowhere to go.

What am I thinking?

Where's the family now eh, and all the wonderful friends? The bastards. They ran a fucking mile when they thought they were going to get landed with me. I mean, who wants to get landed with an ex lifer, a time bomb?

I'll have to get out before anyone sees me. I just can't face them in this state. I can't face anyone right now. I feel like vomiting but my stomach's empty, on fire. My head feels as if it's in a vice but I'll have to get ready, try to get out before they see me. I'm trembling, can't stop shaking. Oh fuck, there's a knock at the door.

– 'Hugh? Hugh? Are you awake?' someone's calling, it's Caroline.

She looks round the door – 'What are you doing? Where are you going Hugh? Oh no, c'mon, let's have some breakfast.'

Andrew's making us all a pot of tea in his studio as we walk in – 'Good morning then Mr Collins!' he grins.

I bow sheepishly in his direction – 'Eh, aye Andrew.'

Caroline's hands too are covered in tiny cuts from broken glass, but there are no stab wounds, fortunately. She takes my hands – 'So how are you then?' she asks.

She's hung over too, but handling it better than me. Andrew's dark demonic features break into a devilish smile – 'An Alka Seltzer Hugh?' he asks.

His penetrating blue eyes flash through my drunken hang-over – 'Well! What a night!

Did you smash everything?' he asks, cheerily.

After all this guy has done for me. An art exhibition, a job at the gallery, introducing me to all his friends, giving me a home.

What do I do?

Wreck the place, almost kill Caroline. Mr Don't Fuck With Me. Sixteen years down the drain. I don't deserve these people – 'Andrew, am really sorry. They daft bouncers in that boozer . . .' I mumble.

Caroline puts her arms around my shoulders – 'Ach Hugh. You've had a bit of a freak out. You're just not used to things out here, that's all. It'll just take time' she says. Andrew agrees with her – 'Yes Caroline. A freak out is exactly what happened. It's all out now. We don't want broken furniture every week but it had to come out sometime or other. I mean, we can't have it happening out on the street. I think prison has done enough damage.'

Caroline thinks so too – 'Yes Hugh, you're going to need time to get all this anger out of your system. You've been psychologically tortured in those places.'

Psychologically tortured? No I haven't. I ran the fucking jail. I did exactly whatever I wanted. I had control.

Did I?

They're being tremendously supportive. Surely they're not scared of me? They know me better than that, or do they, after last night? All those years in prison. Fuck, does anyone know me? Do I know myself?

Andrew laughs – 'Goodness! The fights I've had in the gallery with my ex partner! I have to say, those were what you call fights. That bloody nutcase chasing me all over the gallery with a huge knife! Screaming! Yes! Screaming at the top of his voice that he was going to kill me. He just couldn't cope when I left him. Campaletely mad!' he roars – 'Campaletely mad!'

Andrew's homosexual promiscuity is legendary. He's not camp in any way, quite the opposite in fact. His handsome face is very striking: the black collar length hair lends itself to his masculine features. The notoriously huge prick and the reputation as the dark lusting pleasure fiend make him irresistible. He is always surrounded by both men and women, some with equally wonderful reputations, some too with insatiable drives, all very very beautiful.

I love being in the company of these people. I've had sixteen years of hate. Sixteen years of men. I hate the very sound of men, the sound of their voices, the sound of all that macho bullshit – ME TARZAN! DRAP YER NICKERS!

I want to forget prison, forget that it ever happened. Am I wrong to want enjoyment? Some people seem to think so. Someone said to me in a debate – 'You've never said sorry.' Sorry? Sorry to who? Sorry for what? The only person I can apologise to is dead.

Am I to spend my life apologising to complete strangers who know nothing about me other than what they've read that morning in some tabloid headline? I'm really tired of all the stupid questions and statements from people who, because they have never been in trouble, feel this gives them the divine right to demonise people like me with bullshit – 'Oh I'm from a deprived area and I never turned out to be a bad person.' So what? Do they want a fucking medal?

How do you measure the distance between good and bad? Where does good end and become bad? What is good? If only it were so simple. I used to be bad but I am now a good person. Is that all people want to hear from me? Are they that stupid?

No, I've been punished so have no apology for any of the good people. I prefer to be in the company of the bad. Their punishment? I've been steeled by punishments, by isolation, by batterings by their prison guards. I'm from the gutter. Kill me, that is all they can do to me, but they'd no doubt hire someone else to do that for them. These people don't want to know until it lands on their front doorstep.

All I want to do is try to turn my life around, walk away, but if they don't let me, well I might just turn back, and it might just be their doorstep next time.

Caroline's laughing – 'How could we ever forget those fights between you two! I seem to remember you two having a running battle!' she says.

I look at her hands: they look sore with all those angry little cuts. I don't know where to look – 'Ca . . .' I try to say.

Andrew's laughing but wants the full story – 'What happened anyway? How did it all start? I thought you two were going to kill each other with all the screaming and the banging!' he asks – 'So what happened?'

Caroline mentions Muirhouse. Muirhouse? I don't remember being anywhere at all near Muirhouse.

She assures me we did go to Muirhouse – 'Yes Hugh. They wanted you to be at their annual dance. They insisted that you go, don't you remember?' she asks. Muirhouse? God! That woman! That's right! I was dancing with her! Jesus. It's all coming back. Jesus, I can see it all now. The Muirhouse Festival Activity Centre.

The women all stuck together, huddled around tables at one side of the smallish hall; they're all smiling half heartedly, convincing themselves they're having a great time, but there's defeat etched on their faces. Their faces have that hardened broken look, their eyes filled with pride, and sadness, watching their kids make the best of things. These are life's floor scrubbers, local women grafting their lives away on meaningless tasks, being used as cheap labour, anything, just to get by each day, to get their kids that pair of shoes for school, maybe a new dress.

I watched my granny killing herself doing these kind of jobs and no one ever thanked her for her labour. I'm not being sentimental; poverty and work killed her, and many other women like her.

The men too are jammed in tightly together, hovering over a few free cans of beer, the only reason for being there no doubt. In their prematurely beaten faces, shifting eyes watch every move, scanning the dance floor for any would-be predators, for would-be Don Juans.

Those perusals could well be fuelled by suspicion, but are more likely seeking out the possibility of more free beer, some cans to take home after the party.

I'm dancing wildly with a woman, probably a married woman at that. Suspicious eyes are watching. I feel them bore into my back. There are other people on the floor, but they're probably family.

You don't do things like this. Dancing with their women, it's asking for a sore face. The new slick suit hasn't helped matters either, it almost caught fire in the glare of so many bright coloured polyester shell suits. That burning persual has honed in, found a focal point – 'Chekra fuckin soot maaaaannnnnnn!' a voice roars.

Jenny's boy is swaying around in front of me. The support act is directly behind me buried somewhere inside two shell suits. The three of them are full of temazepam, out of their boxes, barely able to speak – 'Shugs ma maaaannnnn. How ye daen maannn? Am fuckiiiiinnnnn shteamiiiiiinnnn maaaaannnnnn' he slurs.

The conversation is splashing all over my face. I can't fathom out what he's saying for spittle, but he's coming on strong – 'Fight wi eny yous Glesgay cunts' he's saying. Fight? Glasgow cunts? My drunken brain is slowly weighing up the situation. Who is this bampot talking to? Don't take any shite from these pricks, but watch the new suit. My mouth hasn't received the message yet to be careful – 'Here, talk normal son. Wit the fuck're ye sayin? A canny make a fuckin word oot yer sayin son' I explain.

The boy's response is wet and incoherent – 'Amnoagiena-fuck!' he spits.

I took this to mean I am not giving a fuck. Danny, his father, is telling him to listen to me – 'Listen tae Shugs. The man's tryin tae talk sense ya radge cunt ye!'

All these little endearments between father and son eh?

Danny and Jenny have tried to get their son off drugs. Danny seems to think I'll have a positive influence for some unknown reason – 'Ey'll listen tae you Shugs' he says. He'll listen to me? Fuck, *I'm* a fucking junkie! I suppose they think that my being that bit older will make a difference, that the boy will listen to me. I give it a try – 'Look. I think yer Maw and Da huv tried thur best son but ye'll huv tae get a grip. Yer needin a good boot up the arse if ye ask me' I say.

So much for my counselling methods.

The kick up the arse hasn't gone down too well – 'Kick whose fuckiiiinnnn' he growls and spits.

The two pals have surfaced from the standing gouch and fumbling around in pockets. The father disappears as blades are produced: one is jagging up against my balls, the others are still tangled inside the shell suits. The tip of a blade at your balls isn't very comforting. Being stabbed is one thing, but in the testicles? What do you say at the hospital? I fell on top of a knife, landed on my balls?

Fortunately we are all in that dullish state of slow motion between the drugs and drink but things are beginning to go wrong. I try a last bit of common sense – 'Listen . . . Get that fuckin thing away fae ma baws. Am tryin tae gie ye advice but am no shy aboot blades either so take yer pick' I warn them.

Take your pick? Where is all this coming from? Take your fucking pick? I'm seconds away from getting stabbed. My mouth and brain no longer appear to be co-ordinating. The brain is alerting the body to danger, but the mouth is stirring up trouble. Yes, the mouth is working independently. The mouth can't see that the body can barely stand let alone fight. The mouth can't hear those alarm bells ringing in the brain. Run! Run! Run! Run! Run! Run! The mouth is stone deaf!

Three things are happening all at once. The body is beginning to tremble, the brain is fully alert to the dangers. The mouth, however, seems to think that it is in possession of someone else's body, someone who can handle three young hoods, someone like super fucking man.

The slight shift in their stance triggers instant reaction. I throw a punch but somehow manage to brush the guy with my shoulder as my fist travels past his head.

Danny's boy hits the wall behind me, runs straight into it face first as my body follows my arm. His brain obviously hasn't passed the message to his body that I've moved. A face flashes past the corner of my eye, meeting plaster and brick in its momentum.

It is not a pretty sight – 'Grrrr – ummmmmppppphhhhh!'

He's sparkled, knocked himself clean out in the attack.

Women are grabbing my arms, trampling him in the process as he slides to the floor. I see one of the pals directly behind the women, he has a blade. I can't take my eyes off the knife. He only has to reach over, and I will have even more scars on my face. I kick and punch, but these are working women, women with real arms from years of scrubbing and wringing. They're wringing me right now, but all I can see is the blade waving above their heads.

Caroline's face looms before my eyes as my arms are being pulled from their sockets. She has somehow pushed her way through and is screaming – 'Leave him alone! I'll calm him down! Just leave him alone!'

They let go of my arms. Blood begins to circulate, eventually reaching the brain. The mouth? I can no longer be held responsible for the diatribe it's spouting, but yes, it is still wide open, spewing obscenities. The blade disappears out through a side door . . . but the mouth seems to know what he looks like – 'Al get that fuckin bampot. A know es fuckin face!' it's screeching.

Is this me? Do I talk like this?

Caroline confirms that it is indeed me, and that I do talk this way – 'Oh yes, you were going mad, shouting and bawling. They should have left you alone. I'd have calmed you down. They should never have insisted on you going down there' she says – 'It was stupid to think you could simply go back there.'

Andrew's curious – 'What was the dance all about anyway? God. Surely after working all that time down there, you would have seen enough of the bloody place? It's utter madness to think you can go back to that world and just fit back in again. Hugh, you have changed! A wee get together in Muirhouse? Anyway what happened after that? Hold on, the stovies. Won't be minute' he says, checking the pot – 'Right then?'

My face is red with embarrassment. Caroline is reassuring – 'Hugh, there's nothing to feel guilty about. Don't worry about the broken furniture. My Russian things are all in pieces but they can be fixed later' she says.

They're both right. I should never have gone down there but they had insisted. There was the stone to consider as well. The Mother and Child had been complete as far as I was concerned, but there were people who had wanted the form to be more precise or more defined. Some stupid woman going on about the feet – 'Shugs. Wer's the feet?' Where are the feet? Jesus. I had wanted to show the three basic stages of carving to the kids working with me, but no – 'Wer's the feet? A canny see the wumin's feet!'

Three winters battering twenty ton of granite and this headcase wants to see the feet. I'd spent one winter on my knees, frozen in caked mud, praying for summer.

Maureen Scott had formed the community centre in an empty house. She was a rough diamond, but people had taken advantage of her generosity. I'd watched her suffer a stroke. People had then begun to treat her as if she were mentally impaired, gesturing in sign language while they exaggerated each word. I remember the painful look in her eyes. She'd smiled that final day before my release – 'THAT! IS! ME! AWAY! THEN! MAUREEN! O! KAY!' I'd roared – 'CHEE-RIO!'

I doubt if she'll be smiling when I go back to finish the work. The big fight will be my fault. But still, I don't have to take any bullshit any longer, or any of those other snidey remarks about murderers, and my arty friends.

Who the fuck did they think they were?

Some people had derived pleasure from their position. Their attitude had been loud and clear from the very beginning – 'You are a murderer so I can say what I want to you.' All the questions too – Can he be trusted with children? Can he be trusted to be left on his own? He is a murderer after all.

Trusted with children? I killed a man in a square go with blades. I lived in a world of violence, a world they wouldn't last two seconds in. Harm children? I had to take this shit for the duration of a pre-release work placement. I'd dreamed of teaching kids stone carving, give them a chance to get out of their predicament, help keep them out of jail and provide an alternative to drugs, but for those two years – two years of solid graft on a twenty ton block of granite – I had to take all that murderer shit.

Murderer. Will I ever leave this behind? Murder – er. I

hate that fucking word more than ever. Murderer is present tense. How do I leave that behind? How do I leave the past behind? Time: the future, the past, or whatever . . . is right now. Murderer is right now. Will I ever be beyond murderer? Will I ever get there, beyond that past? Will I ever be free?

This placement was to be my introduction back into society.

Caroline looks shattered – 'How'd we get back here? Wis there noa trouble wi some bouncers?' I ask.

She smiles – 'Oh yes, there was a fight, but that was much later at the City Cafe. You went mad when they said you were too drunk' she replies.

I can't believe this. The City Cafe? What was I doing trying to get in there? It's full of young kids most of the time. I don't believe this, but I do remember arguing with all the bouncers in Blair Street.

We're at the entrance to the bar. The doorways filled with black leather and muscle. I have never understood why men wear all that leather gear. I suppose they have to, to appear more professional, but black leather gloves, black leather jackets and trousers to match? Then there's those pony tails too. There is nothing more ridiculous than a balding man trying to create hair with gel – a few lengthy strands glued together into a pony tail. These pony tail hair styles with the receding hairline seem to play a vital part in their image – they all have them.

They look like warders. They have authority stamped all over them. I can't resist the urge to batter one of them – 'C'mon en! Al go fur a walk wi eny ye's!' I'm shouting in the street – 'C'mon! Ye wantey go fur a walk?'

These are huge guys: broad foreheads and hair gel, probably steroid freaks. They're looking mean. One punch and I'll be in need of a blood donor. This is dangerous but the mouth is determined to be tonight's victim – 'Fuckin pricks! Al buy ye's aw a new paira tights! Dae ye's like black tights then? Eh, ya fuckin wankers!' I shout.

I don't see that shoulder move from the last fight knocking one of these guys over but the mouth seems to think so – 'Camooan then! Am jist maself ya fuckin bampots! Ur ye's worried aboot yer make up? Want tae take a liberty wi me then? Eh? Am noa a wee daft boy eh? Al blow yer fuckin brains oot ya cunts!' I roar.

Jesus Christ . . .

The mouth has introduced a gun into its repertoire.

Three hundred kilo of muscle is shifting around on heavy black leather boots, looking nervously around, looking ready to do me.

Being cool is one thing, but you don't just stand there when there's some madman in your face, making noises about a gun. He might just have one.

They're positioning themselves now, watching every move my hands make – 'Dinnae be radge pal. Yer jist drunk, ken wit a mean like' one advises.

The mouth is hellbent on waking up in hospital. The brain can almost smell an odour of disinfectant, almost see that familiar blinding light above the emergency operating table. The mouth has no memory of such places. The mouth just puts me into them. Places like hospitals, and Special Units.

The Most Dangerous Mouth in Scotland.

Where is all this coming from? Is this the real me? Is this what I am? Was my old man like this after he got out? Was he this fucked up too?

No, this isn't me, it can't be. I'm not really like this. It must be the drink, it's got to be the booze, yes, it's the booze that's doing this – or is it? Why can't I just have a drink and go home without all this then? Home? The truth is, I don't have a home. When I got out I was offered a house in Niddrie. The welfare authorities insisted on the move to Edinburgh. This is where they dump most ex lifers – it's an area riddled with drugs and ravaged by economic deprivation. I'd have lasted about five minutes out there – trying to deal with the implications of release, and my own drug addiction.

The gallery was obviously more suitable for my needs. The studio was about the size of a prison cell, but we didn't mind at all. I loved living here with these people.

Why then was I fucking it all up?

Andrew wants to have a look in the studio for structural damage – 'Thank goodness I had all the windows properly barred. Caroline would have gone right through. Look, the frame is completely broken. God. A night out with Hugh Collins!' he laughs. They're both laughing, but it isn't funny. I tug at the Sellotape still dangling from my wrist – 'Caroline, am really sorry . . .' I murmur.

She dances mockingly in front of me, holding up her fists in the way that only women can – 'Hugh Collins eh. We'll have to get you tobered up' she laughs.

I can see her standing there the night before in the very same way, hands on her hips, slightly crouching, blocking me from the door. The two knives are strapped onto my wrists with Sellotape. I'm shouting at her, screaming at her – 'GET OOT THE FUCKIN ROAD! CAROLINE GET OOT MA FUCKIN ROAD!'

We fall to the floor in a struggle as I try to get past her. She's banging my head again and again off the floor. I feel hair being wrenched out of my scalp – 'CAROLINE! LET ME FUCKIN UP! AM GONNY RIP WANNEY THEY FUCKIN BAMPOTS!' I'm shouting.

I'm back on my feet but she's still there, in front of the door – 'GET OOT MA ROAD YA STUPIT FUCKIN COW!' I warn her – 'MOVE!'

I look around the studio. Her Russian keepsakes and other mementoes are broken, lie scattered all over the floor as we stand there looking around the room. A knife's lying beside the bed, one of the ones I had tied onto my wrists. She must have pulled them off before I'd fallen into a drunken stupor on the bed.

How I haven't stabbed or injured her is a miracle. My head's throbbing blindly, my stomach feels queasy with that hollow burning feeling, but questions are surfacing in the hangover.

What if the window hadn't been barred? What if she hadn't stopped me from getting out? What is wrong with me?

Caroline's belongings are lying all over the floor. Why do I find pleasure in mindless destruction? I love destroying things. There is no other explanation for it. Her life is strewn around our feet: years of collaboration, collecting, making relationships, years of work, spat upon. I fumble with a small plastic sculpture. She touches my arm – 'I can fix all these things Hugh. We'll move into a bigger studio' she says.

Andrew confirms other studios are available – 'Yeah, you could do with more space.'

He wants to leave us on our own – 'Let's sort all this out later. I'll call you when the stovies are ready. Why not have a shower, might make you feel better.'

My family wouldn't have handled this, the destructive behaviour. They wouldn't have known how to handle me. What the fuck is wrong with my head? Am I going to turn out like my old man after all? Is this what it was like when he got out?

Caroline hugs me as I try to say something – 'Caroline, honestly, am really sorry. You should jist have let me go. A didnae mean tae hurt ye . . .' I mutter.

She pulls me closer – 'What are we going to do with you eh? You've been battered into submission in those places. But you're here now, you are with me . . . We all care about you. Andrew loves you too so please, don't be afraid anymore. Please, trust us' she whispers.

We fall back onto the bed together, kissing and hugging each other – 'Caroline, a dae luv ye. A don't want tae lose ye . . . ever. Ma heid's dun in wi the jail. A didnae mean tae hurt ye, am really sorry.' I say – 'Honest, am sorry.'

My hand runs down her back; pulling her body in to me. She holds me against her in a warm embrace, but just then . . .

– 'Stovies! Stovies are ready!' a voice calls. It's Andrew.

– 'Stovies! Stovies are ready!' he's shouting.

We jump up, flushed and embarrassed – 'Oops! Didn't realise you two were' he says backing out of the doorway – 'Sorr-ee.'

Andrew's trying to promote his talents as a chef – 'Stovies, absolutely wonderful for a hangover aren't they?' he assures me – 'Wait until you've had this Hugh.'

Caroline and I agree – 'No wine?' she asks.

Andrew has about three quid in his pocket but this doesn't dampen that enthusiasm . . . – 'Yes!' he shouts – 'Let's raid the meters and have some wine! We could all do with a drink after last night! Hugh should write a play about the gallery – *La Poverati*!'

He has that dark look in his eye – 'I must say. You two did manage to ruin a perfectly wonderful evening last night. Completely ruined the most wonderful fuck. Three times and for at least fifteen minutes' he smirks proudly – 'The fuck of a lifetime.'

Caroline frowns – 'Andrew! For goodness sake! We are trying to eat!'

Chapter Five

WE'RE ALL BEGINNING to recover from the previous night, but, it can't go on like this. I'll kill someone if I don't pull myself together, it's only a matter of time before something more serious happens.

Where does it all come from? All that hidden rage. Has prison damaged me, or is the anger something else, something much deeper?

I hide for a few days in our studio, sleeping mostly during the day, roaming around all night, exploring the building, looking at all the paintings.

Caroline's paintings are fascinating. That figure; he's breaking through the bars, he's breaking through from darkness to light, from death to life, crossing the borderline.

Does the figure reflect my own crossing? My black stained soul's struggle?

I *feel* black inside. Is the soul really black with white cancerous stains?

– 'Hugh? Are you there? What are you doing? It's about four o clock. You coming to bed?' a voice calls, it's Caroline.

The paintings blaze like fire in the sudden light – 'Be alang in a minut. Turn the lights aff. Am jist thinkin that's aw, jist lookin oot the windae' I say – 'Al be alang shortly.'

Caroline tip-toes away – 'Andrew's back, been at a club all night. He wants to have a chat before we go to bed. Put the lights off mind. I'll be in his studio' she says.

I nod, saying – 'Aye, be alang in five minutes.'

Andrew's exhausted – 'Hi Hugh. There's tea in the pot there. No sleep again tonight? God. I'm tired too. We have to finalise the accommodation for the Russians. Yes, they arrive tomorrow night. Caroline will you make sure . . .'

Caroline interrupts him – 'Andrew, everything will be fine. Stop worrying will you? The accommodation has been sorted out. Have you decided how much money you will give them? Giniliski and Dema will be fine, but Roitberg. You know what he's like. What? Oh, that's fine. Twenty quid a day should be all right' she says – 'Yes, my parents are coming to the opening. My mum called this morning to confirm. They want us to go down to the house. Hugh? Oh he'll be fine, won't you? Mum's all right now. She freaked out at first. They're all right about things now. She's actually sympathetic now that she knows about everything. Anyway, what have you been up to tonight? Where were you?' she asks.

Andrew's face looks dark, dripping in the candle light – 'Oh just some new night-club. It was all right, we met up with Lillie Bothwell' he says – 'She said she'll let some of them stay at her place. Sacha and Dema could go there. She'll drive them around and things' he continues – 'No. They'll be fine out at her farm, keep them all out of trouble. Oh listen, before I forget, could you go out to the airport tomorrow and make sure that all their paintings are safe and properly packed?' he asks.

Caroline promises to check the paintings – 'Yes, I'll do that' she says.

Andrew's relieved – 'Great. Hugh could go with you. Well, all we can do now is hope that nothing goes wrong' he says – 'John and Elizabeth Smith are definitely coming. Elizabeth called this morning. The show should receive good reviews. The Ukrainian Heat Wave! That's what they're calling it! Yes I read something in today's *Guardian*!' he laughs – 'The Ukrainian Heat Wave!'

Caroline's delighted – 'O that's great! Angels Over the

Ukraine. I think it appropriate to call it that. The Fallen Angel light box should be above your bed! Yes, it's amazing work, hopefully we'll manage to sell something' she says – 'Julian Spalding might buy something for the Scottish Museum.'

Andrew smiles grimly – 'The Dark Angel more like it. God, Caroline. Joe's driving me mad. I feel so bloody depressed. Caroline I do care, but this, this *insisting*. The truth is that he insists that we fuck without condoms. I just can't do it, it's too dangerous.' Andrew tortures himself: being Catholic doesn't help matters either.

I feel so sad for him because regardless of the reputation he does have a conscience. These nightly sessions have become more frequent over the past few weeks, with the three of us sitting up all night drinking tea, talking about politics, prison, religion, art, and the possibility of being infected with HIV.

Would HIV make him a killer? Would HIV make it different to what I'd done? He asks himself this all the time. I don't have any answers but try to rationalise without all the usual emotive arguments.

– 'Naw Andrew. Thur's a big difference. A had a big fuckin knife. Joe knows es takin risks, it's noa as if ey disnae know the score is it?' I say – 'Yer dyin fae the minut yer born anyway. It makes nae real difference when it happens. Life? Andrew, life's jist a moment, a wee sparka light, a pure fluke.'

They both listen as I take a philosophical viewpoint – 'We're aw dyin here, right now. The body's jist an organism, that's aw an it's in a state a death aw the time. Ye don't know when it's gonny happen.' I continue – 'A mean, it's noa sumthin wi a time limit. We aw think we're here for a certain length a time. N'wuv invented religions cos we canny cope wi the reality a death. S'true ye know.' I state – 'Death an life. The same thing. It's the personality, ur the memory processes. S'wit we call the mind, that's wit canny face death. Wit's that?' I ask – 'Well, jail makes ye think. Anyway, we gaun tae bed Caroline?'

After a couple of hours we're all back up again, preparing the exhibition opening with the Ukrainians. Caroline's made tea – 'Are you coming out to the airport with me? Oh, we can get a taxi. No one will see you, you can shave later for the opening. Yes, yes, yes your suit's back from the cleaner's!' she says – 'God, you and your suits.'

I feel like shit, but she's right, we can get a taxi at the top of Blair Street – 'Ca! Ye noa ready yet? Fucksakes man . . .' I shout.

Caroline takes my arm – 'Wow. Wit a mornin eh?' I say – 'A hated the summer in that fuckin place. Aye, it wis fuckin murder. Wit? A wee walk? Ye kiddin? They kept ye in a dinin hall fur two hoors so they could coont the numbers. Two hoo . . . Fuck.'

I try to pull her back round quickly, whispering out the side of my mouth – 'Caroline . . . Don't look. Aw naw. Es seen us. Fuck.'

She's bewildered – 'What? What's wrong? Who's seen us?' she asks.

I pretend to have dropped something – 'It's Jimmy Boyle' I whisper – 'Kin ye see it? A drapped it jist there. Oh hiya Jimmy. How ye daen Jimmy?' I ask.

He looks at me – 'Oh hullo. Fancy meeting you here' he says.

He's wearing a silk suit – 'Yer lookin great Jimmy' I say.

He doesn't even blush as he answers – 'Well, I work hard at it. Here, this is for you two, it's champagne. I hear you're getting married.'

He hands me a bag marked Mappin and Webb. There's two bottles of very expensive champagne inside. I feel like a bug beside him – 'Wit? Oh aye, that's right wur gettin merried next week Jimmy. Eh thanks Jimmy. Eh, aye Jimmy' I stammer.

Jimmy, Jimmy, Jimmy. Why the fuck can't I shut up?

He turns to me – 'How's Betty? Have you fell out again?' he asks.

He knows! She's been on the phone to him! The way he asked, he already knew. He didn't so much as ask, but stated the fact that we hadn't been in contact since the last telephone call. She's been on to him to find out what's happening.

I bow my head – 'Eh, well, eh, ye know wit she's like Jimmy' I say.

For fucksake. Stop calling him Jimmy. It's none of his fucking business.

He pays no attention to me – 'Betty? A wonderful woman. You should give her a call you know. Anyway, where are you living?' he asks.

What? Why can't they call me? Why do I have to be the one to call? When I fall out with her, the whole family fucking falls out with me.

I don't bother arguing – 'Aye, right Jimmy. Am livin in that gallery. We canny get oan the housin list' I say.

He interrupts with what sounds like an accusation – 'There are a lot of people in that position you know' he says flatly.

Jesus. What did I say? They didn't all do sixteen fucking years. Fucking hell man. He looks at the dirty front of the gallery – 'Look, I like Andy Broon. He's a good guy.' he says.

Andy Broon? Andrew will love this. Andy Broon? Aye right Jimmy.

Caroline waves to a passing car – 'Oh, there's my brother Drew and his family Hugh' she says.

Caroline's brother? Fuck. Is this a conspiracy? The one day that I feel and look like shit, and half the planet's converging on Blair Street. I almost run away to stick on a suit. Aye eh, we kin aw wear silk suits ye know.

Caroline suggests going for a drink in Bannerman's. Oh just great. I've got two quid in my pocket.

Jimmy tries to push a bundle of bank notes into my hand – 'I don't know how much is there' he says.

I try my best to resist the bung – 'Naw Jimmy, honest, naw.' Thankfully, Caroline has more sense – 'Thanks Jimmy' I say – 'Thanks a lot.'

Bannerman's is a studenty type of pub, full of big woollen jerseys, combat jackets with ban the bomb logos, burst seams and the odd colonel, but they all read newspapers, even tabloid newspapers at that. Jimmy and I are fairly recognisable as two bad lads from the nineteen eighties – Scotland's Most Dangerous Days.

Jimmy orders a bucket of champagne, and a mineral water for himself. The barman is dropping bottles all over the place. He can't open the mineral water bottle. He can't tally the bill. His hands are trembling. Jimmy fuels his panic, patiently smiling – 'Tell you what mate. Call it a fiver?' he says.

HA! HA! HA! HA! A FIVER! HA! HA! HA! I've never heard such an exaggerated laugh in my whole life. HA! HA! HA! A FIVER! HA! HA! HA! He's drawing even more attention to us, people are doing double takes, it's becoming uncomfortable. Jimmy I guess is used to this sort of thing, being famous and all that. I'm still known as that other guy, the one that was in the Special Unit with Jimmy Boyle.

Jimmy's been out almost ten years now, married into money, a real success story, but me? I have no sense of time, probably a few months at most, and no money. I guess that makes me a complete failure.

Caroline's chatting with Drew, and his son, Stewart. Drew had been helpful in trying to allay concerns with their parents. Drew and I had met many years before when he was a psychiatric nurse visiting the Special Unit. We'd taken to each other immediately, he'd been sympathetic back then, so had been willing to pave the way in my initial meeting with Caroline's parents. This wee gathering must have been an interesting scenario for him – 'Hugh, I'd prefer a pint to be honest' he smiles. Definitely not impressed with the champagne – 'Nae bother Drew' I say. Jimmy wants to have a word in private – 'Can I take him away for minute?' Oh, oh. I can smell the heavy pull – 'It's just to have a quiet word with him' he says.

I can hear my own voice stuttering and stammering – 'Aye, eh, won't eh, be a minute, eh Caroline' I smile.

Why do I let him have this effect on me?

Collie. I haven't been called this in years – 'Collie, look what are you doing? Who are these people with your diaries? *World in Action*? Oh, I see, fifteen minutes of fame. I personally think you are out of order. Well, you're naming people. Look Collie, I'm a million miles away from all that now. I have a wonderful family, I'm a multi millionaire and have just bought my own helicopter. I've spent five years trying to do something out here for other people. Look, people don't let you forget your past you know, it will cast a long shadow in your life' he states – 'A long shadow.'

What's this all about? Naming people? He can talk. I almost burst out laughing with the long shadow spiel, a line from a new book? I look at him. I would have literally killed for this guy. I feel defeated, deflated and fucked by the time it's over – 'Aye. Al phone ma Maw the night then Jimmy' I say – 'Nice seein ye again' I lied.

Caroline reminds me about collecting the paintings at the airport – 'We'd better get a move on Hugh.' Drew and Stewart are here for a few days, and arrange to meet for lunch the following day, before the opening of 'Angels Over the Ukraine' – 'Okay Drew. See ye the morra then okay.'

Jimmy accepts the invitation to our wedding – 'Aye Jimmy, it's on the seventh. It's in Mansfield Church. Aye okay, thanks by the way' I say.

Caroline and I catch a taxi – 'Fuck. That wis really heavy

there. Aye, ey pulled me up aboot the diaries' I exclaim – 'Aye. Wit a fuckin cheek. A jist wish ey wid stop fuckin lecturin me, but it's Betty. She'll be tellin him aw sorts aboot the gallery, an you tae. She's hud it in fur you anyway since she met ye. A noa wit she's like. She's hud it in fur every burd av ever been involved wi Caroline.'

Andrew's busy preparing food and drinks when we get back to the gallery. There are lots of artists milling around, and people connected with the gallery – 'Caroline! They should be here in about an hour!' he shouts.

The place is buzzing with excitement. We sneak into a studio on our own for a quiet drink – 'God! Let's have five minutes alone. Hugh, Caroline, this is for the wedding' he says.

He hands me a thousand pounds – 'I know you have no money. This will pay for the drinks and stuff. No! No! No! I insist! Palease Hugh! It's only bloody money for God sakes!' he exclaims.

Andrew has left himself with near to nothing to pay for our wedding – 'Andrew. Am . . . A don't know what to say.' They both laugh – 'Well! That makes a change!' I almost break down in tears – 'Naw Andrew, seriously, thanks fur this, you've done everythin fur me. A don't noa wit tae say.' We all hug each other – 'Right! Let's go! Russians are on our doorstep!' he cries – 'Let's go!'

Andrew stops – 'Did you say you met Jimmy Boyle? Today? What did he say? Drew was there too? My God! What happened?' he asks.

We're all in hysterics with the bit about Andy Broon – 'Wha-at! Andy Bloody Baroon? I've never been called that in my life! What a cheek! I've never met him Hugh! No! Wait!' he says – 'That time you were on hunger strike! Caroline do you remember? We had asked him to put his signature to a petition supporting your cause. He turned and said there's no smoke without fire!' he continues – 'Yes Hugh! I couldn't believe it. I thought you were friends. That's right! All the newspapers had been saying you were close to death so we were really shocked by his remark.'

Andrew remembers exactly when it was – 'Ye-es. He was trying to get us to buy this champagne, as if' he laughs – 'But yes, definitely 1991.'

No smoke without fire? I'd been railroaded by the prison management, and dumped in Shotts Maximum Security. I'd been photographed, but behind me was a bar, part of the main restaurant at my first work placement in Edinburgh Zoo. I had almost died fighting to get the authorities to give me back my release date after fifteen years. I'd done nothing wrong, other than have a photograph taken with some of the attendants having a birthday party – the photograph had been found in my cell during a 'routine' cell search – and been sanctioned by a governor beforehand – 'Yes Collins. You can go to the party but remember, no drinking or anything like that.'

No smoke without fire? While I'm on a hunger strike?

– 'They're here! They're here!' Andrew's shouting.

The Russians' travel coach is sitting directly below the studio window as I look down into the bowels of the Cowgate. I'm not exactly sure what I had expected, probably moustaches and huge fur hats, but these figures slithering from the bus were utterly beautiful, their elegance absolute. I'm totally stunned by the sheer grace of the men gliding into the studio – 'Andreew! Karoline! Leetle Karoline! Hauw waunderful to see you again! And thees is Hugh?' I'm overwhelmed with bear hugs, kisses and a mass of wedding gifts – 'These are faur you Karoline and Hugh!'

The Ukrainian Heat Wave has arrived – 'A toast! Andreew! Leetle Karoline!'

I had never seen so many beautiful men and women in the same room. The two most stunning of the group were almost identical in black leather gear, with ash blond hair, but the most beautiful of the group was the slinky guy called Sacha Giniliski. Women will go crazy for this guy I thought. He slid into a chair and remained there the whole night staring at the floor, saying very little to people – 'Sacha, you must get an awful lotta wumin pesterin ye eh?' I asked him.

He smiled back – 'I am only a man.'

Andrew gave one of his best deplorable speeches about the connection between the artists of Russia and Scotland. I could feel knickers squelching as the party kicked in for real. Andrew looked like the devil hosting and toasting the scent of all that flesh rubbing up a hot furnace in his lair. I hit that floor half naked, half drunk, but mostly on fire with sheer sexual abandonment. Caroline I saw lounging on a sofa draped in the red national flag of Russia. She was elated to be amongst old friends again, and completely unconcerned with my flailing arms and gyrating hips – 'Hugh! These are our friends! They're wonderful people!' she shouts, smiling, elated.

At about five in the morning I began talking Russian, half Italian – 'So you lika thees leetle citee Dema?' I mean, what do you expect after almost a lifetime of watching 'The Sean' dismantling half the KGB as 007? Dema, the poet, couldn't believe that I actually drank vodka – 'But it is not real vodka Hugh. Don't you like ganja?' All said in perfect English.

While Andrew and Caroline organised the exhibition I indulged myself in the company of the more stylish members of the group. Mansfield Church seemed the appropriate space to exhibit 'Angels Over the Ukraine'. Caroline and I arranged to marry there after the opening – 'Scott Marshall said he'll merry us Caroline. E's brand new. It wis him that wis behind the stane doon in Muirhoos.' I'd said – 'Fuck, did ye see that big light box o'er the altar, Fallen Angel? The *World in Action* mob wur in lookin at it. They want tae dae the weddin as well. Av warned thum noa tae film me wi Jimmy. Well Jimmy said ey wis away fae aw that publicity. Wull see wit happens. Al phone ma Maw up tae see if they're gonny come through fur the weddin. A don't think thur talkin tae me, but al gie it a try okay?'

Chapter Six

WHEN DEMA AND Giniliski had hung their paintings they wanted to wander around and look at the city. Wee Scottish nippy faces beamed at the sight of the amazing people floating around their city. The City Cafe low life surfaced from behind painted nails to claw the burning leather searing the bar of their local haunt. Volody and Lera his bird looked scary with their identical ice cool appearance. No one went near them after dark. Giniliski fell prey to the usual mauling, however, whenever he exposed his neck to the occasional set of rotten teeth in the men's toilets, the tight arsed Crimplene slacks squealing in his ear – 'A jist wantae suck ye, ken wit a mean doll!'

Black Bo's was no better. Lesa, Giniliski's German girlfriend, wanted to go there one night. I couldn't believe it. I'm standing there with them – 'Two Nooky Broons mate an a mineral water fur hur. Ye sure at's aw ye want Lesa? Wit's at pal?' Some guy is on my ear. I can't make out a word he's saying – 'Wit? Canny hear ye mate.' I say.

– 'Do you wa me to fif k uk yu?' he's saying.

Giniliski and Lesa are in hysterics laughing.

I try to ignore him – 'Wit's at? A canny make ye oot mate' I say.

I just can't understand a word the guy's saying between the general bar noise and the loudish music in the background. Giniliski and Lesa seem to have cottoned on to what he's saying though – 'Wit issit, a drink? Naw yer bran new mate. Wuv goat a drink so nae bother. Wit's at?' I ask.

Giniliski and Lesa are doubled up laughing. What's so funny? What's the big fucking joke? The para's starting to rip out of me. I'll knock this cunt out if he's gettin wide I think to myself. *No you can't, you're on licence*, flashes back.

He's in my face again – 'Dae ye want me tae fifk yu?' he's saying.

I don't have a clue what he's saying, but then it clicks in – 'Wit wis that? Wididje say there? Fistfuck? Wit the fuck's that? Naw look pal wuv goat a drink okay?' I say. Lesa has tears streaming down her face. A fistfuck? I've never heard this before. Is it a drink or somethi . . . Here wait a fuckin minute. A fistfuck? In the arse? He knows he's bloomered. The flush of embarrassment from my toes just registered on his face. This fucking low life. I've had sixteen years with headcases and not one of them has ever said anything like this to me. Fistfuck?

I'm raging, but a voice in my head is saying – *Don't touch him. Don't lay a finger on him, he'll put you back in the jail. Walk away, let it go, just let it go, c'mon now, walk away.*

I want to wring his fucking neck. DON'T! DON'T! DON'T!

Fistfuck? I can't let it go – 'You tryin tae get wide?' I snarl, picking up a bottle. He's squealing that I've got it all wrong. Fucking right it's all wrong. He's heading to a flight of stairs, but I block his path. My head is fogged by conflict. In jail I could bust him and spend a night in solitary. Out here, this prick can put me back in there for at least five years, an average recall for breach of licence.

FUCKIN TAN UM SHUG! TAN THE FUCKER! *NO DON'T! HE'S PURE JAIL BAIT! JAIL!*

I don't care. I'm not taking this fucking shit out here. I didn't take it in jail – 'Ye callin me a poof?' I sneer in his face.

He manages to struggle past – 'Please! Please! I apologise!

I'm sorry, ple-ease!' He backs out the door holding his hands up. I let the beer bottle drop to my side to let him see the danger he's in, to torture him.

GIE IT TAE UM! STOAP FUCKIN ABOOT! FUCKIN CHIB UM! FUCKSAKE! HE'S JIST CALLED YE A POOF FUR FUCKSAKE MAN! TAN THE FUCKER!

The look of fear on his face breaks the drive – 'Beat it! Fuckin mo-oove!' I watch him run up the street before returning to the bar. People are glancing over at me but I'm having the pint before I leave.

BIG DEAL EH. AM HUVIN MA PINT. NAE CUNT TELLIN ME WIT TAE DAE EH. The barman's looking at me – 'S'up wi your face stupit?' I snarl at him.

OH GREAT! TAKE IT OOT OAN THE BARMAN NOO EH! THE BIG SHOT EH! The barman backs off to the far side of the gantry – 'Nuthin mate, nuthin' he says. Giniliski and Lesa have quietened down too – 'At's awright en innit! C'mon let's fuck off oot ey here, place is fulla pricks.'

I feel stupid once we get outside – 'Ye's okay? C'mon, let's go back tae the gallery eh an see wit's happenin. Andrew'll be wunderin where ye's ur enywiy. Listen, Caroline isnae tae know aboot eny ey this okay Sacha?' I tell them.

Sacha and Lesa smile their reassurance but I've ruined the night for them. Why do all these gay guys think they can just fire in at you? Andrew's never tried to fuck me ever since we've known each other. I don't go around asking women if they want fucked do I? Fucking men. I fucking hate them at times. I mean this has to be a male thing hasn't it? Heterosexual men feel they have to proposition any woman who happens to stumble into their field of vision, their territory – 'She wis in the pub wint she? Wearin a mini skirt wint she? Askin fur it wint she?' Fucking bampots.

These gay men are doing the same fucking thing. They just move in on you no matter what you say. Oh no, you're a latent homosexual, a repressed potential fuck. I'm sick of all the faggot bullshit about that fucking life sentence – 'Oh you must have thought about it, surely.' The thing is, if you say anything, you're in denial. I'm a compulsive, obsessive, a sociopath, institutionalised. Now I'm a fucking homosexual? What is it all about? Homosexual? Heterosexual? Is sex the relationship? Sex, is that all it is? Caroline and Andrew are having a meal with some people in his studio. I look in and say hullo but head straight for our studio. Dema has transformed our old one into his studio for writing. He's reading when I look in – 'Okay Dema? Heard ye goat a joab.' I smile – 'Sounds okay, ye jist butterin rolls? Startin the morra? That's good. Get ye some cash in hand.'

Dema is a laugh. I liked him a lot. He point blank refused to work – 'No Hugh, I am a poet.' Sure Dema, whatever you say. Andrew had arranged for a job in one of the local sandwich bars to get him some cash to assist in his defection. Dema was going to defect rather than be conscripted into the army back home – 'No Hugh, I am not a soldier. I am a poet.' Dema had never had to pay a bill in his life, none of them had in fact. In Communist Russia people didn't pay rent, electricity, hot water, telephone bills. They thought everything was free in the West. Andrew was getting desperate in his efforts to support them financially. He was really at breaking point trying to make the exhibition a success and look after everyone else at the same time. Dema wasn't making matters any easier. When he hadn't shown up for work the following morning people began to panic that he had got lost in the city. The last place we looked was his bed and there he was, writing poetry – 'Andreew, it is no problem. The man loves me. I will see him later today. Does he want rolls buttered now?' he asks.

Andrew was at his wits' end finding ways to support him but the last straw came later that day. Andrew had given him about forty quid to buy food to feed himself for that week – 'God! Bloody Russians Hugh! They're driving me mad! The show will be all set for tomorrow night. It looks absolutely wonderful, and generating great publicity so let's hope nothing goes wrong now. How are you and Caroline? Everything ready for the wedding?' he asks – 'Wonderful. I'm so happy for you both. Right! Let's go for a drink! The City Cafe will do. Oh Hugh! No one will look at you, will you stop all this nonsense for goodness' sakes. You would think every gay man in the city fancies you!'

Andrew orders a drink at the bar while I find a table – 'Andrew! O'er here. Right, ta. Ye seen Dema?' I ask, smiling, looking towards the door.

– 'Palease! No Russians! I've given him money to get some food. Where's Caroline by the way? GOD!' he splutters – 'DEMA!'

Dema looks an apparition from a fifties movie. His hair is slicked back flat against his skull, and he's immaculately dressed in a white starched shirt and a black ballroom dance suit with black patent shoes. His presence brings the bar to a complete silence, apart from an odd murmur – 'Check that guy oot man!'

Andrew is staring at him in amazement – 'Dema you look fabulous . . . but where did you get those clothes and the tails?' he asks.

Dema doesn't bat an eyelid, but slips in behind the table – 'Oh, I buy clothes with the money you give me today. Is this not a beautiful suit? Do you like to wear it Hugh?' he asks.

Andrew recovers his composure – 'I don't believe this Hugh. I just don't believe this. This man is campaletely fucking mad' he exclaims – 'Campaletely fucking mad.'

I can't believe it either but there's a guy. He's moved to the end of our table, and he's staring straight at me, malevolent sneering eyes. He keeps exploding into hysterical laughter. He looks Italian, thirtyish, and fucking crazy –

'HAAAAA!' he squeals. He's staring directly at me again – 'HAAAAA!' he screeches.

That fucking laugh startles me again – 'HAAAAA!'

Andrew doesn't appear at all bothered by his antics. Who the fuck is he? Oh Jesus, he's coming over – 'HAAAAA! We can all wear big white woollen jerseys you know! HAAAAA!' he screams at me – 'HAAAAA!'

Andrew finally turns to him – 'Oh Sam, c'mon now. Hugh, this is Sam, Sam Piatricini. Sam, Hugh Collins, highly dangerous I might add' he says.

Sam looks at me – 'HAAAA!' I'm trying to be super cool, but this guy is terrifying the fucking life out of me – 'HAAAA! Have you seen his Persian Missile?' he roars.

Andrew's prick? Who is this guy? I'm lost for words – 'HAAAAA!'

The Nooky Broons are taking effect. Andrew too is getting drunker. Who can blame him? Sam appears to be on water alone – Jesus. Dema has a leading writer crawling all over him with bony nicotine stained fingers teasing and groping beneath the new suit – 'Do you like to wear my beautiful new suit?' asks Dema. Black lungs gasp – 'I'll wear wit ever ye like son.'

Shit. The *World in Action* team have walked into the bar. I try to move along a seat, pretending to be looking for someone, someone not in this company. Fuck, they've seen me.

I'm not a poof is screaming out of me. Please for fucksake, someone walk over to me, speak to me, a heterosexual macho coalman, a bricklayer will do, but please, make it a heterosexual – 'Oh, hullo Bill. Wit ye daen in here?' I ask – 'Me? Wit, ye kiddin? Am waitin fur ma wife, eh ma burd, fucksake man, am waitin oan Caroline.'

– 'HAAAAA!' the voice screams.

Bill Lyons is the chief researcher, an observer, nothing passes his eye – 'Hi Andrew. Would you like a drink?' he asks.

Andrew invites him to join the company – 'Sam, Dema, Alan, Sacha. Bill Lyons, he's filming Hugh for *World in Action*' he explains.

That Italian – 'HAAAAA! The Persian Missile should be filmed. Gone through half of Edinburgh! HAAAAA!' he's laughing.

Bill sits down, soaking up the scenario. This won't look good for my image. What will people think? Sitting here with all these poofs? – 'The film crew are meeting here at some point Hugh. We can plan tomorrow's schedule. Glasgow might be a good idea. Do that and then finish with the wedding. Oh by the way, I met up with your old arch enemy, Albert Faulds' he says.

Albert? – 'Albert! You met up wi um? Wit fur? Widdae say aboot me? Wididje want tae see um aboot? Checkin oot ma side ey the story eh?' I ask.

Bill's smile is unflinching – 'Well, yes! We are investigative journalists Hugh. Do you think we just accept every story we hear and start filming? Oh he confirmed it all, but asked why you didn't just bring all his gear back. Jack Cousins died you know. Well, apparently it was just drink. No, Albert didn't kill him. I quite liked him. I don't think he's afraid of you, but doesn't want any trouble, he's changed it seems' he says.

Jacky Collins, my brother, had told me this too. Albert changed? Doing marathons to raise money for charity causes. Still super fit and going strong. Where the fuck did I go wrong then? How can he change and I can't? How do you just stop being violent after a lifetime of being a thug?

– 'HAAAAA!'

I'm less startled this time by the barking laughter, but this guy's off the leash. Sam is on the bar, gyrating his hips and screeching – 'HAAAAA! HAAAAA! HAAAAA!'

Andrew's locked in deep conversation with the leading writer, columnist, although he himself seems locked inside a pair of dance trousers. Where the fuck am I? What am I doing in this fucking place? It's full of poofs. Bill is watching my every move. Fuck him too, fuck his documentary. I don't give a fuck what happens in jail. The Special Unit? Fuck them too. Barred? I fought for that place. And now I have been barred? My dirty diaries? Aye fuck them all.

– 'Here Bill. Am noa daen enymer filmin' I declare.

That woke him up – 'What?' he gasps.

– 'Am noa daen enymer filmin' I repeat.

Bill's all over me, whispering gently – 'Hugh, what's the problem?' he purrs.

– 'Am noa gettin paid. That's the fuckin problem. Aye, an am barred!' I state.

He tries to be even more gentle – 'Hugh, we can't pay ex lifers' he says.

– 'Well wit ye's filmin me fur? You're gettin a fee int ye? You're gettin money int ye?' I reply – 'So wit aboot me?'

Bill withdraws and stares at me before leaving. Was that an angry man's look there?

I can't quite figure it out – 'Here Andrew. Thur nae clubs through here? Am noa gaun hame. A want mer drink' I say.

A pair of legs in hot pants looms before my eyes. Andrew leers at me – 'Hugh. Meet Lillie, Lillie Bothwell. Lillie, Hugh Collins' he leers.

– 'HAAAAA! LILLIE FUCK WELL! THE HEAT SEEKING PUSSY! HAAAAA!'

Jesus Christ. This guy is relentless. I'm bursting for a piss but too afraid to move just in case he shouts something at me. I don't think I'd handle his abuse. Andrew is now head to head with sexy hot pants – 'Wit's that Andrew?' I ask.

Andrew's leaning over, grinning – 'Do you want to go to a night-club?'

– 'HAAAAA! A NIGHT-CLUB? HAAAAA!'

Oh Jesus Christ. Some cunt get this guy under control. He's sneering a malevolence into my sweating face – 'You going to FUCK the talking CUNT then MR COLLINS?' he asks – 'HAAAAA!'

I have to get out of here. I can see the door, but will my legs make it? Glasses hit the floor as I steady myself against the table. Can I make it? C'mon. That's it, one leg at time. WOOOOPPPPSSSSS! Whole table nearly went there. Ach, fuck them – 'Witsat pal? Aw sorry er, sorry. ANDREW! AL BE BACK UP! OKAY? HAAAA! FUCK YOU!' I roar at Sam – 'HAAAAA!'

Sam and I later become great friends – still terrifies me though.

Caroline's handing me an Alka Seltzer – 'Ta. Time'd a get back tae the gallery Ca?' I ask.

– 'Oh quite early. You wanted to go to a club with Andrew. You could hardly stand. I carried you up the stairs. No, you were all right. No, you were laughing but going on about prison all night, until I put you to bed. Andrew was in this morning but he's out with the Russians. Everything's ready for tonight. Oh, you'll be fine, just have a long lie' she says.

The long lies in bed are becoming more frequent, the hangovers worsening. I hate drink, but there's nothing else. I never know how it's going to hit me. Sometimes it's white wine, but mostly it's these Newcastle Browns, Nooky Broons, Mad Dogs. I can't bear the taste, but you can't go to a pub and ask for a glass of white wine, definitely not on your own, you would be taken for a poof. They blow me away but what do you do?

A Martini please, and a pair of knickers!

No, I'll stick to the pints, real men's stuff, a bevvie, blootered – SHE WIS ASKIN FUR IT! Caroline hands me a coffee – 'Remember to call your mum Hugh' she says.

My Ma. I'd better tell her about the wedding. I'd forgotten.

I dread them coming but have to ask. Caroline's family will be there. I can't bear the thought of all the in your face socialism being fired at them because of their middle-class background. It just pours out of her like poison whenever she meets something she doesn't understand – 'Post natal stress? That's fur the middle classes. A loada fuckin crap if ye ask me.'

God. Why is she so fucking angry?

I suppose I should call her right now, get it over with. We've hardly spoken since my release. They don't call – and I won't be controlled any longer. A Mexican stand off. Well, here we go, it's ringing – 'That you Ma? It's me, Shooey. Sorry av noa phoned but . . .' I say.

– 'Humph . . . Ye signed oan yet?' she asks.

No, please, please don't do this to me – 'Ma, look, honest, am sorry. Av jist been. Am gettin merried the morra. Gonny come through Ma? Please Ma . . .'

I feel tears fill my eyes – 'Am afraid yer Ma's goat ur wurk tae go tae. Alex and Jim ur wurkin aw day. They'll be knackered tae' she says blandly – 'Am afraid we canny be afforded the luxury a takin time aff wurk.'

I put the receiver down, bury my tears in the pillows – 'Nae bother en Ma. See ye eh' I say.

I dry my face. The bastards, I think. That's the last time I call. I hope she fucking dies. I hope they all fucking die. My fuckin Da as well, him especially.

DIE YA BASTARDS!

This is my home now, and this is my family. I'll never make any contact ever again, I swear, never again. They can tell people whetever the fuck they like, fuck them too. C'mon get a grip, I tell myself. Get up. Don't let them do this to you. You're free now remember? You can do whatever you want.

They bombed *you* out, remember?

That's right, they bombed me out. At least I have a bed here. That's more than they ever offered.

I'd had to sleep on the floor during my home leaves. Alec too fucking selfish to offer a bed for a night to the Big Bruvva.

No, that's it this time, no more calls to them. Caroline and Andrew are my family. I'm finished with that mob through there. Her and her fucking boyfriends. That Jim Smith trying to do his daddy figure 'Noo Hughie. Ur ye oan smack son?'

Son? You're just *fucking* my Ma. *You're* the fucking lodger. I remembered his face that day – 'Wit? Wit if a am Jim? Wit the fucks it goat tae dae wi you? A kin blow ma fuckin brains oot if a want, it's nuthin tae dae wi you' I'd said to him.

The fucking headcase. You on smack? Son? Where's that fucking shaving gear? I'm getting up. Fuck this. Lying here fucked up – 'Caroline! Didye collect that new suit fae Smith's?'

The Mansfield Church foyer is tightly packed with loads of people when we arrive for the Russian exhibition – 'Angels Over the Ukraine'. The Russians are stunning, every one a star! The paintings look really amazing on the church walls with the famous murals above painted by Phoebe Traquair. One painting in particular is magnificent. It is of a black horse rearing on hind legs, giving the viewer the impression of being below, looking upwards from underneath the horse. The head of the stallion transforms itself into the head of God. All around the head are tiny wispy angels blowing horns. The artist had been a lover of Caroline's in Russia. She had been the real link with Soviet and western artists. Oleg Gholisy had died in a tragic accident just days before the others had come to Edinburgh. Giniliski had been his closest friend. Oleg's works to me were by far the best I had ever come across but this one especially had transfixed me, he'd called the work *Adagio*. He had wanted his paintings to fly, and fly they did. Andrew and Caroline had hired a rig which carried the paintings across the floor, floating towards you, from almost invisible wire threads. The effect looked like angels swooping down from the heavens. Oleg's paintings *are* angels.

Andrew's voice boomed from the pulpit, of all places – 'I would like to welcome all of you to the exhibition!'

He's in full form, magnificent. There is only one Andrew Brown, I smiled to myself. The Fallen Angel box was lit up, directly behind him, just over the altar. Old Lucifer himself would have been proud of his speech – 'Most of all, enjoy!' he roared.

The wave of the hand signalled that the show was now open. The hall, filled with the artists and friends, felt amazing, like walking on air. The coolness of these fashionable people, all in one room together, left me breathless – 'Wow! Fuckin brilliant! This is absolutely amazin!'

I turned to find this beautiful tall lady, dressed in see through fabric, gliding down the steps from the altar. Liz Rankin, a former ballet dancer. Now doing performance art. She had a huge thick dildo strapped on to her hips. Alan Scott Moncrief's handsome face behind her, clad in skintight black leather, chains, slithered, almost explosively, in pure sexuality. Sophie, another girl, appeared to be shedding silk fabrics, dropping them to the floor, one by one, until she was naked.

Together, they flowed, melted into the packed hall. I've never seen anything like this in my life. The sound of voices rang through the hall, like the sound of chandeliers, cheerful ringing noises and glasses chinking.

The Male Nurse band began to rumble, their instruments like some weird awakening, screeched into a mass of twisted burning wire, with strings stretching dangerously to breaking point.

Keith, the lead singer, burst through the middle of their peaks before the band finally let the throttle go, breaking down just as it had begun, one by one, until silently, they just walked away, melting into the crowd.

– 'Hugh! Hugh!' Shirley's shouting and waving, the big blonde hair, flying around in a mane – 'Hugh! You've been summoned! John Smith wants to see you!'

Jesus. John Smith's the next prime minister. He wants to see *me*? Has Shirley had too much to drink or something?

I look at her puzzled – 'Me? Wit fur? Is there sumthin wrang?' Caroline, I knew, was a friend of his wife, Elizabeth. I had never met either of them. What is this all about? I wondered.

Shirley drags me by the arm – 'C'mon Hugh. He's a lovely man! Ye-ees! He wants to meet you!' she's shouting – 'C'mon!'

John Smith's beaming face is smiling at me 'Hugh! Elizabeth and I are insulted that we haven't been invited to your wedding!' he beams.

I find myself half bowing, terrified to put my hand forward – 'Oh, ehm, well you are, Mr Smith. But don't come because all the tabloids know about it. John Major might use it' I say.

He looked at me, bemused – 'John Major? Oh, poor old John. He'd shoot himself in the foot' he laughs.

I shift around, one foot to the other. I feel lost for words. I don't want to bring dirt to this man's private life – 'This is my lovely wife, Elizabeth!' he says.

I almost genuflect before her to kiss her hand – 'Oh eh, hullo' I mumble.

She's a strong but gentle looking woman, her face and eyes smile warmly at me – 'I hope you're coping then?' she asks.

These people don't have to talk to ex-cons, lifers. Their kindness touches me, reaches inside me – 'Eh aye, eh, yes' I reply.

Caroline appears by my side; lets me back off discreetly, bowing all the way, with a smile that doesn't hurt my face.

– 'Andrew! Andrew!' I whisper excitedly – 'John Smith jist

spoke tae me! Honest! A jist met um! Ey said, eh, said eh, the weddin an aw that. He said *hullo*! Tae *me*!'

Andrew feels illuminated by some invisible energy force. He's coasting – 'Oh Hugh! isn't this absolutely wonderful I'm so happy for you to be here with all these people! John Smith is a wonderful man! They both are! Oh Hugh!' he shouts – 'Get Caroline Hugh! Lets make a toast together!'

Caroline, Caroline, my beautiful wee missus. She looks absolutely stunning – 'Aye! A think ey wants the three ey us tae make a toast!' I tell her – 'C'mon, es o'er here.' We hug each other, kiss and hug all over again. This is a special moment for me. To be in the company of these two very special people – 'Cheers!'

Auld Cathy, how I wish she could be here, how I wish she could just see me, for once not in trouble.

I don't know how I manage but no matter how drunk I am, I somehow always manage to fold my trousers, hang my jacket and shirt, even my shoes. Prison habits are much more complicated than people imagine. I don't know if this is one from prison or just another neurosis, like the incessant cleaning and tidying, the drive to establish order, which is actually disorder. I've caught myself tidying something just tidied. In jail my cell was empty but for a steel bed. This was to make sure they couldn't read me, but I somehow managed to find something in an empty cell, something that wasn't just the right way, something needing moved. Now there's magic. Paul Daniels couldn't even do that, find something in an empty cell. The habit was the shifting.

My life is habit.

Andrew and Caroline are in his studio with lots of other artists – 'I need a holiday to recover my energy' he's saying – 'What a night! Morning Hugh! What did you think of the opening?' he asks – 'Yes I agree, it was a success. We did it Caroline! We did it against all the odds!'

There is no stopping this guy, he thrives on pressure. Caroline on the other hand is a cool, composed creature – 'Hi how are you?' she asks – 'Coffee? Oh we're just going over last night. Bill Lyons called. Someone from their end is coming to see you later today. They're in a panic about the filming.'

Andrew can't believe that they are not going to pay me – 'Tell them to pay Caroline!' he shouts.

That's an idea, but I want to push the issue. People want the story, the work, whatever, but it's always this shit about paying ex-criminals. What have I to do? Go through my life working on stone and never be paid? How am I supposed to pay for material? It never ends, all this nonsense about rehabilitation. I'm physically out, but they're not finished with me yet – 'Oh, Julian Spalding will meet you next week about the Christ statue' he continues – 'I think he'll buy it you know. I've told him sixteen thousand, a thousand for each year in prison. I hope you don't mind.'

Caroline believes the statue should be part of the works in the Museum of Religious Art in Glasgow. Spalding is the director of Glasgow Museums and Art Galleries – 'It should be there, where it has a place' she says – 'I mean, the Special Unit is part of the culture in Glasgow. The Christ statue was an amazing feat for someone in prison with no formal education or experience in art. The Museum should be proud to have such a work but in that context, religious culture.'

Andrew has been financially wiped out by the exhibition. The gallery too I discover is on its last legs, having had no financial support from the Scottish Arts Council.

I had no idea things were so pressing. Andrew's laughing – 'Hugh, I'm quite sure we could do with your assistance, don't you have any old friends in Glasgow? Oh, just a couple of bank robbers would be fine!'

Caroline pulls her jumper up over her face – 'Right! It's

a stick up!' She's up with the invisible gun now. We're all roaring with laughter – 'What do you say? Right! Hand over the money! Doof! Doof!' she laughs.

I can't stop laughing at her antics. Doof. Doof? What is that? I ask. She puts up her fists and comes at me with a Glasgow accent – 'Al doof ye up ya bampot ye!'

The place is in hysterics, but there are pressures. Andrew says he's more tired than anything else – 'No, it's not purely financial' he explains – 'We could meet that front. We're all just worn out Hugh. This has been our lives. India!' he roars – 'I'm going to India! Caroline! Could you look up the flights and things. God! I'm so tired but we did it didn't we!'

The Scottish Office should consider itself fortunate that this guy didn't turn a hand to crime. He'd have taken any jail I'd ever been in, shagged the place twice as they say in there – 'Oh don't look so glum Hugh. We're not talking tomorrow. I mean we have much more work to show for goodness sake' he states – 'Now! While we're all here. Tomorrow's Hugh's stag night.'

He roars with laughter – 'I can just see all Hugh's friends. Coming through here from Glasgow to have a stag night in a gay night-club!'

I do a double take. A gay night-club? – 'What? Of course I am Hugh! Where did you think we were going? The bloody rugby club or something!'

Why not? What am I so fucking uptight about? – 'Anyway, you love all the attention! Caroline! Honestly, he is unfortunately heterosexual but what a big flirt with the men! Glasgow hard man? Indeed!'

Chapter Seven

ANDREW DID ARRANGE the stag night, in a gay club – with all his gay friends. I couldn't believe it at first, but then again, so what? The Russians all seem androgenous amid the wee harshly pinched gay faces of Scotland – 'Well, it makes a change fae aw the jail hash parties, fulla murdururs eh?' I say in agreement.

Caroline doesn't bat an eyelid – 'Oh you'll be fine, just don't get too drunk. You can't handle it, and get too aggressive. What? Oh yes you do! I'm the one on the receiving end so don't give me that Hugh Collins!' she says.

I laugh reassuringly, saying – 'Al be fine s'long as ma arse stays in wan piece.'

She smiles – 'Well, it'll be in safe hands!'

She's quick – 'Gettin wide McNairn? Here. Al jist stick oan ma denims the night. Ma suit an that ready fur the morra?' I ask – 'Wit ur you wearin? A dress? V'never seen ye in a skirt huv a? Wit's that?'

She wants to know if my family are coming to the wedding – 'Naw Caroline, thur noa cumin. Ach, she said sumthin aboot huvin sumthin already arranged. Alec? Naw, he canny make it either, eh, wurkin ur sumthin. Eh? Naw, naibdy fae ma side'll be there but ach well' I say – 'Here! Wer ur you gaun the night by the way? Don't want ye's turnin up at oor party. Well, ye never kin tell kin ye? Suppoased tae be bad luck ye know! Lorraine and Shirley gaun there tae?' I ask.

Caroline and her friends are going somewhere special, a

restaurant and on to a night-club – 'Naw a don't mind where ye go. Lorraine's brand new, Shirley as well so don't be daft. Goan huv a good laugh, might be yer last! Merried eh! A canny believe it! A wis always tellin the guys in the jail *never* tae get merried when they goat oot as well! Wit a fuckin cheek!' I laugh – 'Na a luv you, that's the difference. Yer a wee bam, but a luv ye!'

I dodge the flying shoe – 'Right! Al see ye the morra then! Wit's that church called? Hauw! Don't throw that! Am only kiddin – Mansfield Church. Right, okay, huv a good night the girra wi yer pals an al see ye at the altur. Geeza wee kiss afora go. See ye the morra Caroline!' I say waving goodbye – 'See ye in the mornin hen.'

Millionaire's is in Niddrie Street – a dark lane. The muscle bound bouncer on the door is covered in tattoos under his leather waistcoat. He won't let us inside. Andrew is losing his patience – 'We are a stag party for goodness sakes! WHAT? NO! WE JUST WANT TO HAVE A BLOODY DRINK!' he's shouting.

I push forward – 'Wit the fuck's happenin man? We gettin in?' I ask.

The bouncer backs into the wall – 'Sorry! Sorry there! A didny ken it wis you! Listen jist go in, thurs nae problem, honest!' he stammers – 'In ye go mate!'

I'm as puzzled as Andrew – 'You don't know him Hugh? Well, he certainly knows you, or of you. Wonderful, absolutely wonderful, just what we needed!' he laughs.

Pink suits and black leather fill a dry-iced alcove – 'Champagne! Hugh, champagne?' he's asking – 'Champagne?'

Andrew knows how to spend. His extravagance knows no bounds – 'A Nooky Broon? Hugh you must be joking! O well, if you insist! All right everyone, a toast! To Russia! The 369! To Hugh and Caroline!' he says, raising his glass – 'Cheers everyone!'

– 'CHEEEEEEEEEEEERRRRRRRRRRSSSSSSSSSS!'

Six Nooky Broons later, I'm on the floor, dancing like a maniac, surrounded by young men. One of them is black, called Alf. Is this a guy? Is it a lesbian? I mean, Alf? The dykes all call themselves Alf, don't they? I can't tell if this is a man or a woman that is dancing with me. Who the fuck cares – check that arse! – 'R'you a burd big yin?' I ask.

Brilliant white teeth flash back – 'Only one way to find out isn't there?' he grins, or is it she grins?

Is this a man or a woman? That difference has been blurred by booze, dance music and sexual urges. Isn't this what men always say when they get captured with their hands down the wrong pants – 'A wis steamin! A didny noa it wis a guy!'

Alf is becoming blurrier and blurrier. That tight arse is grinding itself into my groin . . . Full, black lips are on my neck, nibbling wetly at my ear – 'C'mon, come with me. I'll suck you' they're whispering – 'Let me suck your cock.'

There's a tongue probing my tonsils, fondling hands, unzipping my jeans – 'O-ohhh.' I feel those *tight* buttocks, but then . . . those balls – 'Fu-uck!'

I yelp – 'Jesus!'

I pull back from . . . *him*, holding the guilty hand in the air – 'Aw fucksake man! Euchh!'

I continue yelping – 'Euchh! S'a paira fuckin baws!'

Andrew has gone with the others, left me on my own, stagging – 'Here Alf! D'ye wanta pint?' I ask – 'Na, don't be daft, everyhins okay man. Me? Ye fuckin kiddin! Am gettin merried the morra!'

Alf's asking if I know Andrew – 'Aye. Andrew Brown? That bastard. Na, av known um fur years. Naw am jist oot efter a lifer' I explain – 'Witsat? Aye, sixteen stretch. Wit? Naw, listen, don't start aw that fuckin shite. Am noa a poof awright? Furfucksake man. Leave it oot wull ye, fuckin hell man. Naw, naw, it's awright' I laugh.

He's okay, doesn't get uptight at all with me, a nice guy in fact – 'Listen Alf. D'ye want anura pint en?' I ask – 'S'noa bad in here innit? Apart fae aw they poofs an at. Well, you're awright. A thoat ye wur a burd man! Aye! Fucksake eh! Anyway, am headin off' I say – 'Av git a weddin the morra. Here see ma burd by the way? Bran new, aw a wee diamond. Dead laid back an at, noa wit a mean man? Witsat? Aye, nae bother, am off anywiy, see ye again okay mate.'

God I feel wasted but yeah what a stag night. Andrew you old devil you, exposing me to my own homophobia. All those hidden terrors when my old wanked out dick would simply refuse to jump to attention – 'Arrggghhh! Am a poof!'

Men. Here. Who's that blue chinned face squinting at me from the bar? I wonder – A face from prison? He's too clean cut for an ex-con, a straight peg.

Now this *is* male without a doubt. No blurred tight buttocks here.

No, this is decaying white once upon a time bum flesh, hanging together inside tweed trousers, probably bunched up into a ball of dough, a bluebottle trying to escape.

He doesn't look comfortable. That too-tight collar neck stretching men do. Scanning the bar in case someone recognises them.

This is 'I'm straight' poof antics but the face? I know the face but from where? Jesus he's doing that fly squinting again. Oh, oh. Here he comes – 'It's Collins isn't it?' he asks gruffly.

I do the best bricklayer voice I can muster – 'Aye. How?' Ohho. Eddie Campbell. No let me rephrase that – GOVERNOR Eddie Campbell – 'Oh hullo. Wit ye daen in here?' I ask.

That too-tight collar almost chokes him. He splutters out, but, authoritatively mind you – 'Hummpphh! I'm meeting my grandfather! What are *you* doing in a place like this then?' he states.

Oh I see – 'Tryin tae nip a rent boay! Seen any yersel *Eddie*?' I ask.

– 'What? I *am* waiting for my grandfather!' he splutters.

Aye Eddie right – 'Och take it easy. Think am gonny run tae the *News ey the Wurld*?' I ask, laughing.

He physically comes apart before my eyes – 'You know that Ferris! I locked him up in Shotts!' he wails. Jesus, he's in tears – 'He left my sister, in the middle of a road with her legs broken! The little bastard!'

I look at him – 'Ferris? Know the name but . . . Ye still in the prison service?' I ask.

He clutches his drink – 'No I . . . retire . . . had a nervous breakdown' he gasps.

I buy him a drink but there's no more gossip coming my way – 'Time's yer granda due *Eddie*?' I ask – 'Am headin off. Merried the morra. Naw don't be daft. Why would a want tae tell any cunt ad met ye in a gay bar? Might think am a poof tae. Al see ye again' I say, waving – 'Cheerio.'

The homing device in my brain somehow delivers me back to the gallery, unharmed, but drunkish. I have a few hours to pull myself together, get shaved, showered, and dressed.

Andrew looks into the studio – 'Where have you been? Looking at stars? God! Thank goodness you're back! You were going mad on the dance floor. No! No! We tried to get you home, but you were having none of it. Incidentally, did you . . . Oh never mind, c'mon we don't have much time!' he says, rushing around – 'C'mon hurry!'

Time? There's something about time out here. I have no sense of time at all. I keep thinking when it gets dark that it's nine o clock – lock up in jail time. A few hours later I think it's still nine o clock. I become trapped in a time warp where it's nine all night. Then the sudden change in the sky throws me into a state of panic, that I have to be somewhere, that I'm late for something. I keep expecting a light to be switched off to signal that it's time to put down that book, to finish that joint, to prepare for that next day of jail, but out here there's no light, no next day, no time – I'm free.

Andrew's back in again – 'Hugh! Come onnn. The taxi's waiting! Yes! Yes! Yes! The suit looks fine. You look fabulous! Now come on!' he's calling – 'Hurry!'

We make it to the church with just ten minutes before the ceremony. The church has been searched three times for tabloid journalists. I down three whiskies in a bar just across the road before heading back – 'Cheers mate! Here we go.'

I'm suddenly standing at the deconsecrated altar, looking straight ahead – *You're not in court. Relax. You're standing to attention. This is a minister, not a judge.*

Scott Marshall, the minister marrying us, is speaking – 'Do you, Hugh Collins, take this woman, Caroline McNairn, as your lawful wedded wife?'

The Lucifer light box is directly above his head, clashing with his bearded image and religious garments. The heat from burning candles, the burnt fragrance of incense, is filling the air, creating atmosphere, elation – 'I do' I say.

Caroline is beautiful. Those huge brown eyes, filled with light, looking at me, smiling at me. Her presence brings tranquillity into the ceremony, her little voice – 'I do.' My hands trembling as I put the ring on her finger – 'I now pronounce you man and wife' says the minister.

Caroline's tears, damp, wet on my cheek – 'A luv ye' I whisper as we hug. Andrew's hugging me now, bringing me round again – 'Congratulations Hugh. Oh Caroline. I'm so happy for you. Shirley too is crying – 'Oh Hugh, look after her' she whispers.

My dizziness begins to clear – 'Caroline, we better let the guests in. Ma wee missus, eh, Mrs Collins!' we laugh – 'Mr n Mrs Collins!'

Koscha puts two beautiful hats on our heads – 'Karolyne, Hugh these are my wedding gift to you. They bring luck to the future for you.' He then punches a huge fist on my chest. – 'You will look after leetle Karolyne. Yes? She very special friend to Russians' he growls.

I'm overwhelmed, tears filling my eyes – 'Aye Koscha. Al look after ur' I promise. Caroline and I greet guests as the old church fills with friends, and other people from both our lives. Anne Goring kisses me on the cheek – 'Anne? Jesus!' I haven't seen her in years. Jane McAllister lifts me off my feet – 'Oh Hugh, I'm happy for you. You old devil!' Jane and I had been lovers, and had become great friends, an amazingly warm, loving woman – 'Aw Jane. Thanks fur cumin pal.' I smile – 'Thanks pal.'

I feel a rush, a surge – I'm really out, free from that whole culture of hidden pain.

The *World in Action* film crew are here too, hanging around, waiting for opportunities, watching for a unique shot.

Bill Lyons hands me a crate of expensive champagne – 'Compliments of Jimmy Boyle Mr Collins!' he says.

I take the opportunity to explain the situation – 'Bill listen. Nae cameras oan Jimmy. He disnae want eny publicity so leave um alane okay? Tell the crew the score tae so thurs nae misunderstandins. A don't want um thinkin av set um up okay?' I say.

Bill's like a detective, never stops analysing, never stops asking questions, examining each and every detail – 'He farted? What did it smell like? How did it sound? Loud? Were you in close proximity? How close? A foot? Two feet? Closer? How close? An inch? Two inches? Three?'

He's at it now – 'Did Jimmy say that? When? Where? Why? In Bannerman's? That a bar? What kind of bar? You met him there? When? Why?'

OH FUCK OFF BILL!

Caroline's parents arrive with her sister and brother. Drew's family are here too, Susan, his wife, and their son Stewart. Caroline's mother asks me – 'How are you then Hugh? Are you coping?' Caroline's father quietly observes the murals. He seems more interested in art than in people – 'Hi Hugh. It's a wonderful setting, don't you think? How's Ca coping then?' he asks.

My family's absence is conspicuously obvious, and shamefully embarrassing. I mean, almost everyone here knows them. What do you say to people – 'Oh. They couldn't be here tonight.' None of them? At my wedding?

Someone bumps into me, it's Jimmy – 'Oh sorry there. Oh hi Jimmy! Thanks Jimmy, thanks fur comin, an the champagne. Wit'sat? Naw, she coodny make it' I say. Bill manifests by our sides. Spotlights and cameras zooming in from nowhere. They have been waiting for the moment, the two of us together – 'Here Bill! Fucksake man. A thoat a told ye, nae fuckin cameras! Wit's this?' I shout.

Jimmy launches straight into a spiel – 'What I'd like to talk about is the decline of the Special Unit' he's saying.

I'm taken by surprise but try to focus – 'Oh aye, Wullie Bennett' I echo.

He doesn't pause for breath – 'Well, there was more than one guy there' he says.

What? More than one guy? What's that supposed to mean? Oh I get it. The decline is being put down to me now. Jimmy's *the* only success story and all that. Fuck me. He's trying to discredit me, at my own wedding? Bill joins me at a distance, watching the performance – 'Didje hear that? A goat left wi that cunt Bennett! *He* waits tae es *oot* an *en* publishes that daft Pain a Confinement?' I say – 'A ended up knockin that cunt oot because ey *his* fuckin book. Wee sparras sittin oan the windae an aw that? A huda five year battle wi cons, defendin him an noo it's aw ma fault? Dae ye see wit a mean noo Bill?' I ask.

Bill's smiling – 'Interesting' he smiles.

His assistant researcher joins us – 'Man's an egomaniac! He can't stop talking about himself' he laughs – 'I wouldn't worry about it, won't be shown. Oh, by the way, did you know we have shown your diaries to *Granta* magazine? No? Well, Bill Buford's coming to see you about doing something with them' he says – 'Yeah, they're literary publishing. Yeah, Bill's looking forward to meeting you, fascinated with the diaries.'

I feel stifled – 'Bill, al be ootside. A need fresh air, al huv a fag.'

A huge bunch of flowers are walking towards me as I leave. A head pops round from behind them – 'Are you Hugh Collins?' it asks.

Three tabloids journalists have been thrown out already, found hiding up in the clerestory above the murals, trying to get photographs. The flowers hardly disguise this one – 'Naw mate, he's in there. Daen an interview. Guy wi the black silk jaikit. He's gaun grey. Denims an a tee shurt. Looks a bit like Boyle. Aye, nae borra mate. Yer fae the *Sun*? Magic!' I laugh.

When I return from the fresh air, the man who changed is *still* giving it the decline of the Special Unit to the camera lens – wonder if he's at the bit about the helicopter? I have to laugh, a helicopter? What for? Going for the morning papers – 'Be back in a moment darling, there's some news of my wonderful life in the *Sun*!' WHOOOOOSH. Caroline's parents I find looking at the murals – 'Early nineteenth century. Oh hi Hugh' her dad's saying. This man lives and breathes art from every pore. His whole life has been art in every sense.

Caroline's mum takes my arm – 'Goodness Hugh! What a noise!' she exclaims.

The Male Nurse? What are they doing here? Who let them

in? This is our wedding! They have revved up that inimitable sound – 'HERE! KEITH! KEEEEEE . . .' I roar.

The music collapses into a faint screech – 'Hi Hugh! Eh?' he asks – '*You* invited us! The Ukrainian Show? Remember? Said we were brilliant?'

I look to the floor – 'Oh aye, ehm, at's right. Well, ehm kin ye keep it doon the noo eh? Caroline's parents ur here. A mean ur Da's eighty odds. Aye, later oan. Aye, at's nae problem' I say.

Phew!

Caroline has a surprise – 'Hugh! Shirley's given us the key to her flat, for two weeks! We can have our honeymoon there! Yes, it's in Leith!' she exclaims.

Oh Caroline, how I'd love to have given you more, how I hate to land you with an ex-con, a murderer.

Leith? Well, Leith's as good as any other place. There's the docks, there's the shore, and the people – 'Great Ca! Tell ur thanks! S'thur a telly? Brulliant! We kin jist stay in bed aw day an watch the telly the gither aw night! A real double bed tae?' I ask – 'Fuckin excellent! A real bed fur two whole weeks. Naibdy chappin the door, jist the two ey us, fancy sneakin away jist noo?' I suggest – 'Av had enough. Your parents ur leavin in a wee while. Let the rest ey the guests dae wit they want efter that, okay?' Caroline agrees – 'Yes, they're fine. I'll just let them know that we're going to leave, in case things begin to get a bit wilder. You never know what will happen. Andrew's been fantastic hasn't he, but he'll want to have fun, and you know what that can lead to. No, he's been wonderful, hasn't he? Lets thank people for coming, then leave. It has gone well hasn't it? How do you feel being married then?' she asks.

I hug her – 'Yer ma wee wife McNairn. Aye, it's been great eh? In Glesga, the square gos usually start aboot noo. Ye kiddin? Ye canny huv a weddin withoot aw the men gettin the shirts aff fur square gos roon a backcourt! Aye, honest!' I laugh.

We eventually disengage, and head off into the night to begin our honeymoon, down in Leith.

Shirley's place is a one bedroom flat with an inside toilet and a bath. The 369 toilets have one shower in the ladies, situated on the cold, draughty stairs of the second floor landing. That desperate trip during the night is often jeopardised by the endless procession of subterranean pale white faces and fluorescent orange hair prowling the gallery for crash out space. Shirley's bathroom has soft carpeted floor, the toilet seat covered in pink fabric, bottled blue bubble bath, lilac-perfumed scented salts, plastic liquid-filled jars, huge bouncy sponges and soaps – 'Caroline! Am gonny be in here a wee while! Jist in case ye need the toilet ur enahin awrite?' I shout.

Caroline transfixes herself to the televison, watching soaps and chat shows without a word. I emerge two hours later looking like a freshly boiled lobster – 'Aw Jesus. Wit a bed eh? That's the best bath av hud in years ye know. Dae ye fancy gaun fur a wee walk? Huv a drink ur sumthin? Eh? Dae ye fancy . . . Hauw! McNairn! Ye wi us? The planet earth calling Caroline McNairn!' I laugh.

Caroline looks up, startled – 'Oh, sorry, sorry. Yeah, we could go for a walk along the shore, it's such a wonderful evening. I'll pop in, have a quick bath. Did you leave the water in?' she asks.

The Shore Bar is packed inside, but has tables and chairs dotted around outside, near the water's edge. We find a table and order a bottle of champagne – 'This is amazing isn't it Hugh?' she says.

This is the first time we have been alone in weeks – 'Aye Caroline. It's great jist sittin here innit. A feel as if wur in anuther country, know wit a mean?' I reply.

Her face is smiling at me contentedly – 'Yes Hugh, I do

know what you mean. One day we will go abroad' she says – 'Travel together to Russia and to New York. Chicago's fantastic. You will love it there, meet all my friends. I love travelling. Yes, I've been to most places with my work, but I've always loved Russia. You'll love the Russians. Yeah, one day we'll go there together.'

The blinding twinkling sunlight bouncing from the water turns her blonde hair to gold, her rich gentle voice melting into me – 'Are you happy Hugh?' she asks.

Happy? I don't know where I am. I don't have the words – 'S'like bein in the movies ur sumthin. As if am dreamin this is happenin. A don't even know how long av been oot' I say – 'A keep thinkin al wake up in a jail bed. Aye, fancy walkin back tae the flat? Am beginnin tae feel a bit cauld noo tae. S'been good cumin doon here innit? It's quieter an calm tae. Nae bampots in yer face aw night. Aye, we kin lie in bed an watch the telly eh?'

The huge double bed makes a change from the mattress on the floor. I roll from side to side across the broad span – 'Magic! Av noa slept in wan this size fur a long time! Here listen. The late film's cumin oan, fancy watchin it? Aye, the bold Norman Bates! *Psycho*!' I laugh.

Caroline throws me sometimes – 'Oh Hugh, no! I don't like these films, psychopaths and all that. They scare me, give me nightmares' she says.

I look at her – 'Sykapaths? Caroline, yer in bed wi wan' I say.

After a few days, the tiny flat begins to creep up on me, the walls close in, furniture is crushing me. I'm tripping over things constantly, banging into table lamps, elbowing wardrobes. I can barely breathe – 'Wit the fuck is this!' I kick bedding, shoes, clothes out of my path – 'Fuck! Get me tae fuck ootey here!' I feel trapped by things, barely able to move – 'Caroline! Get this fuckin stuff! Get the fuckin door open!' She pulls me out into the stairs. My breath? What's wrong? I'm hyperventilating – 'Hugh! I have you! Calm down! Breathe slowly! Calm down! That's it. You're all right. Slow down. That's it, slowly, nice and slow, relax now, you're all right' she's saying.

I sit on the stair, sweating and shaking – 'Jesus. That fuckin place. A canny go back in there. Fuck Shirley. Wur gaun back tae the gallery Caroline. A canny go back in that fuckin place. A don't know wit happened there. Aw that fuckin stuff lyin aw o'er the place, an they stupit fuckin lamps' I moan.

Caroline is laughing as we head back home to the gallery – 'Goodness I thought you were having a heart attack! All that shouting and swearing!' She mimics my accent – 'Karaline! Fuckin, fuckin! Al batter that fuckin wardrobe! Am fuckin tellin ye! Oh! What are we going to do with you Hugh Collins?' she sighs.

Shirley's fine, but obviously concerned – 'God! What happened?' she asks.

Caroline believes I've had a panic attack – 'Yes, the same thing happened one day on Princes Street. I had to get him into a lane and calm him down' I hear her explain. Princes Street. I remember that day. All those daft umbrellas poking me in the face, in the eyes, streams of people rushing blindly, banging straight into each other.

I had felt the same then too, people, brollies, heavy bags, parcelled boxes, like waves coming at me. I'd begun pushing the brollies first to get them away from my eyes. At first I'd tried to step constantly aside, but no matter, something was rammed into me. Caroline'd been startled by the first burst of pushing back, but when I began throwing people out of my way she grabbed me – 'Hugh! Hugh! What are you doing?' I threw brolly holders off the pavement. I knee'd a head-down barger in the balls – 'Agghhh!' My hand locked on a throat, snarling – 'FUCKKKKKK OFFFFFFFFFF!'

Caroline steered me into an empty lane – 'Hugh! For Godsake! Calm down!' she was shouting – 'Calm down!'

I didn't know what had happened – 'Fucksake! Cunts jist fuckin walkin right intae me! Fuckin ignorant bastarts! Widnae last two fuckin minutes in the fuckin jail! Fucksake a kin hardly fuckin breathe man!' My breathing is laboured, trapped in my chest, like an asthmatic – 'Fucksake Caroline. Am wringin wi sweat. Look at ma hauns, a canny stoap shakin man' I'd said.

Shirley's helpful – 'Oh, I'm so sorry Caroline. I hadn't realised. I just wanted the two of you to have some space together' she says.

Poor Shirley – 'Naw don't be daft Shirley. It wis great doon there, honest! We went doon tae the shore wan night, an watched the telly maist ey the time. It's noa the size ey the flat, it's me' I explain – 'Same thing happened at ma maw's wan time. It's the furniture, it jist seems tae get bigger an bigger tae a canny breathe. Naw, honest the flat wis bran new, we hud a good time an that big bed! Oh well, wul noa go intae aw that then, but naw, it wis great tae get away fur a few days, an anywiy, we kin huv a honeymoon later so nae problem' I assure her.

She seems more reassured – 'Oh by the way, Hugh. There was a call for you from the film people. Bill Buford's coming to see you. He's the editor of *Granta* magazine. He said he's flying up next week' she says.

Chapter Eight

I'M RELIEVED TO be back in the security of the gallery. I enjoy walking around but can't bear the aggression out here. The faces, the fashions and attitudes fascinate me but I think my brain has been moving in a different direction to most people. In prison and other institutional systems, internal values develop, cultures are established, shaped by the nature of the regime. People do become different through time, they adapt to survive in whatever environment they happen to find themselves, or perish. In prison people become more acutely aware of themselves and their environment, developing paranoid anxieties, psuedo personalities, reputations, and images. I've developed in an alternate environment, and become super sensitive to things that have no place in the real world. I worry about always fitting into situations, making everything normal, perfect, orderly, square, controlled. I explode when it goes wrong. What am I going to do out here? Am I too old to change? Do I have the energy? I *have* to change if I am to survive. It's funny, all those years in there thinking – 'Jist wait tae am oot. Then al *really* enjoy maself!' All that time, wasted, squandered. I projected a future, lived there, in a non-existent place, manufactured in my head, while real life passed me by in a flash. And now? Right now? At forty seven I'm beginning to live in the past, in a series of selected memories, those sepia tinted good old bad days, the ones that have pleasant endings. Just waiting to enjoy myself doesn't exist here. No, I've abandoned that old future. Now I'm in danger of looking back, of living in the past, living another life in my head. The future for me now holds dread, decay, and death. I don't want to live there any more, I don't want to look forward, thinking – 'Jist wait an *then*!'

No, I try to focus in the present, in *now*, but this feeble, deteriorating, forty seven year old brain doters on memories, on the past – 'Aye, a kin remember the time when . . .'

Writing too poses this problem: manufactured futures, and interpretations of the past. I mean, you can't write about the future unless it's fictional, and most historical books or biographical works are an interpretation of the past. You can't actually write in the present tense, it's an impossibility. We all live in that little world of tomorrow which is merely a fiction, a projection of something better than today.

God. Why did I let myself get involved in all this? I've let myself be trapped, tied to a machine, interpreting my own memories, my own muddled up past. What happened to all that – 'Wait tae a get oot'? All that – 'Then al really enjoy masel.' I have to be either masochistic or going completely mad.

The honeymoon becomes another week of wandering at night in the gallery, but as a married man. Nothing changes really. Andrew's nightly crucifixion sessions, drinking sessions, fucking sessions. Caroline doesn't behave like the little 'conventional' wife we men expect in a woman after that ring has been welded onto her finger. There is little chance of me being the conventional husband either for that matter. No, but, we are in love, and lovers. She has total faith in me. Something few people have had in me. I can't let her down, I can't turn back, the point of no return is *now*. She is my wife, not some fuck, some handbag for a blade – 'Wisa? Aw fuck huv a slept in again? Eleven?' I ask – 'Oh, sorry. Thoat ad slept in fur the meetin wi that guy Buford. Dae a need tae go? Kin you noa jist gie um the diaries Ca? Ey disnae need tae meet me dis ey? Aye okay, okay. Makin me a wee coffee an al get up?'

Caroline's been up having coffee with Andrew – 'Dis he never sleep?' I ask – 'Fuckin sex machine. Right right. Al be alang in a minit okay. Goan make me a wee coffee eh. Here, check the size ey this hing! No fancy cumin in here fur a cuppla hoors?' She just laughs – 'A couple of hours? Let's not flatter ourselves then Mr Collins. Now c'mon! Up!' she shouts – 'Bill Buford will be arriving soon so get yourself showered and dressed. We're meeting him for lunch at one, down in Le Sept.'

Le Sept? Oh no. I hate restaurants, all that carry on with the cutlery, menus written in French. I always order the wrong thing, a crab, staring at me from the plate, then pretending not to be all that hungry, in case I crunch teeth into a leg – 'Naw, honest, I like aw the hard bits!' Fuck . . . Still, two hours later we're there, drinking champagne, and needless to say, strange tiny eyes staring at me, from the huge oval shaped plate – 'Hello, wit's your name? You the chef's pet ur wit?'

The thick, black hairy wrist stretching across the table has a strong, square hand. The texture is dry, but not callused, not sweaty and nervous either – 'Hi Hugh. I'm really pleased to meet you. I think we can make a great book together. I'm Bill Buford.'

Billy the Kid. *Enfant Terrible*. These are his first words to me – 'I think we can make a great book together.' The American drawl, the blue, twinkling eyes, the genial smile, the confidence, are eating me alive. He's the chief editor of *Granta* magazine. Author of *Among the Thugs*. Will Self, Martin Amis, Salman Rushdie, the literary jet set, are his buddies – 'Great book together.' My loathsome ego, whimpering, orgasming, at his feet – 'Great book? Aye Bill! Aye Bill! Aye Bill! Suck yer dick Bill!'

I pull myself together, get off my knees, regain some composure, find my Special Unit voice – 'Ehm. Well av been daen a bitta wurk oan the diaries fae the time in the unit if ye wantae huva lookit thaem furst Bull?' I say in my best serious voice.

Bill's more interested in the forty page document that I'd written when I first arrived in the Special Unit in 1978 – 'I'd like you to work on *that* Hugh. Well, the diaries, um. No, those forty pages are more interesting Hugh.' More interesting? I was off my fucking head when I wrote them – 'Aye. Well, eh, they wur ma life story, noa wit a mean?' I ask.

I feel totally disarmed by that smile – 'Fuck. Ad never dun enahin like that in ma life so that's how thur a mess. Wit's that?' I ask – 'Rewrite thum?'

He's got to be kidding, surely?

No, he's serious – 'Yeah Hugh. The diaries are, umm. You become too self conscious in them. The first document is raw, uninhibited. Yes, we should do a short story with the magazine first, and then begin working on a book. Have any other publishers had a look at them?' he asks – 'No? Great! We can get a short story ready for the next edition. I'm flying back down this afternoon to London. Umm, I'll call you okay?'

Caroline displays her literary knowledge, lifting the dialogue to a level that leaves me looking out the window, furrowing the eyebrows with an affirmation whenever anyone looks in my direction – 'Aye, at's right. Hmmm, sure, sure. Fuckin disgrace so it is.'

Even the crab's looking away with embarrassment – 'Oh just eat me!'

Bill's departure fuels the future with literary dreams – 'Well Caroline, Hugh, it's been a pleasure meeting you both. I'll call in a few days. Let's do a great book!' he drawls. The Armani suit disappears through the restaurant tables with a wave – 'Bye then you two!' he calls as he leaves.

I'm stunned – 'Caroline! Fuck me man! Didje hear um? A great book? Fuckin hell man! A great book! Wait tae a tell Andrew!'

Andrew's delighted – 'Wonderful news! Wonderful! *Granta* magazine! I'm impressed Hugh! Didn't Angela Carter publish with them Caroline?' he asks – 'And Saul Bellow too! You are in with literary giants Hugh' he says – '*Granta* has this great reputation with literary writers. It means you will be taken seriously as a writer. I mean, there are writers who would do anything to be published by them. What's he like Caroline? Oxford? Hmm. Yes, he started the magazine there didn't he? Well, wonderful news isn't it?'

Caroline agrees – 'Yes, it's fantastic. What did you think of him Hugh? Yes, I think he liked you. He'll never have met anyone like you. No don't be silly, you were fine. No no, honestly, you were very articulate. Wasn't interested in little me was he?'

Andrew's curious – 'Why? What did he say?' he asks.

Caroline laughs – 'Oh, London lads and all that. Salman Rushdie's a friend. Bill was his best man when he got married' she explains – 'Oh, he didn't say when that was. Yeah, Martin Amis and Will Self. They all play poker together, you can imagine. Yes, he's brilliant, I like Will Self. Maybe Hugh will meet them all one day eh, you never know. Bill was nice, a nice face, yeah, ruggedly handsome. Hugh's story fascinated him. He wants to do a short story first, and then do the full book.'

I look at them, asking – 'S'Bill Buford famous? Oh, a see. N'Will Self, is he a writer? Ye never hear ey these people in jail. Na, it's aw murder stories an assassins. SAS an aw that. Nae wunder thur's stabbins o'er bars a soap every day. Litrature? Wit dis the wurd really mean?' I continue – 'A know that it's tae dae wi writin, but wit is it? Is aw writin litrature? Witsat? Aye, great. You pick the right books an al read thum, aye an then al know wit the difference is wi litrature an ura books. Shakespeare's literature int it? Eh? Av read some ey his stuff in the cells oan solitary. Aye. Av read *Hamlet* an *Macbeth*.'

They're listening as I elaborate – 'Aye *Macbeth.* Aulder guys in the jail wur intae aw that kinna stuff. A went wi a burd fae the Scottish Ballet. So ye hud tae be able tae read that kinna stuff tae impress thum, that wis aw, but thur only books. Aye. Burns as well. Ma granda usetae read his poems oot tae me when a wis a wee boy. Burns is brulliant but it wis good fur impressin the burds, writin poems tae thum in letters.'

Andrew turns suddenly, exclaiming – '*World in Action*! Isn't it on tonight?'

He's right – 'Aye! It's the night! Ad furgoat wi seein Bull Buford! Great we'll watch it alang in oor studio!' I say.

There's something about seeing your own image on a screen or in photographs. You are nothing at all like the image in your head – 'Issat wit a look like? Fuck!' After so many years of seeing only your face in a small metal mirror, the rest of the body takes some getting used to – 'Check they fuckin feet man! Issat the camera angle, ur is that wit a look like in real life?' My face looks haggard, battered and weary. My cracked vocal cords sound smoke filled, like someone else's, not the voice inside my head – 'Jesus. I talk like my old man' I say, watching the programme.

I can hear *him* talking, *his* voice, not mine, not the clear, crisp articulation in my own mind. The voice I delevoped for the visitors in the Special Unit, the 'How do you do?' as opposed to the usual 'How ye daen?'

Funny that, all that energy poured into trying to put on a front for people when all the time they knew that I was a murderer, as if an accent would change my past – 'Oh he can't be a murderer, he speaks polite after all.'

Why am I so naive?

It's like writing, I mean the machine transforms all the words in my head into standard English.

The *World in Action* film became nothing more than a segment of my release. What it didn't show was the state my head was in, or my nerves. Shots of me walking across a bridge with millions of starlings swarming around overhead, making it all look like a dark sky scene from Hitchcock's film *The Birds*.

A knife blade flashes slowly across the screen every time the angle changes to a new sequence, with yet another face appearing from my past. A police inspector who had arrested me for murder – 'The Shamrock were a particularly vicious gang.' He looks much older but I can still remember his face, and the gun pressed against my temple as he challenged me to make a run for it from the car – 'Go ahead gangster. C'mon! Huv a go! Al blow yer fuckin brains oot!' He'd seemed disappointed that night when I remained in the car – 'Get this bloody *thing* tae the station an get um charged!' he'd sneered.

Perth prison looks different from the hill we're looking down from, almost humane at a distance. I'm looking down, pretending to be remembering for the camera. I hear myself say – 'Aye, a enjoyed stabbin they screws, every minute ey it.' I'm playing to the audience, to prisoners possibly watching the programme, but to prison officers in particular to let them see that sixteen years of jail hasn't dampened my hatred – 'Aye a took great pleasure fae every blow that day. They tried tae kill me, tried tae kill me in a dungeon in C Hall. Well, here a am.'

Saughton prison looms up. Those huge steel gates. There I am now. My big moment is on screen right now, and yet the day seems a million miles away, gone a long time down the track. I try to read my face – 'How do you feel?' asks a voice from behind a camera lens.

How do I feel? Was I meant to feel anything?

– 'How do you feel?' the tripod lens asks again.

Caroline touches my arm – 'What do you think Hugh?' she asks.

I'm not sure what to think – 'Eh, aye it wis okay, nice colour. The Christ statue looked better oan screen eh?' I say.

Andrew feels the programme was successful – 'I mean, you can't lock people up and expect them to be rehabilitated in those conditions. Prison simply doesn't work. He would have been killed, or killed someone else had it not been for the Special Unit. I know he comes across like a bag of rusty nails but he has changed. Hugh? Hugh do you agree?' he asks.

I'm miles away – 'Wit? Ehm, aye, aye' I reply.

My head's in that cell again. How did I get here, to this point in time? I crawled out of that dungeon, but how did I get to here? The Special Unit, Saughton, my release, it's all a blur. So many fronts, so many faces, all for other people. I don't know who I am any more. Why the fuck did they have to let me out? Why didn't they just kill me too? Where is Wullie Mooney? He's been written off as a statistic, an acceptable murder. A dead thug in another gutter of Glasgow. What does that make other murder victims? I preferred the blackness of that dungeon, no one could look at me in there. I *feel* like a murderer out here. In that black hole I had freedom, the freedom to look away, look elsewhere, certainly not at my own actions. I don't belong out here, a murderer.

The documentary is searching for reasons, motives, a cause, something that explains killing, but in real life these things just happen. Murder happens at lightning speed. Wham, you're gone! No story, no slow motion, no last words, or that final prayer. It's shockingly upon you, stunning everyone. Film isn't actuality, it makes stories, a yarn, a tale, but nothing describes that cold finality. You stand up from some gutter with a dead body attached to you, stuck to you for the rest of your life. You learn to live with that dead person, let him kill you too, kill the life in you. There's no getting away from him. He's there in every aspect of your life, haunting you through other people, those people who want to know what it is like to kill, who want to feel the thrill from danger, to feel the release from fear, the pleasure in surviving violence, or not surviving. You stand there in situations knowing you will be asked, someone will ask what do you do but drugs helps there. No matter what people think about heroin – for me it has been a shield from having to face this aspect of my life.

A great book? What is a great book? Some bullshit fairytale about the good guy and bad guy. Is this what I'm being asked to write? I'm a cunt, but not as big a cunt as he is? Is this the story? I've killed a guy, but have to provide logical reasons, create this fairytale, something for all those good people to understand, to be able to take home, take to bed, make sense of it for them, make it more entertaining, more palatable.

The truth, to write the truth. That will make them revile me even more, hate me, stare at me in the street, in a bar. Do I think this will change anything, the politics of prison culture, the perception of any individual? A great book? I'd have to be off my head to write a book. I'm beginning to hate the sight of myself. I hate to be looked at. Why the fuck did I let this happen? Challenge Michael Howard? Fuck Michael Howard! He can do whatever the fuck he wants. Who am I? A fucking murderer, that's who. That is all he has to say – 'Who are you to question me, a politician? You are a murderer.'

Jimmy Boyle may be able to face all that, the political debates on the causes of crime, the statements about deprivation, but I can't. I can't blame other people for what I've done, blame my parents, my granny or anyone else. I fucked up, no one else. Wullie Mooney and I played with fire. He got burned – I'm still burning.

All I want to do is float through life without touching the sides, do all those things I've wanted to do, have been doing for the past sixteen years. Have the heroin protective lining insulating me from the past, from your eyes upon me. See pals from jail, have a blether, a few joints, a walk. You can't imagine what it's like to walk around the city with another long-termer, especially at night in a city like Edinburgh. Half of the faces walking past have no idea where they are, but long-termers are overwhelmed by that feeling of time, the smell of history down the dark narrow closes, by those lights that have been glimmering from the same windows since the fourteenth century in the Old Town of Edinburgh.

You can't imagine the feeling as realisation sweeps through you, that you are walking in a street, that you are no longer projecting imaginations from a steel bed in the dark, that you are here right now somewhere in your own future walking on cobbled stones in an ancient place, having conversations with someone who remembers somewhere else in time with other people, other killers lying in the dark, masturbating on steel beds or just staring blindly, projecting that fantasy future into the dark.

The 369 is changing. The Russians are going to different places. Andrew is going off to India. I feel the end of something, but at least for once I've been in the right place at the right time. Caroline and I become alone for a while. She cares about me, this wee Borders lassie, I really feel it inside, a belonging. Why I don't know.

I don't want to go to bars, and then I do. I feel I'm missing something exciting, a good time, and yet the good time is right in front of my eyes, in her, in Caroline. Together we begin to explore the city, going for walks, talking about art and dead artists. Are there any other kind?

I'm looking at a gravestone in a sort of garden just off the Royal Mile. The stone was erected by Robert Burns to commemorate the poet, Robert Ferguson. The inscription brought tears to my eyes, still does whenever we go there. Robert Louis Stevenson later had the stone cleaned and added the inscription 'From one Edinburgh lad to another'.

I don't know why, but don't these words say something to you about all artists, about the poverty, about their lives?

There's rarely money in art, particularly in Scotland. Most artists go abroad to earn some kind of living as an artist. Those boasting success should be viewed with some suspicion; paintings provide laundering fronts for dodgy dealers, turning dirty money into legit currency. Still, these gestures between artists can break that tiredness, and the long hard slog.

I don't know what I am but I feel that same tiredness almost every artist experiences. That – 'What's the point!' that wakes up with you every morning. Lying in bed all day and worrying, working all night.

This is being out. Lying in longer and longer each day, asking yourself – 'What's the fucking point trying to change? Who gives a fuck?'

I'm transgressing each moment to the point of being called the head in the bed. How I wish I could give people that 'Hug a tree' line, or a book about that sense of freedom. A walk with a pal. That's all there is to it – and die. A book? Those forty pages that I wrote were necessary for me to get rid of something, not for entertainment, bed time horror tale – stick to ghost stories and Dracula.

Caroline's excited – 'Hugh? Hugh? There's a flat! A flat in the High Street!' I roll out of the mattress – 'Eh? A flat? Wit aboot the studio? The gallery?' I ask.

She's not wearing it – 'C'mon! Hugh! We can't live here. Wait till you see the view! It's fantastic' she's screaming excitedly – 'C'mon! Get up! Come and see it! It's just up at the Tron!'

A flat? Where is the money going to come from? I haven't even signed on yet. You need two months' rent in advance before the housing benefit will support your claim with the rest of the payments. The studio's an inch from the pavement; the difference between home and homeless, but there's no stopping her – 'C'mon! Come and see it with me. I have the keys! Hugh, the view's absolutely fantastic!'

The Royal Mile? – 'Okay. Geez five minutes an al be ready' I grumble.

Jesus! She's right! What a view! The Venetian windows look across the Forth Water towards Fife, and beyond to Perth. Aye, and over there, to the left are the humpbacks of the Forth Bridges. Wow, is that Ben Ledi? The other four windows look up to the Castle and Calton Hill. Down below looks like something from a fairytale with all the turrets and monuments – 'Lookit the Scott Monument Ca!' I say – 'Wow.'

I look around the room, and take in the distressed look with the pink curtains and the green painted woodwork – 'Eh Ca, where's the bedrooms?' I ask – 'Aw a see, it's jist the wan room, but it's massive innit?'

I love the kitchen too, small with an old hob but a window where again you can see everything, right across Princes Street Gardens – 'Caroline! Check! A bath! Look at this! Wuv goat tae get the money fur this. Am noa leavin! Am huvin a bath right noo! A think this wis made jist fur us eh? Look at that fireplace, issat wit ye call a, wanney Adams?' I laugh.

Caroline's parents pay the deposit for us in the end. The last thing they needed as an in-law was a murderer, but they've grown fond of me, and have an understanding about my background. I wouldn't have let my daughter marry a convicted murderer, and yet they have tried to understand what happened, tried to support us at every turn. That term, it has become a permanent feature of my life, no matter which way you turn it's there all the time – makes you suicidal at times.

Suicide? Sometimes I think of wiping myself out with one nice smooth line of smack, leave with a painless smile on my face. I've had no desire to hang around waiting for old age to cripple me, but enough of that. Now I *am* finding reasons for hanging on a bit longer, simple reasons like the amazing view.

The flat is a retreat, an eyrie in the sky, red sunsets and blue mornings, even winter is amazing with coal fires, it reminds me of those cold nights sitting at the fireside, with my granny, Auld Cathy.

By the time the fire was turning to embers we would hear a taxi arrive in the street, it was like clockwork – 'Maw! It's ma Da!' I'd shout.

The shouting in the street usually signalled that he was refusing to pay the fare. That night the street was filled with black taxis because he'd refused to pay the fare. She knocked the driver at our door clean out – 'Get the hell outa here ya swine ye!' she'd roar.

Then him lying drunk in the end room singing all night, the same song over and over, or fucking some bird he had met. I hated those noises, but the singing was worse, the same words over and over.

> We seem .... no-oww
> Funny .... can change.
> We .... insepar-aable.

Who was he singing to? Was it my mother? I can see them harmonising somewhere in a house, singing that same song. When was it? Was it before or after the ten year sentence he served? What happened to him during that sentence? Had he had a flat like this would things have turned out differently? Somehow I don't think so. Houses don't make people. People make homes, families, communities, shelter. What I have here is a chance to make a home out of a house, a chance to rebuild something that's never been there, never been built in the first place, my own home with Caroline. We love the place, and immediately set about organising moving our bits and pieces from the gallery, there's not much, but it's a start, a beginning – the beginning of an end, an end maybe, to all of all those previous lives, those violent and liberating pasts.

The Old 369 Gallery. I'll be forever thankful to her, to the people there, the artists and others who took me on. Andrew and his lover have found a cottage down in the Borders. That pink suit is sure to raise quite a few eyebrows, but I can just see him down there strutting around the countryside in tweeds and brogues – 'I'm going down there to paint!' he'd announced, magnificently – as always.

Chapter Nine

ANDY'S COMPUTER IS beginning to look like an ornament. What am I going to do with it sitting there? Looks good for the occasional visitors – 'Oh you're writing a book?'

I keep looking at it, piling up intelligent looking books at either side, piles of paper in old folders, folders full of those diaries from the Special Unit. Andy, what did he mean about writing the way I talk? Those diaries just full of big words, learning to spell, the whole sob story. I can't even look at them without cringeing. Still, I guess they got me through madness, the Special Unit. The forty pages though – they're raw, uninhibited. I haven't looked at them since they were written in, what? Almost fifteen years ago? God. What was I like then? – 'Eh Jimmy. Widje hink ey ma docyament?' I'd always ask.

He must have been demented at times with me. No wonder he pretends not to really know me, but why? Why does he do all that? Those public statements, laying blame for everything on deprivation – 'But if *I* can do it, anyone can.'

Do what? He first claims he didn't kill anyone, and yet signs a parole paper admitting to the first question that he did murder someone. That is the first thing you are asked by the parole board. Then he claims that he's innocent, that he was fighting a brutal regime, *after* his release. Then there's the contradiction – 'I've changed.'

This comic hero mentality damages the cases of men inside who *are* innocent. Men who have refused to sign that damning parole paper. Men like TC Campbell, Joseph Steele, Stuart Gair, and Raymond Gilmour.

They have refused to sign the parole paper, after years of mental and physical torture not only against themselves, but against their families too. Victim support groups feeding off a need for revenge, consider the families of perpetrators, well, they must be criminals too.

I'd want revenge, but that's why we have a democracy, to prevent any miscarriages of justice. You only have to look at the cases of Hanratty and Bentley. Revenge took their lives, but when do you hear of the support groups calling on their families? They strike me as a vengeful organisation with no real purpose.

TC Campbell, Joe Steele, Stuart Gair, and Raymond Gilmour. They would have been hanged, dead, but they're only working class.

Lord Lucky Lucan. He leaves a pair of shoes at the water's edge, case closed, *forever.* Why didn't I think of that? When the upper classes kill, it's described as a tragedy but what about those other prisoners with no excuses? Surely the truth is preferable to a lie. I killed a man and don't know why. *I don't know*. Isn't that the brutal truth? Isn't honesty better than a million fucking reasons? None of us know why.

That deprivation line slapped my granny in the face. Why couldn't I have been left in that hole in the ground? I hate sitting here, staring at the fucking computer screen. In there I could live inside my memories, live with my deprivation, with my poverty, with my hole in my shoes.

Why couldn't I have been left alone in the dark, in my self pity, in my ignorant malice, with that wound of hatred in my heart?

A book? Now I'm going to have to face something that I've been trying to run away from for almost seventeen years, that night on Sauchiehall Street, armed with a Bowie knife, and killing Wullie Mooney.

Why couldn't you just have been an inch away from me, from what was going to take off, what was going to erupt in all of our faces that night, then and forever?

None of us there that night will ever be free. I had the knife but we all killed you. All I can do now is just keep walking, walking around with 'murderer' stamped on my forehead, but keep walking until it all ends one day.

Yeah, sure, I'm liberated, walking down cobbled streets of history, but trapped there, standing still in time, with you still in the gutter, Wullie Mooney. Would you, I wonder, forgive me for what I did to you? Accept what I did to you? Would I have accepted a chunk of my life being stolen by you? Patronised you with my forgiveness?

Maybe this book will let me take that first step out of there, to then look back, face my past? Look back? There's looking back, catching fragments of what you may have in your mind of what you might want to think happened, but to go back there means the truth, going behind the so-called facts, finding the real ugly truth.

How do you write a book? What do you do? Sit down and write words? I've heard a lot of writers have disciplined routines of four to six hours each morning. Does their brain plug into auto – bang, bang, bang, words, words, words, rat-a-tat-tat?

Bill Buford says – 'Write in the present tense.' Go back there into the past, relive it all but make it in the present – 'Aye Bill nae problem. Wit wis that again? The past?' Write it as it is, say it as it is, is all I can do.

Twenty years or so ago is when it all began. My disintegrating brain has distorted a lot of the facts, transformed them into a picture, a story for other prisoners. Do I write about those two and a half million years, those recorded in my organism's memory, in those hundred billion neurons sending signals throughout the brain, through each of those go-betweens of each neuron, those minuscule sparks of energy, of light, of life? What do I call it? *Autobiography of Protons, Neurons and Electrons*? Why not begin with *Autobiography of a Murderer*?

Now I have to write about writing a book. that's three past lives; that first deadly past dealing with killings and jails, the second past about freedom, which is gone, moving still. Write down those two pasts, do it here now, in the *real* ever shifting present. What will my family say? My family? What family? Auld Cathy's dead. My mother is alone, my father is alone, strangers to each other, each and all of us. I'm alone to all of them, just another stranger, pretending to know them, pretending to love them.

Yeah, I've taken a few wrong turns in life, but feel I'm about to turn one more of those corners with this, face what has been done in those previous lives, the previous pasts – all of them.

What more can happen? What will the authorities do – punish me for writing words? Will they retaliate for exposing the beatings throughout the years, or the time when they tried to kill me – when it was all right to murder a killer?

While in between those previous pasts, I will flip into day to day 'real life' fiction as it passes us by in the book. Like today, while sitting in my chair, being screen blinded, a murderer is at my front door. Honest, I can hear him knocking, hear my wife calling – 'Hugh! Someone at the door for you!'

What do I do? He'll drag me back there, back to jail talk. Caroline? She's cool. She has faith in me. You? What would you do? Call the cops? Me? I've no choice, I've lived with these guys, shared hate with them. Want me to recommend your address as an alternative counsel shed? Give them the sorry routine – 'Sorry, I've changed, fuck off.'

My brain doesn't receive government funding per lifer, per junkie. This is what walking away involves, so walk with me awhile, read on reader, and wake up to the New Deal.

Boney! Jesus! – 'When didje get oot wee man? Wit? Yesterday! Yer jokin!'

This is his first day out after a life sentence – 'How dae ye feel?' I ask.

What? Did I actually ask that there? – 'How do you feel?'

He's twenty five, and a good hairdresser, which will give him a chance of surviving on the outside. What will he want first? A drink? A bird? Both? – 'Wit's happenin in the hen hoose? Issat right? Thank fuck a goat oot when a did. Fancy a pint? Oh, by the way, this is ma wife, Caroline. Caroline, Ronnie, or Boney' I say.

Caroline smiles – 'Hi Ronnie. How are you?' she asks.

– 'Fine' is his response.

The quiet man still. One word and silence as long as night. It's why I liked him in the jail. He rarely spoke, still doesn't by the sounds of it. He learned fast, never gossip, or mix it for other prisoners – 'So? Wit's yer plans? Caroline wer's ma jaikit? Right. Al be back aboot nine okay? See ye later. Ye eny money left?' I ask.

The Burke and Hare. They've got strippers – he'll enjoy that. A few beers, a bit of nice pussy – 'Wit ye hivin? A lager? Right. Here! A lager an a Nooky Broon! Check that! Check that fuckin pussy!' I exclaim.

The stripper's spotted his eyes too. She's waving her cunt right in front of his young face – 'Wit's your name then!' she asks.

Boney can't believe his luck – 'Eh Ronnie. Wit's yours?' he asks.

That was at least a full sentence, must be excited. Six Nooky Broons later I can barely walk, but manage to stagger back down the Royal Mile. Ronnie has the bird hanging on his arm – 'Aye. We kin go tae ma flat. Get the keys fur wanney the studios an then al see ye the morra okay' I tell them.

Caroline's on her way down the stairs to look for me as we are on the way up – 'Oh is this your little fuck for tonight?' she sneers.

Jesus. She's right on the roof, raging at the time – 'A didnae realise that wis the time. Anywiy wits the big fuckin deal? Al cum in wenever a want' I declare – 'Fuckin real yin, embarrissin me in front ey peeple. Naw Boney! Ye's ur fuckin stiyin the night an at's it!'

I kick a lamp table up in the air, almost breaking my toe – 'A told ye, never get merried coz iss is wit it's fuckin like. Ye canny move wi'oot hivin tae check in every time ye go oot the fuckin door! WELL! FUCK YOU!'

Another table goes up in the air – 'Am fuckin sicka hivin ey be sumthin fur every urra cunt oot here! That's wit it's aw aboot Boney. Bein sumbdy else. CUNTS!' I shout. Somehow the bout ends. I awake with guilt in my mouth, glimpse around from under the bed cover. Boney's on a sofa with the bird. They're sneaking out without making any noise. Let them go, I tell myself, the music is still to come. I'm not even going to ask myself how it all happened. This is just me, that's all there is to it – end of story. I turn around later to find no Caroline. She's in the kitchen – 'Ehm look. A don't kno . . .'

I try to say.

Caroline's becoming worn out with the eruptions – 'Hugh, you'll have to stop drinking before something serious happens. Look at the mess of the place. This is our home!' she cries – 'Look at it!'

The drink? No it's not, it's *me*.

She suggests a walk – 'Let's go and get the shopping in at

least. Why don't you make a start with the writing for Bill Buford? Do something constructive for once!'

Wullie Low's is the cheapest and not far along the Bridges – 'Aye, okay, let me get a bath first, but am sorry okay?' I whimper.

Shopping. I hate it, feel like a shoplifter. Every time I walk into shops with the scarred face I feel the assistants watching me – 'Al wait ootside Caroline, huv a fag.'

– 'Shug! How ye daen Shugs! Wen didje get oot?' shouts a voice.

I know the face, but vaguely – 'Eh, how ye daen? A know yer face but am hopeless wi names' I explain – 'Tam! That's right. Eh, a few months ago. Aye, am daen no bad. Wit aboot yerself? Long ye been oot? Wit? Tems? Aye, kin ye get thum?' I ask.

Temgesics, painkillers. I loved them in the jail, but didn't think anyone bothered with them out here on the street. They're a jail drug, cheaper but a bit like heroin – 'Aye, a kin get as many as ye want. Twenty quid a tray, ten inna tray. Geez a buzz the morra an al get ye thum. A noa a geezer wi a script' he says.

Caroline appears laden with shopping bags – 'Caroline this an auld pal, Tam' I say.

Being described as an old pal has his face beaming with pride. He served six months over in the prison reception area; the job's usually reserved for failed crooked lawyers, and first offenders, the type who never see the inside of a cell – 'Aye, how ye daen Caroline? A usetae gie um the wire wen ey wis bringin in the hash. N'case the screws wur gonny nip um, eh Shugs?' he winks.

News to me, but he's got a source for tems, 'Jimmies'. 'Aye, Tam wid gie me the nod if the screws wur waitin tae turn me o'er at the reception, aye, when a came back in at night fae ma placement' I lied.

He's determined to get the recognition he feels he deserves for that six months in the nick – 'Long wis at ye dun Shugs? Sixteen stretch? Av jist goat oot, two weeks ago, thank fuck. Nae mer big yins fur me. Ye'll be gled tae be oot eh?' he asks. Glad to be out? Fuck, if only he could see inside my head – 'Ye stayin in Edinbra? A see. The Royal Mile? Must be loaded ya cunt ye eh?' he asks.

How I wish – 'Naw Tam. Am dodjin the bullets. Glesga? Fuck, thur aw shootin each urra through there, fuckin headcases. Am too auld fur aw that. Sixteen wis too long, still fit, but fucked, burnt oot' I laugh – 'A like Edinbra. Well anywiy, geez a buzz the morra okay, see ye later.'

Tems, Jimmies – thank fuck! They'll keep me off every other substance, including the booze.

Caroline's laughing – 'God! Who was that? I could barely understand a word he was saying' she laughs.

I know what she means – 'Ach, jist a jail punter. Tems? Ach, they're a sorta painkiller keep me affey the drink Caroline. Anyway wull see wit happens in the mornin' I say. Tam comes up good – 'That you Shugs? Goat that message fur ye. Five minutes? Al watch fur ye at the windae mate' he says.

I do the biggest part of the next three years looking up at that window. I don't know if it's the window or the tems that become the habit, but whatever, they take me away from the drinking, give me a confidence to face openings, the few dinner parties that we can afford, without shying away from who I am – a murderer.

You fed up hearing that word yet? Murderer? Try living with it almost every moment of your life – MURDERER!

Wee Tam though has me by the balls after a few weeks on the tems. The comedown is nowhere near the heroin sickness, but fuck me, your veins feel filled with the North Sea. A couple of days and it's over, bar the head craving, the 'what's the point being straight' conversations in your head, painful just the same but bearable enough to cut the habit. Somehow though, just as I get there, there's the phone call – 'Shugs? Wee Tam here! Listen a fun wanney they wee hings in ma pocket!'

My resistence just collapses into that – 'Be there in five minutes.'

The following day that geezer he knows, just happens to come up with another fifty of them, and just happens to be the day my giro arrives.

Now after three years the coincidence begins to wear a bit thin, but what do you say?

He's an earner, it's *his* script, and he's earning off my back – but so what? I like him; he tells lies, but the lies are entertainment, fantastic – 'Shugs. Mind ey that time in Peterheid' he'll say.

This is after only two pints of peev. Now there's a word – peev. I asked where it came from but he came out with some lager tale, truth is peev means black beer in Russia – 'Russia? Na, na. Nae danger chav. Russians drink *vodka.* Black beer? Shugs, iss is Edinbra!' he'd claim – 'Russia? Na, na chav.'

The Captains Bar fortnightly sessions get more surreal by the regularity of the giros.

That nine months he done has become ninety years – 'Shugs' he whispers – 'Listen, tween you an me. Am known up here as the Wee Godfather.'

The Wee Godblether more like it, but I need him, I need him to escape, escape from the writing, escape from Hugh Collins' *Autobiography of a Murderer.*

Oh I'm writing that book, during the darkness of night until dawn, drugged out my old skull. I tried the disciplined six to eight hours in the morning shit, but prefer the burst in my brain of a flashback from the drugs, prefer the distance from the dialogue that's spewing out of my guts. I see daylight on signing day, and of course the view of that five minutes away window day just up from the Royal Mile.

How else could I write it?

Caroline sells the odd painting to sustain her work, our lives, but me? I do my best to be nice to everyone, be someone else for them, to prove to them I'm not me, that I'm a rehabilitated ex murderer. I mean, I've changed, surely?

Mr Mellow, that's me. Mr Temgesic, the pacifist – 'Goodness! Hasn't he changed?' Is this change? I have three silk suits. Elocution lessons, and I'm made – 'Witsat Ca?' I ask – 'The phone fur me? Who is it?' Caroline looks oddly at me – 'It's your Mum.' My Ma? Something's wrong. Crisis or death has been our only communication these past three years. One of us just can't change the pattern, and of course that has to be yours truly, regardless that I have finally stayed out of trouble all this time.

– 'Aye Ma, wit's wrang?' I ask.

It's after midnight – 'Listen ye better get through here. That Denis wan wis in the pub shoutin the odds at me the night! The cheeky bastard!' she says.

Denis? Denis is one of my best pals. We did Borstal together, the young offenders, and the Special Unit. Denis was my Ma's pal in there too – 'How? Wit happened? He threaten ye ur wit?' I ask.

I can feel my insides twisting, and turning – 'Naw, naw. He'd a parcel behind the bar. That manageress opened it an he went fuckin crazy. Ye noa wit es like wen es drunk. The next hing es shoutin at me! Ye better get um soarted oot Hughie!' she says.

My immediate instinct is to look for a blade, but, I can't, I can't go back to that killing, murderous way of thinking. Denis had always been hot headed, and frustrated. He'd been given a life sentence for a carrying a dead body from a party with another guy, but hadn't been involved in the killing. He'd thought the guy had jumped out of a top storey window to escape a fight with the other guy. The tabloids as always came up with the grossest depiction – 'Keep Glasgow Tidy Murder'.

Denis had been dragged down like a dog. His frustration and anger landed him in a lot of trouble with the authorities, until eventually they put him in the Special Unit. He had harmed no one, and now? I'm supposed to fire through and stab him?

That manageress is an ex copper, but shouting at my Ma?

What the fuck do I do here? Denis is a pal. I'll phone him and see what's happened, but be cool about it, no threatening him. I take a few deep breaths – 'Hullo? Denis? That you?' I ask.

He's been waiting for the call – 'Aye how?' he grumbles.

I stay calm – 'Betty phoned, sayin ye wur in shoutin at ur?' His raspish voice sounds agitated, hypered up for trouble – 'Look, am noa diggin ye up Denis. Am jist tryin . . .' He explodes into that old rage – 'Wit? How'd you get this phone number?' he roars. I try to calm him down – 'Denis. Listen you gave me the number a cuppla weeks ago, remember?' I say.

He's too hyped up for this – 'Listen! You an that other cunt through there urra cuppla grasses! Aye, you an yer pal Boyle!' he screams down the line.

The hook catches me like a fish – 'A grass? Am noa a fuckin grass. Witsat? Al come through any time ye want ya fuckin bam!' I shout back – 'Blades? Al blow yer fucking brains oot ya cunt. Blades?' I laugh – 'Away ye go tae yer bed Denis. Wit? Aye, nae bother, eny time ye want!'

A grass? I've never grassed, not that it makes any difference these days. Grassing is just pulling a stroke, a wide move, trading with coppers. Denis and I are out of touch, just two old dinosaurs. I thought I knew him, but obviously not. Blow his brains out? Who am I trying to kid? I wouldn't even know how to load a gun. I almost broke my jaw trying a bluff on enemies with a sawn-off shotgun when it went off accidentally in a hotel just weeks before murdering Wullie Mooney in 1977.

Caroline hits the roof – 'What? They want you to go through? Is one life sentence not enough? You're not going anywhere near Glasgow. I mean it Hugh!' she roars.

Denis? I've just lost another pal, made another enemy, and for what? I'd valued the friendship we'd had. He'd sung in the strong cells, rebel songs, and *Positively Fourth Street*, just like Bob Dylan.

Poor Denis. I regretted the call. I don't know what his experience has been, but I don't imagine it's been easy.

Now we are nothing more than strangers; strangers from the same previous past, but I'll remember it all in my moments, my privacy, those rebel songs, and the Bob Dylan numbers – *Like A Rollin Stone*.

Chapter Ten

I CRUSH TWO tems in a piece of paper to forget, turn off the telephone to get sleep. I feel that initial gag, almost vomit – 'Tea Caroline! Make tea!' Much better, I think, but the hit's rapid, rouses my brain into thinking, remembering songs in cells, songs with the images from the forty pages. I look at them, and begin another fourteen hour shift, to get rid of them, while they're clear in my mind, taking me almost there, back into the streets, into that first previous destructive past, that killing period we all had.

That's how it is.

Barry's due for release next week. That window up the street may have to go without the giro, maybe he'll give me fifty on tick. I want to be at the gate for Barry. Waiting there with a nice car, a hire will do. The suit I got him fitted to a tee, another giro has served the prison system well. Wee Tam, The Godblether is another matter – 'Tam? I need fifty Jimmies.' That five minutes has become three, he meets me half way these days – 'Goat tae be careful Shugs. They hornies are watchin me.' Hornies? Oh I get it, the coppers – 'Listen Tam. There's sixty quid. Geez three an al get the other wans the morra. Big Barry's oot so al need tae hire a car. Av money cumin in the morra so thurs noa problem, okay?' I say.

That six month jail smile wanes slightly – 'Shugs, av cuvered these so a need the money the morra, it's hur message money, ken?' he says.

I assure him that I'll cover the money – 'Aye, nae bother

wee man.' We drift into the usual lies about the world of crime – 'How's Paul?' he asks. Paul? 'Paul who?' I ask. He grins, knowingly – 'Wee Ferris. Av heard he's behind a lotta shootins throo there' he states – 'Supposed tae be you that's daen thum fur um.'

Paul Ferris. He's never met the guy – 'Witsat? Och Tam, be careful wi yer mooth coz stories travel. He's noa shy aboot cumin through here, d'ye know wit a mean?' I ask.

– 'N'me daen shootins? Thurs too many gangster videos through here, honest.'

The threat penetrates; his face changes – 'Naw naw, naw mate. A jist heard some daft stories. Ye ken the wiy aw these radge cunts throo here rattle thur gums. Naw Shugs ad never spread stories as ye noa' he says – 'A wis jist sayin, at's aw mate. Right en, see ye the morra, jist geez a buzz an that message'll be there. At's forty quid still tae cum eh? Okay mate, you take care.'

Paul Ferris. Last time his name cropped up I'm being asked to shoot him and another guy, while I'm being held in Shotts Maximum Security. I'm on a downgrade for being in a photograph taken while on a pre-release work placement at Edinburgh Zoo. A photograph that put me in a strong cell on Christmas Eve.

Santa had no chimneys to drop down that night. What a downer I had for Christmas. 'Jingle bells, jingle bells, jingle all the way!' Aye, the cuffs jingled all the way. Three days later I'm put up amongst the population, next door to an old pal, a lifer from the gang days, John Smith. John and I were altar boys together at St Roch's Primary School. There are other similarities between us – we are both murderers. Shotts is a young man's jail. At that fortyish stage of our lives, we don't belong here. We should be in a home for burnt out lifers.

I'm into my fifteenth year of going nowhere, but things could be worse I guess. John shot a guy in an accident involving a gun. Still, the future doesn't look good for him. The lawyers claimed it was an accident in court. The judge, oddly enough, accepted this defence as a possibility, but had no choice but to give him a lifer – it's mandatory apparently, depending on who you are that is – 'Ad sat it oan ma knee under the table tae look at it an it jist went aff! Bang! The bullet went throo three urra guys at the bar. The backey the bench blew aff wi the guy at the table across fae me, blud an splinters every fuckin where. A didnae even tipple the thing hud went aff.'

The parole board wouldn't be looking at his case for a long time regardless of what a judge might have said about it possibly being an accident. The parole board have no interest in accidents, only murders, murderers, and serious time.

– 'Aye, John, ye'll huv tae keep tellin thum that's wit happened.'

I have my own problems: nine months into this downgrade, and still no signs of these people giving me back my release date. I'll have to do something drastic to get their attention, a hunger strike, a protest, something. I can't just sit here, and watch my life ebb down the drain. I'll have to do something fairly soon or go insane in this fucking place. I *hate* this fucking place, worse than the hole in the ground in Perth Prison. In there I had blackness, I couldn't see, or feel anything. Now I have to be something for these young guys – 'Shug an John. They've dun the business wi screws.'

Fuck. Do any of them know what it's like? Hating yourself, hating your life, hating all your family, hating the guy you killed for dying? They know nothing about real hate.

Shotts Prison is a fucking nightmare. There are incidents every day: stabbings, fires, smash ups, lock downs every day, it's complete fucking chaos. At every meal you get an account of some other incident. I don't want to know. Neither does John. But we have to listen, the politically correct prisoners, that's all we want to be – we just want out of Shotts.

My head's done in but what do you say to someone just starting off a life sentence? You can't sit around moaning all the time but that's what happens in jail. All the old stories you hear about prison culture – the 'Us and Them'. It's all bullshit, finished, a long time ago. There's no culture, it's anything goes. Each day is drug fuelled, drugs affect all aspects of prison life. Conversations are dominated by possibilities, chasing these possibilities twenty four hours a day, every day. Conversations are half a dozen guys all talking at the same time – no one listens in jail anymore.

John doesn't take drugs so it's all the more painful for him. You have to go along with things and listen to what he's saying, show some interest in his case, reassure him to the point of lying, that it's not the end, lying to him – that's all we're doing – 'Aye John never gie up hope.'

You lying bastard, tell him the truth. No, don't, because they'll think you put him up to it – remember, survive this. That's all that the mob want to hear – 'Shug Collins talked him out of it. John stabbing one of us.'

John's head's done in. Some bampot has planted it in his head he'll be better in the Special Unit – 'Am gonny tan wanney they fuckin screws. Am noa bein left tae rot in iss fuckin place Shooey.' Shooey? No heard that for long time, but jail *is* time. No one leaves here normal, sometimes not alive, sometimes, feet first in that old suicide box due to death from restraint – nothing changes in here, in jail *time*.

He's been told this guarantees an automatic transfer there. I should let him do it but I know from experience that they'll kill him. They retaliate and with extreme force, it's an opportunity for them to try out the new riot gear, and martial arts training, to see if it all really works – he's only a killer. Yeah, I should give him the go ahead. Why not see one of them stabbed to death?

– 'John, listen. A stabbed three screws in Perth. Aye, an a

enjoyed every minute but believe me, they'll try tae kill ye so don't kid yersel aboot this. They know the public don't gie a fuck aboot prisnurs. *They* kin get away wi murder, but noa us. Thuv dun a few cons in an never been dun. A few bogus investigations an that's it, cleared. They tried tae kill me' I say – 'Ye know the script so be careful aboot makin any statements cos ye know wit happens later if ye don't perform. The cons? Oh aye, they'll be right behind ye, it's entertainment but wait tae it happens. Think this through. They aw ran away when a went ahead wi the screws, honest, John.'

John knows this isn't bravado. He knows I wouldn't lie to him, knows the strength of me. Fuck, we were altar boys, at school together, St Roch's, we were the Shamrock. Caroline breaks the past – 'Hugh, your Mum's on the phone' she says.

I close my eyes – 'Tell ur tae fuck off. Tell ur thit av tanned Denis. Keep ur happy the night eh' I sneer.

An hour later I'm back there, back in my head, back in this fucking book – in Shotts.

John's staring at me as he's talking. He looks like an ex lifer: that cropped iron grey hair, the gaunt unshaven jaws, and thin sneering lips. Those penetrating blue eyes, they can twinkle, but not too often. I look much the same, but my eyes are grey. Was he staring at the guy he shot in the boozer, I wonder?

– 'A know aw that Shug. Am jist noa spendin the rest ey ma life in this place. A mean wit wid you dae in ma pisition? Na, they better dae sumthin cos am no wearin eny mer ey this fuckin shite. Am deadly serious. Wit've a goat tae lose?' he asks – 'Ma life? Fuck!'

I try to change the subject – 'Want mer tea? Fore the worksheds cum back?' I ask.

John's head is back in court. He's just sitting, staring into space. He'll be going over the judge's summing up. That's all that's holding him together. He's hanging onto any thread of hope. He'll have gone over this so many times in his head, he can switch it on like a video – 'A mean, the judge even said it wis an accident' he'll say. I was the same when I was first sentenced, going over and over what had happened.

He'll become convinced he's innocent within a few years, winding and rewinding the same old video in his head, it's a common feature of long term isolation, and the deep fear of confinement for life, until you're an old age pensioner, or even that final death.

The worksheds are back. You hear the shouting before you see anyone. The hall fills with mindless screeching heads, screaming out the sides of their faces. John's cell is suddenly swarming with prisoners – 'Any tea bags John? Any sugar John? Awright en Shug? Awright en John? Here? Yous two cunts noa wurk at aw en? A right paira auld gangsturs eh? Here you ya cunt ye! Nae cunt daen ma arse! Two auld poofs!'

Ricky's first with the day's gossip. Who's been stabbed. Who's getting stabbed. Who should next be stabbed. Prison sort of stifles any other dialogue. What else can you talk about? I mean, economic, social debate is more direct this side of Lanark. Dope, tablets are behind most stabbings and slashings, but not always. Occasionally you'll get straightforward paranoia. That – 'Who you fuckin lookin at' sort of thing, first thing in the morning, usually, someone who had nothing for a nightcap the night before. The traditional square go types do still happen, but occasionally, very occasionally.

– 'Stab eny cunt the day en Richard?' I ask.

Ricky laughs, thinking we're joking but he's the jail rocket. He's behind most of the stabbings, active in almost all of the violence in the prison. He fuels his drug habit by taking on contracts. You can get someone slashed in here for two Temgesics, worth a fiver. A freelancer, if you like, willing to mark you for life, for five fucking quid. Screws don't care what happens amongst prisoners, and sometimes mix things, to keep them fighting with each other. They don't want the focus to be on *them* – not with a young population sharing home made works, and the invisible stalker, HIV. Would you want some guy strung out with a needle in your face – 'A BETTER GET FUCKIN DRUGS!'

These things don't happen? I spoke to a young guy about the dangers of sharing the needles and catching HIV – 'AIDS? So what? It's that ur the Joab Centre!' he replied. This isn't bravado. These young guys just don't care what happens to their lives. The fact that families are infected as a result doesn't enter their heads. Why should it? We are *all* in jail. The next parcel, the next hit is important. Drugs today, right now, is all this population cares about. This is our existence – it's all we know.

Guys are coming in and out of the cell. There's one conversation; that craving driven dialogue, all talking through each other at the same time, and yet within this there lies information, a sublime input – who's copping, who's getting fucked, and who's onto a wee nightcap. A nightcap; to become deaf, dead to those losers screaming out of the windows every night.

– 'Here! Guess who'd a visit last night?' whispers the bold boy, Richard.

– 'A noa. A heard tae. Fifty tems an a half ounsa saft black! A think es goat smack' someone else says.

– 'Fat Thomson's haudin tae. Wants five phone kerds fur three tems. At's noa bad by the way. That urra cunt's daen two fur five kerds! Fuckin arsehole, he's gettin tanned as soon as es in oor hall, am takin the fuckin face right aff um, five phone kerds? The fuckin prick! Issat ma tea ur yours Shug?' asks Ricky T – 'Yer runnin oota tea bags by the way John.'

– 'Aye Ricky, it's you that's usin thum aw ya cunt' replies John.

– 'Here, by the way! Didje see that daft screw's face this

moarnin at the tea brek? Av lit a joint in the can anra next hing es gonny case me? Big fuckin rookie. Here! Ye's shooda seen es face! Wee Platty threw a steel bolt at um, the cunt! Jist missed um wi a cuppla inches tae! Kin a take anurra tea bag fur the dub up?' asks Ricky – 'Kin a get a lenny at shurt fur ma visit the night by the way?'

We watch him – 'Aye, nae borra. Wan fuckin joint? Issat right Ricci? Ey wis gonny case ye?' asks John.

– 'Aye! A daft joint' he replies – 'Here you cunt!' he calls after someone passing the cell – 'You owe me two tems by the way! Don't hink av furgot! Here. Gen up. A hink that cunt o'er er's a fuckin beast. Him in that furst peter, the wan next tae the screws' oaffice. Am noa sure, it's jist sumhin aboot um, readin aw they daft fuckin books awra time, noa wit a mean? Didje see um the urra night wi aw the new trainin gear oan? Aw here! Ye wantae a seen um by the way. Wee skin tight shorts, right up between the cheeks, wigglin the tight buttucks aw the way alang the corridur. Cunt wants it up the arse, the cunt.'

John laughs – 'Big Spartacus eh! Here! At's yer last tea bag by the way!'

This is the dialogue, twenty four hours a day, every fucking day.

How do I feel? Any tea bags?

The harsh voices. I can hear them so clearly, even now, as I write this book, the book about that first killer book.

Spartacus? I'm sure we all know what he means. This is, however, the sort of general conversation you hear at dinner break. By tea time it will be at fever pitch with the hysteria mounting over those paranoid possibilities and vindictive suspicions.

I notice someone looking in my cell. A young guy, overweight, in a huge brown dirty jersey down to his knees. His back's to me, but I've an idea who he is – it's 'Fat Boy', Arthur Thomson Jnr.

The *Godfather*'s boy.

Arthur Thomson Snr was the genuine article, a real gangster. He had an outfit of the younger generation working for him from his base in Glasgow's Blackhill. He would educate them in all aspects of criminal activity, including every method of extortion – you didn't fuck about with this guy. The very mention of his name was enough to put the shits up most people. The young team, however, were moving up, they were fast earning reputations of their own. The education had begun to backfire.

Paul Ferris – his most promising protege, had recently had a fall out with Auld Arthur. A slightly built young guy, in his early twenties, but already a major player within the criminal world.

Things had begun to happen, quietly at first with rumours and then into full scale war with shootings and car chases throughout the city. The city? Guns are everywhere! The tabloids, as always, exploited the situation to sell their porno rags, manufacturing Godfathers, and an Underworld. Fantasists and petty criminals actually believe in all this stuff – 'Aye! S'true! Wis in the *Sun* an the *Daily Record*! A red it oan ra bus the s'mornin.'

I suppose this validates their existence in some way, making it all a bit more real. The truth is that it's all tabloid fantasy, bullshit to sell papers, business, money.

The Underworld?

What Underworld?

Tabloid journalism, that in itself creates the so called Underworld.

Auld Arthur had been shot at from a passing car. A bullet had hit him in the groin. The feud then became earnest, became the talk of the jail. Everybody had to be in on the act: they all have to know someone who knows somebody who knows either Arthur Thomson or Paul Ferris.

Thomson Jnr was hanging around my cell. What could he want with me?

– 'How ye daen? Ye want sumthin?' I ask.

'You Shug Cullins?' he asks.

– 'Aye, how?' I reply.

– 'Your gettin oot shortly int ye' he says.

This was more of a statement than a question. He looked in bad shape, for the son of the Godfather. His face is covered in spots. Most guys in jail don't take any interest in their appearance apart from visits, but this is abusing the privilege.

Apparently he lived on a regular diet of Mars bars, Mars bars, and more Mars bars. His father had tried to straighten him out, but to no effect, he liked his sweeties. He had even arranged for a guy to go to jail to look after his son in Barlinnie.

Fat Boy, as he was known, had his personal dealers and runners in the jail. Bampots who imagined the association would lead to a step up the criminal status ladder. I think it's interesting the way the criminals would mimic the aristocracy with their own hierarchy of faces and codes of honour – not so any more.

You spot these guys a mile off though, the swagger – 'Eh, a wurk fur Arfur Thomsun!'

That right big shot – any tea bags then?

I can identify with him though, the boy. A father who is a gangster. I too had the same misfortune, the same run of luck. I can well imagine the pressures. Looking at him it is easy to see that here is a young boy who only wants his sweeties and action video tapes all day. His father had pushed him into a trade – a gunsmith: could tell you anything about guns. In my case it was razors.

What chance does this boy have? A fucking gunsmith?

I look at him – 'Eh, am due a release programme, but fuck knows when it'll be.'

He's all business – 'At disnae matter. Yer away shortly int ye' he says out the side of his face.

– 'Am noa sure. How? Wit's aw this aboot anyway pal?' I ask.

He grins – 'Al gie ye thurty grand apiece fur Ferris an Tam Bagan.'

– 'Thurty grand? Wit ye talkin aboot, shootin thum?' I ask.

– 'Aye. Thurs a motur innit fur ye tae, an sixty grand up frunt. Ma auld man'll get ye a pump action, urra haungun, witever ye want.'

I'm looking at him. Is he seriously asking me to take on a contract? Murder these two guys? Here, does he have any tems on him? Could string him along, get a freebie?

– 'Ehm, ur ye talkin aboot in the legs ur wit?' I ask.

He dismisses my question with a look of contempt – 'Na-aw. Fucksake man. Ye'll get the same pressure fae the coppers fur shootin thum in the heid. Thur's nae difference is thur?' he asks – 'Wan in thur heids an ye walk away wi sixty grand man. Yer skint anywiy so wits the difference?'

Paul Ferris lived just up the road from my granny's old house in Royston Road. John too knows the family, we grew up together. Wullie Ferris was in our class at school. Fuck, I know these families, they all know each other, and here's one of the families, here's this boy asking me to kill one of them. Tam Bagan? I know nothing about him other than the usual tales about who he's supposed to have chibbed, shot, or maybe shagged.

I smile at him – 'Naw son, listen this isnae fur me. Am jist finishin a lifer. Wan murder wis enuff an anyway a know the wee man's faimly so jist furget we hud this talk.'

The wee man? Where did that come from? I've never set eyes on him but I do know the family. Do I know somebody who knows somebody who knows somebody?

– 'Fucksake! Honest!' he exclaims – 'See aw yous auld yins, man! Ye's dae years an fur wit? A daft fight? Sixty grand an yer sayin yer noa interestit? A canny make ye's oot! Wan thra heid an at's it! Thur's nae fuckin difference!'

He has a point. Why don't I take the offer? Ferris means nothing to me. I am indeed skint. He's still ranting about the shootings – 'Gangsturs? Aw kiddin thursels thur aw tryin tae shoot each urra. Glesga! S'fulla deid moturs!'

I watch him wobbling down the corridor, still mouthing off about bogus attempts with guns and murders, and dead cars – 'Aye! Glesga! Fulla deid moturs!' he's shouting. A week later he's shot while on his first home leave – two in the head, four in the back at point blank range, and his balls kicked off, literally. Murder's never like films, that slow motion sequence; Bruce, and Big Arnie killing the low life of that Underworld: Paul Ferris is later charged with murdering him, and subsequently found not guilty at the Glasgow High Court.

The tabloids devoted themselves to every bloody detail of the trial, and the following tit for tat revenge shootings during the aftermath of killing, until eventually a massive heart attack ironically cheated them of a few more sales, and took out of the picture Auld Arthur, the Godfather. A fucking heart attack! – 'We Wus Robbed' says the *Sun*. Anyway. Where am I?

Shotts – in the past – 'A cuppa tea John? Thank fuck the wurksheds are away. Nippy bastards eh. Ricky gave me a cuppla tems. Think al write a cuppla letters, thur good fur writin, an gettin a good kip' I say.

John's staring – 'Aye Shug. Here, at's anurra thing a meant tae tell ye aboot. See when that judge wis daen his summin up he . . .'

Caroline breaks into the past with a coffee – 'S'that the time already?' I ask – 'Aw ma back's killin me sittin at this machine aw night. How long's that been? Twelve hoors? Two mer an then al finish aff fur the night. A wis jist writin aboot Shotts. Av goat tae get back tae *this* book, the present tense stuff' I explain – 'Witsat? Ach. S'hard tae explain. Ye done any paintin? Great! Kin a come an huv a look? Time did ye get tae bed?' I ask – 'Sorry ma heid's up ma arse wi aw this writin. S'that Bill Buford. A wish ad never met um. This is crazy, writin aboot a book av already written. Still, it's gettin there, well a start anywiy but am knackered, needin a cuddle.'

I smile at her – 'Yer a wee darlin McNairn. A don't know how ye put up wi me. Fancy a walk later, efter av had a wee sleep? Right okay. Two hours an a kip, an then we'll have a look at your new paintings okay pal? Wee kiss?'

Caroline gives me a cuddle – 'Oh Wee Tam phoned last night. I didn't want to disturb you' she says – 'He sounded a bit huffy. All right, two hours, and I'll wake you about two, let you get some rest.'

Wee Tam? The huff? I'll phone him later after I've had a sleep. I'll do one more tem later and leave the writing out. Barry's big day tomorrow. Stuart Swanson, Ca's pal's hired a car, a big Rover. It was all they had left for hire, and still a cheap price. That fifty quid that's left from the giro can cover a bottle of cheap champagne. Caroline's bought film for her camera. I'll show those bastards at the gate. They threatened to take his release date if he was found to be associating with me. Wait till they see me with the champagne bottle, the flash Rover.

Jesus, do I need sleep – 'Oh God. Tems, painless, relief, sleep, rest.' I hit the bed in a state of satisfaction. I managed a good chunk there, but no more remembering for the rest of the day, no more of that previous past.

The tem and exhaustion are easing in now, easing me into a stupor, melting me into a shape, a memoryless blurry form, distanced from those forty pages, from those lines I wrote in anger, those thousands of words, that blood splattered hatred.

I'm an addict in some, in *every* form, from tying laces to where I am now in life. I can't help myself. I say this because I can see it, smell it coming a mile away, a bad scene, coming hard at me, in some shape or form, something bad about to happen, because of this book – I'm scared of what might happen. I have to hide, find some place, hide from the fears, the terrors of tomorrow's unknown. Bill Lyons' last words to me were – 'Hugh. Mooney's boy has vowed to kill you.' Who can blame him? He wants revenge – the book may be the trigger, literally. I prefer to dull the fear, than prepare it with a weapon. Fear dictates – get in first, kill him. He has every right to hate me – to want me dead. Does he think I'm proud of what I did to his father? I sometimes wonder.

Nothing was planned to kill his father. I didn't premeditate his death. We happened to be there together, during personal violent exchanges with other men. I didn't mean to kill his father – it just *happened*.

Revenge will make him no different to any other killer, not in jail – or to a parole board. Forgiveness? The only person who can forgive any of us there that night is dead.

Forgiveness I believe is the dilemma of almost every killer in jail.

Temgesics? Painkillers? These are the least of my addictions.

Words, truths, are more addictive – maybe fatal.

My fear is an addiction.

Chapter Eleven

A VOICE IS ringing in my ears – 'Hugh? Hugh? A wee coffee. How are you, get some sleep?' she asks. It's Caroline – 'What? Yes, it's after two. We could go down to my studio if you like. Yes, I've been working all day. Well, we'll see later what you think of them.'

Wee McNairn. What a sight, covered in paint, those leggings, the arse hanging down to her knees almost, and that pink cardigan. Mad as a brush, but I love her – 'Did you walk up the road like that Ca?' I ask, laughing – 'Here, geez a cuddle, fancy cummin in wi me fur a wee while? Aye, okay. Al huv a quick bath, an en we can have a wee walk doon tae the studio. Am dyin tae see thum. Pink? Ye've never used pink afore huv ye? Right, al noa be long.'

The painting of the figure breaking through the bars is still there, put aside to give her room for these new works. The dozen or so works on the walls are half way while the other remaining blank canvases wait patiently against a wall to replace those already hanging, being worked up into a form. Somehow she works on all of the paintings at the same time. She doesn't complete them one at a time, but together – 'These are in the first stage, but what do you think of the pink?' she asks – 'I'll put blank canvases up later tonight. I think there's enough going on just now with these ones, so? What do you think?'

I can't take in the strength of the colours in one session. I have to keep coming back to absorb the shape emerging within the colours. She is a colourist. In two of the big canvases, they can be arranged in any order, in any configuration, any way you want. There is no statement, no meaning to be unscrambled, no secret code hidden, there's no story – this *is* painting.

You can create one for a moment, a story, and then let it pass. The next story will be different, in a different time, but just as true. These and other paintings are not what you would call finite, static objects with meanings, but the means to visit a place, see somewhere within us all, a path from darkness to light – 'Ehm, a kin see wit ye mean aboot the pink. Issat the wee hill we wentae that day when a wis released?' I ask of one particular painting – 'Aye a kin see a lot aboot that period in these paintins. Ach, a don't know enough about . . . That me an you? There, in that big canvas? The pinks work in well though. A wish a could paint ye know, paint like this. Naw, the carvin suits me' I say – 'Aye drawin's okay, but even wi that, am locked in on that chocolate box stuff, daen wee flowers, an aw that "I'm normal" paintin. Caroline, you'd get sent tae see the jail psychiatrist if you were in the nick, honest! They'd jist say that ye wur disturbed if ye wur daen these paintins in there' I explain – 'Na-aw! Honest! In there it's aw that – "Wit's it mean?" They need tae see a picture, a face, urra flower, sumthin they can understaun. Naw these are great. Wish a could see without lookin fur a wee picture. Well, ye heard me a minute ago askin if that wan there wis us two. Naw, naw, am too auld tae to go tae art school. Anyway, c'mon let's go fur a wee walk, an then settle doon fur a nice tea, an *Brookside*.'

Brookside. My life's becoming a series of soap operas, night after night, and writing until dawn. I'm losing parts of my former selves, those habitual drives to be out, to be in bars, to be not missing anything. Tems, soap operas, and writing leave little room for anything else – but there is a comfort in working and vegetating up here in the sky with my memories, it's not all hell. I love looking across that same sky, love being at the kitchen table, decent food to eat, talking to people, having a tem, watching those soaps with my wife. After three to four years I feel I have a life, but that long shadow, does *that* follow you around. God. Time though helps leave it behind, circumstances, people's tolerance, and good will. These things can work it out, rehabilitate, change your situation, your viewpoint – your life.

Barry, I wonder what he's going to make of all this out here? There's twelve years of frustration, hunger, and anger, waiting to hit the streets. He'll be projecting onto that blank ceiling during these final hours, projecting that future he has lived, fantasised a thousand times before, but for one last night – I wonder how he feels?

The Rover screeches to a halt at the gate, just as the first step through that narrow slit of light brings him into daylight, into freedom – 'Here Barry, Champagne! A toast tae freedom! Cheers! Aw the best Barry!' I shout.

The gatehouse window has four sets of seething eyes burning into my back – 'Barry' I whisper – 'Don't even look at the cunts. Don't look back.'

Caroline is catching that broad handsome smile, on camera, forever – 'Okay Stewart?

I smile – 'Let's get the fuck away fae this shithole. Ye goat everyhing big man? Okay Stewart, straight up tae oor flat. Thur's a wee breakfast waitin fur ye Barry.'

Revenge? I know the burning faces at the window, but I feel nothing towards them. I don't hate them, feared them probably, but they're powerless now, have no control to wield over me. I don't remember their names, but they're the jail's dogs, bastards.

Barry's feelings are more important right now, not mine. He needs to say – 'Fuck you!'

He's delighted to be free – 'Shug! Didje see thur fuckin faces man? Thur fuckin ragin!

Sick bastards' he exclaims – 'Aw Shug, yer sum man! Thanks mate. Caroline, sorry pal. Shug knows wit a mean. The bastards want ye tae walk oot wi yer heid doon. A Rover tae! Thull be sayin there's that animal loaded as well noo. Fuckin hell man, yer sum guy, honest Shug.'

He pats down the new suit we'd bought him – 'The suit looks the business tae eh' he grins.

Barry's been to the flat a few times for a meal while out for a couple of hours from the training for freedom hostel in Saughton Prison – 'Check that view big yin! Check they hills o'er there. Ye can go there whenever ye want. Yer a free man Barry!' I smile at him – 'Here, gie yer maw a phone an let her know yer here. We'll drive ye hame but thur's a few things tae dae first, daft things but ye'll enjoy thum. Okay Caroline, a wee toast! Tae freedom! Tae huggin trees! Tae they blue skies an aw that! Great tae see ye big yin! How dae ye feel?' I ask.

Caroline's breakfast is light but wolfed down in a matter of minutes – 'Right, let's go a wee run an we'll show ye some things Barry' I say.

Barry can barely contain his elation – 'Caroline, thanks hen, yer a wee darlin. A don't know wit tae say.' I break the possibility of the tears behind those sensitive eyes – 'A think we should get moving eh Ca?' Stewart's enjoying the excitement of it all – 'Aye let's go. I can't imagine how this must feel for you Barry. Whatever, or wherever you want to go, just say the word. I'm ready to go whenever' he says.

Barry's bewildered at first by the hill until I point downwards to a familiar spot – 'Check doon there big yin.' He doesn't believe this is happening – 'Caroline! We stood doon at they windaes every night, lookin up here!' he roars – 'See that wan there? That wis mine. We wur next door to each other wint wi Shug? Fuck me man!'

Caroline's catching every single moment on camera. The two of us standing here, no longer projecting forward, but back to that place – 'Time tae get you hame big yin but we dun it eh, stood up here oan that wee hill lookin doon at that place' I laugh. Barry has one last look before getting into the car – 'Bastards. Didju dae this tae wen ye goat oot Shug?' he asks.

Well, Barry, it's a long story – 'Caroline brought me up here that very first day, but that wis different. Mind ye phoned the gallery that night?' I ask – 'Ach, it's aw in the past. Ye awright? C'moan, let's go, get ye hame.'

Barry's mother has food spread across a whole kitchen table – 'Honest, jist a wee cup fur me' I tell her – 'Caroline might eat something. Naw honest, a coodny eat enymer. Barry, tell yer maw, wit like wis that breakfast? Anyway we canny stay long. The car's a hire. Wit? Ye kiddin? A Rover?'

Bill, Barry's father, shakes hands with me – 'Thanks son. How you managin yersel? A think a mighta knew yer Da. The Locarno. Yer gaun back a bit noo' he smiles. 'Ey shood never huv got that ten years, everybody said that at the time.'

The handshake is made of iron, it's a workman's hand, callused and rough textured.

His mother's a lovely woman, polite, gentle. How did Barry get into trouble? This is a good family – 'Barry, listen, we'll huv tae get movin. Ye want dropped aff anywhere?' I ask – 'Yer burd's hoose? Okay nae bother. Caroline ye ready? Aye, well it wis nice meetin you tae hen' I say, leaving – 'Right Bill! nae bother, good meetin ye. The big yin's heid'll be nippin fur a wee while but he's a good big boay so jist gie um time tae settle. It's noa easy, specially fur the famlies, so don't worry too much. He'll be bran new. Right okay! Cheerio then! Wul see ye's aw again eh.'

Barry acknowledges the palming during the last handshake – 'A cuppla quid. Keep aff the drink' I say – 'S'pure fire water by the way. Naw a don't drink at aw noo. Canny handle it, it's too dangerous. Anyway geeza phone when yer ready tae come through. We jist go fur walks aw the time, it's brilliant. Anyway goan get a good shag an al see ye in cuppla days okay? Aw yer noa gonny start greetin ur ye?' I ask, laughing.

Barry punches my shoulder – 'Right Stewart. Let's go, get back tae Edinburgh. See ye in a cuppla days Barry!'

On the drive back, we pass my granny's old house at the very top of that steep hill of Tharsis Street. That hill killed her, climbing up there every day after work, laden with heavy shopping bags, those huge washing bags, bed sheets, tied into damp bundles, strapped across her shoulders, climbing that hill, for her family, for us all.

I get out of the car, kick a can around – 'Check that left peg eh McNairn! A sculptor? Shooda been playin wi Celtic! Look, there's ma old close where we all lived.' I look up to the window, half expecting to see her there, leaning out on an old pillow. She's where she was before she was born, free from that harsh life of work and those seven kids. Where has everyone gone? The close fronts are boarded up, the windows too, boarded, filled with ghosts, old dead pasts. I don't know where any of them live. I never thought I'd come back to this place, but deep down it seems like an inevitable journey. Nostalgia sweeps over me, smells, women's voices, faces of people. I do the few touches with the tin can, and bang – a goal! It's mad, we played football, across a steep hill, every day after school, unconscious of the slope – 'Did ye check they wee touches there? A played ootside left when a wis a boay. George Best, Eusebio, Pele, Garincha, that was us, the world's best!' I laugh.

Caroline catches glimpses from that early period of my life on camera, but I'm losing parts of those previous lives, losing those pasts buried deep down, like those familiar habits, the habits of other lifetimes, like kicking old tin cans, hooked into my instinct to go back, to return here, filling the hole in me, that longing to go somewhere, some place no longer here.

Yes, I'm walking, walking away.

Abandoning them, leaving behind these things, being prodded by forces, and counter forces. Yes, I'm walking. Walking beyond these old ghosts, talking with living people, living there in those places, through writing only, through memory, remembering.

My instinct is to keep the knowledge, hang onto the habits of those lives, those pasts, preserve the dry clay of my shape, resist change, but that deterioration, that shedding is inevitable, irreversible. I'm losing, forgetting, merely walking into new experience, new old memories, as each moment is moving and gone – sunk in past tense.

I get back into the car – 'Caroline remind me tae phone that wee Tam. Ad forgot this mornin but when we get back tae Edinburgh. Wis ey in the huff right enuff? Wunder wit's the matter wi um?' I ask – 'Stewart, there's money tae fill the tank, but you can huv the car for the rest ey the day and take it back later, issat okay?'

The telephone's ringing incessantly just as we get into the flat. You can almost sense when there's a pissed off caller by the tone. Debt collectors somehow manage to get across that cold, matter of fact, dialing tone. You just know when it's one of them but no, this is one of those 'C'mon I know you're in' types of tones. I grab the receiver – 'Hullo?' I gasp, panting from those four flights of stairs.

– 'That you Shugs?'

It's wee Tam – an agitated wee Tam – 'Aye Tam, am jist back fae Glesga wi Big Bar . . .' I almost finish.

– 'Wit's happenin en?' he snaps at me.

– 'Ach, probably hit the bed, feel shattered wi the journe . . .'

– 'Naw chavvie. Wit's happening wi that fuckin message?' he growls.

That message? Fuck, the two trays of tems! I'd completely forgotten all about them, and worse, we're skint – 'Fuck Tam. Listen a wis let doon wi money but a kin . . .' I try to explain.

– 'SCANLOUS! FUC – KIN SCANLOUS!' he screams.

I think he's shouting at one his two boys for a moment, but no, it's me. Scandalous? Fucking Scandalous? Three years and never missed a payment, or had a lay on off him, or that Geezer. Who does this arsehole think he's talking to? The Godfather? I think he's beginning to believe his own lies – 'Here! Ur you shoutin at me there? Al be up in five minutes ya fuckin wee real yin ye. Scanlous? Al fuckin scanlous ye ya wee cunt ye!' I snarl down the telephone.

The two pints he's had have suddenly evaporated with reality – 'Naw Shugs! Am noa shoutin at *you* mate. Naw, naw, naw. Ye've goat it aw wrang mate. Naw, ma missus wis oan ma ear, ken? Ye noa wit thur like mate. When a hudny heard fae ye a thoat ye wurny that interested' he explains – 'Naw, av held ontae thum fur ye. That's wit a mean. A wis jist worried when a hudny heard, that's aw. Shoutin?' he says – 'Na-aw mate. That wis hur oan ma urra ear at's aw. Shugs! Ye ken am yer mate. A ken aw that. Naw a widnae get wide wi you, ur ye aff yer heid? Shugs! C'moan noo, ye noa me better than that. Na-aw! Two pints an that's the truth. A ken, a ken wit yer sayin. A ken that' he repeats – 'Na-aw, ye've never acted like a gangster wi ma faimly. Ma faimly ur your faimly mate. A apologise if a sounded like wan, an a ken, a ken. Aye, yer dead right. Shugs, thur's naibidy kens that better than me. Right well listen! Dae ye want me tae bring they things doon the noo?' he asks – 'Naw? Right. Okay al see ye the morra, an listen, a ken a wis in the wrang there but ye ken wit these wumin ur like, never aff yer ear. Okay you take care mate, an al see ye the morra. Right then mate, same tae you mate, take care mate.'

Cheeky bastard! Scandalous? Wee Scanlous – that's it, his new nickname. I'll take a walk up anyway, in case he gets paranoid. Wee Scanlous. Barry'll love this one, but I do feel a bit out of order. He's a wee guy, harmless, fantasising, entertainment – so why growl at him? God, I'll get a packet of biscuits or something, say sorry. I should have phoned him at least. My head's up my arse. The writing, doing my fucking box, but I'm getting there, it's almost finished. I pull a jacket on and head up to his house. As I walk up to see him I spot a face, a jail face. Who's that? Joe! – 'Oh. Hullo there.' Joe McGrath. Fuck, the last time I saw him he was cuffed and surrounded by screws, must be on parole – 'Aye. Ehm, long ye been oot?' he asks. The tension between us is laden with past deeds, old tricks from the Special Unit days. He'd taken about a dozen hostages after getting another ten year sentence not long after his release. He had been the Unit's first ambassador on the freedom front, released straight from the Unit having served a four or six year sentence for armed robbery on a jeweller's shop in Glasgow. He'd been bad a boy in those Special Unit days, a stroke puller, switching camps, trying to play double, double, *double* games – or treble wide, you might say, in the Underworld.

– 'Eh, three years ur sumthin. A thoat you ended up daen a twenty? Aw that hostage kerry oan? How did ye get oot, ye oan parole?' I ask.

The film of sweat is immediate, glistening in a sheen over his skin. That balding forehead, shining always in grease. He never could pull off the thug act. He looks about to burst into tears – 'Look Joe. The Unit an aw that. It happened a long time ago. We wur aw at it so don't get paranoid, let's bury the hatchet okay?' I say.

He accepts the handshake – 'Ach Collie, ma heid's up ma

arse. That mob slung me oot a cuppla days ago. Paroled me. Am stayin wi a burd, she's loaded. Wit aboot you?

How long ye been oot?' he asks – 'Three stretch? Huv ye been oot that long? Three years? It's fuckin murdur innit' he says – 'A canny sleep ur nuthin, am fulla Valium. Witsat? Ye'v got Temgesics? Fuck me! Thanks Collie' he says – 'Wit? Right, Shug then. Seriously Shooey, it's really good tae see ye again. A canny talk tae eny cunt oot here. Wit huv you been daen? A book? Ye gettin it published? That's great!' he exclaims.

Great comes over more like – 'Bastard!' – 'Aye Joe, nearly finished. Am tryin tae keep the trainin up as well but it's heavy gaun oot here' I say – 'The best thing tae dae is get intae some sorta routine right away. Keeps yer heid straight. Huv a smoke, tems ur whatever yer intae, but bodyswerve drink, it's fuckin lethal, pure Jekyll and Hyde. Dae some trainin Joe' I suggest.

What? I don't believe this, tomorrow? Not slow is he – 'Aye, okay, nae bother, al see ye the morra then. Ten o'clock, ootside the Commonweath?' I say, agreeing to meet him – 'Naw, jist the punchbag, yoga an at' I explain – 'Ye shood try Tai Chi. Naw, ur ye kiddin, weights? Naw weights ur fur aw they headcases. A wee wurk oot n then take a swim, okay? Right see ye then.'

What have I done? I've just lumbered myself with another ex long termer. And an old enemy at that. Ach he'll be late or something, or won't show up. Anyway, he can't do me any harm, we'll see what happens. It's up to him what he does out here.

That Wee Scanlous! I'd have been in the house, never have even met Joe! Bastard! Bastard! Bastard!

Joe's there the following morning at ten o clock on the dot. He's been hugging those trees by the sounds of it.

The new Voice of Scottish Prisoners?

Jesus. He's definitely serious – 'Jimmy says *am* the new voice fur Scottish prisnurs' he's saying.

That telltale film belies the coolness of the statement – 'Ach, huv anurra tem Joe.' I say, pushing him towards the punchbag – 'C'mon Joe, two minutes, an en a swim, an at's it fur the day. Fancy a walk later, huv a wee joint an a blether?'

He's determined to stress the importance of his new role – 'He gave me six grand tae start a communication magazine fur cons. That governor as well, Dr Coyle. He wants me tae gie speeches tae, aboot brutality an aw that in jail' he adds excitedly.

Six grand? That'll mean four, he'll have two added on, to impress himself, to impress me – jail mathematics never add up, but he has it all worked out already – 'Aye Collie, al buy a kilo a hash furst an en put the money back in wance av punted the hash. The profit kin cover the next parcel. Here, Collie. Sorry a canny help it. Right, Shug! Naw but seriously, dae ye need a grand?' he asks – 'Gen up. Ye don't huv tae pay it back. There's no rush.'

Did I catch just the hint of an elocution lesson there? – 'You intae silk suits Joe?' I'm tempted to ask.

That forehead – 'I'm highly intelligent, but fucked up' – is screeching across the water at me – 'Jist geez the wire if ye wanta grand.'

The Voice of Scottish Prisoners is just taking the locker room horrors, that wee, small object experience, full on – 'Eh Collie! Fulla poofs eh! Cunts aw starin at ye eh, eh' he's sneering, while covering up his private parts.

I'm listening, but thinking. Caroline? I wonder if she has been paid for that painting?

That'll pay those two telephone bills, cover next month's rent, maybe afford us a wee holiday? Nah, fuck. That fucking community charge. That will have to be paid, we've had a final warning. Fuck, how are we going to survive? I wish I had taken that sixty grand – 'Wit Joe? Gap's? Aye nae bother. Ye lookin for linen troosers? Gap's have a lot of good gear an it's cheap. Right then . . . ready? We kin take a walk alang, it's noa that faur fae here.'

Princes Street proves dangerous, brings home my vulnerability – 'Collie. Green. Try tae find olive green. Linen wi turn-ups at the bottom' he says, gesturing, a sweeping hand – 'O'er there somewhere.'

Joe literally disappears. I look around – 'Joe here's linen . . .' He's nowhere, vanished. There's no sign of him. Oh well. I'll bump into him. Here. Olive green, turn-ups too, two full racks. Where the hell is Joe? Oh. Oh. What are they staring at? I'll bet they think I'm shoplifting. These fucking scars, they . . . Oops! – 'Joe? Wit ye daen?' I gasp. That bald forehead, the telltale film, hidden between the racks, is shining – 'SSShhh, geez a smuther' he whispers.

I freeze, looking down and across at the assistants in one cruising sweep. Joe's down on one knee, ripping off alarm tags, and stuffing trousers into his jacket – 'Wit waist? Wit size ur ye Collie?' he's asking.

Jesus Christ. Twenty quid a pair? Tabloid headlines flash through the panic – 'KILLER SHOPLIFTING! KILLER STEALS LINEN TROUSERS! BUT THEY WUZ OLIVE GREEN!' Don't panic. Stay calm – 'Joe. Wit the fuck ur ye daen?' I whisper out the side of my face. – 'Put thum back. The whole place is clocking us ya *fucking* nutcase. Get up an jist walk straight to the door, kid on yer tyin yer laces!'

I feel like a bug, bowing past the assistants – 'Ehm, sorry hen. He's under community care. Am the welfare wurker. Aye, he's clean, everything's cool eh?' I beg, cringeing. Joe's full of apologies when we get outside the shop – 'Collie! Sorry man, sorry. Jist auld habits. Ye know wit it's like.'

I'm stunned – 'Joe! Fur fucksake man! Am a fuckin lifer! Twenty quid troosers? Are ye aff yer fuckin heid? Wur ye jist gonny let me walk oot cauld? Eh? Aw c'mon man. Knock oot the security guard? Joe look, I'm tryin tae keep ye straight, at's aw. A wid rather walk aboot skint. Fuckin hell man. C'mon let's get a coffee. Head up that hill, up towards the High Street. Aye, go up by the Mound.'

I feel like telling him to fuck off, but I can't – 'Joe listen. I know wit it's like gettin oot. Aye, it's fuckin murdur, but ye'll huv tae rethink every . . . Naw, naw. Listen tae wit am sayin. Stop *thinkin* like a criminal. Dae a tem, huv a walk, a wee workoot, but stoap thinkin like a prisnur. Yer oot man! Joe kin you imagine if we'd got caught there, the fuckin headlines? A know ye didnae mean tae put *me* on the spot. Aw furget it, fuck. Jist use yer fuckin brains man.'

The Mound. How I hate climbing this hill – 'Witsat Joe? Aye, thur's a toilet jist alang at the corner. Al wait ootside fur ye' I say assuringly, almost apologetically, for what he will feel was a sherricking.

Twenty fucking quid? I still can't get over what might have happened. Jesus, what a state this guy's in. Fuck, what's keeping him? That's about ten minutes he's been in there? Oh Jesus, what's this? There's this guy, a real bear, right behind Joe – 'Poof? Don't you ever talk tae me like . . . Wit?' he growls at me – 'You stay ootey this pal, am warnin ye!'

I feel the strength lying below the surface of those huge biceps. He's a working man with working muscle, forged by hard graft, probably bends steel – 'Nae problem big yin' I whimper – 'He's jist ootey the hospital. Honest, don't take a liberty wi the guy' I beg – 'Aye! Aye, a noa wit ye mean. Al get um up the road. Nae problem. Sorry if he offended ye mate, honest. Naw, a noa yer noa a poof' I say – 'Right big man, nae bother. Right Joe, c'mon, move. Aye big yin, it's okay. He didnae mean anythin, naw e's jist a wee bit paranoid . . . jist back fae Northern Ireland' I lie – 'Nae bother big yin, see ye again mate!'

Joe finds his legs, recovers his composure – 'Collie! Ey wis starin at me. Eyin up ma arse! Aw a said wis – wit ye lookin at?' he explains.

I don't know what to say – 'Joe yer gonny huv people *right up* yer arse oot here. That guy widda wiped the two ey us oot! Didje see the size ey es fuckin erms man? Joe a don't know wit yer gonny . . . A blade? You're kerryin a fuckin *blade*?' I blurt out – 'A don't believe it man. A fuckin blade? Joe look . . . A blade? Jist in case? In case wit happens?'

I look at him, then the blade he'd been hiding, it's an open razor – 'Fuckin hell! Joe!

A fuckin razur? Am tellin ye . . . Look aw it takes is sum arsehole right in yer face. Joe that's wit it's like oot here. People don't gie a fuck who ye are.'

His head's down, embarrassed – 'Collie, honest . . . am sor . . .' he says.

I'm relentless – 'A don't even go near pubs, especially wi bouncers. Thur burstin tae batter sum cunt. It's too danjerus. A blade? Ach Joe, don't gimme aw that shite, fur protection?' I say, sneering at him – 'Protection, fur fucksake.'

I laugh, but put him in the picture – '*You're* the wan that's dangerous wi that thing in yer pocket. Anyway, look am gaun up tae the flat. Al be there at ten, but am bein up front wi ye. Av goat good people roon me noo an am noa sacraficin that fur nae cunt so it's up tae yersel Joe.'

He's listening, but – 'Joe, am noa gaun back. It makes me a cunt, makes a fool ey aw the people that huv helped me. Ma wife's family, friends, genuine cunts. Boyle? Fuck him an aw es magazines. How're you gonny help prisoners? Look at ye fur fucksake man. Getta fuckin grip ey yerself Joe. Yer oot man! Walk away fae it, an then maybe that'll help urra prisoners if that's wit ye wantey dae.'

Blades? Shoplifting? What the fuck am I doing with this guy? Time to bodyswerve him, ease off, back away. I'm not equipped for this kind of thing. He'll put me straight back to jail. I can smell it coming. I'll push him during the training, grind him into the the ground, burn him out until he can't go on, force *him* to bodyswerve *me*. He'll give it the torn muscle, the back problems, the old damp brutality line – 'They punishment cells. Aye, fucked me up. Damaged ma joints, that fuckin dampness.'

Caroline agrees – 'Yeah, just back off. It's terrible these men are coming out in such a state. Barry's different, he's intelligent. I think you need each other to get all those things into perspective. He listens and has a natural curiosity. University would have made such a difference to his life. Prison simply starves the brain and he does have a brain. Joe tries to sound intelligent but . . . could he be gay do you think?'

Homosexual? I'd never considered this as a possibilty – 'Nah es stayin wi sum burd, a wumin ey met in prison. Loaded apparently, got a flat up near Arthur's Seat. Well, a don't know. Anyway, Barry's coming over on Friday' I say, changing the subject – 'A boys' night oot! Naw, wull be doon in that new bar on the High Street, EH1. Sorry but this is a boys' only night, nae wumin. Joe? Naw, ye kiddin!'

Caroline laughs – 'Oh, I see. All the men discussing their feelings? Who else will be there?'

I don't take the bait – 'Big Norrie Rowan, he's a good big guy. Ca wit a fuckin size ey a man! Al show ye a photograph ey um durin es international rugby days, when ey'd played fur Scotland! Jesus! Built like a tank! Barry likes him tae, e's a man's man' I explain – 'Never eny bullshit, a big diamond. Wee Alan Muir's comin wi us as well.'

Caroline jokes – 'The Hole in the Wall Gang! Yeah, I like big Norrie. Alan's nice too, he must earn a fortune as an advocate.'

I pause for a moment – 'Alan? Aye, they're paid a fortune up there. Organised crime eh. C'mon. Who's kiddin who?' I laugh – 'A don't know what es all about. Well, an advocate oot wi two murderers? Ach a suppose he's bein friendly, open minded, who knows eh? It pisses people aff anyway. Well, am noa supposed tae huv friends like him, advocates an lawyers. Aye eh. D'ye remember that first time we met him? Aye, that time your friends wur o'er fur the Festival, Kim an Terry fae Chicago?' I ask.

How could we forget?

I think this had been my second experience of the Edinburgh Festival. I'd have been out about almost eighteen months, and still off my head.

Caroline's friends are here for the Festival. Terry and Kim are artists from Chicago.

– 'So, are you famous then Hugh?' asks Kim.

Kim's talking about those press cuttings about me. Caroline likes to pull them out for a laugh at dinner parties – 'KILLER'S MILLION DOLLAR FILM DEAL'. If only . . .

Kim is Danish but grew up in Chicago. Grew? He's still growing at six feet seven. He *is* big. Terry's dwarfed beside him: thick black framed spectacles, and a plain sensible suit gives the impression of a straight peg, but he's funny, and cool.

Both of them are highly respected artists in America.

I'm staring at the bottle of expensive wine on the table. Who could have ordered it? I don't know anyone in here. What am I going to do, I have about six quid in my pocket. Who the fuck is Alan?

I have to look up to answer Kim – 'Witsat? Nah Kim. Scotland's jist a wee village. A newspaper is like a local rag, adult comics. They'll write anything tae sell papers and a mean anything. Eh Caroline. The wine, who ordered it? Who's this Alan?' I ask. Kim and Terry are fascinated with my broad Glaswegian accent. They've been having difficulty with it all day, and me doing my best too with standard English.

– 'Yais! Aiy kim frim a little town called Glaiysgow!'

Chraiyst! I'm even saying 'little' instead of 'wee'.

We Glaswegians describe everything on earth as either ded wee or ded big. Big Tam or Wee Tam. Big guys, wee guys. Big burds, wee burds.

Glasgow's mini celebs always amaze me. One minute going on about socialist roots – actually boasting about being poor? How they'd all played in the middens as weans – then give them a few quid and it's elocution lessons – 'The little middings we played in as kiddies!'

And let's not forget those celebrity ads for the BBC – Billy Connolly's *Dark Places*.

Dark places? Gimme a fuckin break. This another fucking *Underworld*?

– 'Jistawee? Where exactly is that Hugh?' asks Terry.

Caroline translates the dialect of that *Dark Place*.

– 'Terry, Hugh's from Glasgow. They speak, they talk, well . . . differently!'

Kim had loved the flat but wanted to go to a bar – 'Hey guys! Let's go to a bar! Yeah! Let's gerra cold beer! Heeeyyy! Lirrle Caroline! So good to see ya again! We wanna hear what you've been doing since we last saw you. C'man let's gerra beer you guys!' he'd roared.

The Bank Hotel is law faculty territory. Advocates, lawyers, procurators, and the odd judge haunt this place – it's *their* boozer, a few yards from the courts.

– 'Who did ye say ordered the wine hen?' I ask again.

The waitress indicates towards the bar but I don't know any of the barmen. Is it paid? This will be embarrassing if they hit me with a bill – 'Yes. Alan. Alan Muir. Yes he's wearing the braces at the bar . . .' she says.

Braces? None of the barmen are wear . . . Hold it. Who's that at the bar? *He's* wearing braces, designed with the black and white band of a police hat. Who is he? This guy is immaculately dressed – a lawyer? The accused usually wear Armanis. The braces, could he be a procurator fiscal? A procurator wouldn't send me over expensive wine.

– 'Honest Caroline. A don't know the guy' I whisper.

Alan Muir? He does look familiar though. I don't want to embarrass him by staring. I do know the face: a handsome, dark featured face, a sort of rugby player build. That distinctive scar running from his hairline, through the temple, to the corner of his eye. The image is definitely Glasgow – scars and Armanis.

– 'You sure you're not famous then Hugh?' persists Kim.

– 'Naw Kim! Av never met the guy! Fuck, here ey comes!' I say.

Alan leaves his friends to introduce himself, there's quite a crowd of them standing at the bar. I suppose this is what's meant by passing the bar for a law degree – 'Hi Hugh. Alan Muir. We met years back when you were in still in the Special Unit. I was with a group of law students. You probably won't remembe . . .'

Shit! I do remember – 'Jesus! We hud a big debate aboot capital punishment? Aye! That's right! A dae remember ye. By the way, yer due an apology. Ad wound ye's up tae get ye's tae talk. Law students wur the maist difficult in they days. Wit? Ach, am daen okay. You a lawyer noo?' I ask.

Alan is an advocate, and he *is* from Glasgow. He laughs – 'Well, you certainly got the students talking Mr Collins! I hope I've made up for the bloomer back then?' he asks. The bottle of expensive wine!

– 'Thanks! This is ma wife Caroline. Kim an Terry. They're here fur the Festival. Aye, Alan came tae the Unit years ago' I explain – 'Said we shooda aw been topped, hung fur murder.'

Alan laughs – 'Well, Hugh lured me into that one but it

was a day to remember. We'd all been terrified going into that place. Your husband didn't help matters but it was a good experience' he smiles.

Caroline laughs too – 'Oh I can well imagine. You're an advocate you say? Are you based in Edinburgh?' she asks.

I sense eyes at the bar, disapproving eyes, looking in our direction.

– 'Alan, listen' I whisper – 'A dae appreciate this, but look. Ye might feel different in the mornin. Don't feel compramised in eny wiy okay? Yer a barrister. You canny be seen talkin tae guys like me, murderers. The gesture's appreciated though so thanks.' Alan looks over his shoulder – 'Oh I wouldn't worry about that lot Hu . . .'

Terry – 'Cannybeseen? This where you live Alan?' he asks.

We all burst out laughing.

Chapter Twelve

CAROLINE MISSES HER friends; marrying me hindered her travelling – 'Yeah, Kim's living in Chicago. But that bottle of wine, yes' she smiles – 'Is he married, Alan Muir? Oh just curious' she laughs – 'Anyway Lorraine and I might go out. There's an opening tomorrow night at at the Fruitmarket Gallery.'

– 'Aye, ye shood go' I say – 'Al no be oot late ur that, definately no drinkin, the tems dae me so al noa be drunk. Barry'll want tae go fur a walk anyway, he hates bein in pubs. N'Big Norrie jist likes huvin a blether an a laugh.'

Caroline asks again about Joe – 'Naw, ey won't last long. Al ease aff, see um less an less. A canny jist tell um tae fuck off' I say – 'The trainin'll kill um. Am too fit for um so a canny see um lastin much longer. Ey'll bump intae sum urra guy jist oot the jail an team up wi thum. Ey disnae actually like me. Am jist a convenience, a kinna short cut intae wit he imagines is anurra Special Unit world. Thinks we're loaded coz you're middle-class' I continue – 'Middle-class burds wur a status hing back in they days in Barlinnie. Ye hud tae huv a girlfriend who wis a somethin, middle-class, a rich family urra professor or sumthin like that. Es heid's still locked intae aw that. Aye a noa, a hud tae pick wan that wis skint!' I laugh.

Wee Scanlous has a lot to answer for. Had I just ignored the telephone, answered the call later after we had settled down. Joe – What the fuck are you going to do? Voice of Scottish Prisoners? Six grand? Kilos? You'll probably blame the world, but a fall is on the cards, you can't live without that past life – you are pure jail bait.

Ca's cool about me going out – 'Yeah, sure. Just be careful' she smiles.

I do the usual call – 'That you Tam? Shugs here. Listen, kin ye see that geezer wi the wee things fur Friday? Aye Barry's cumin through, he's lending me the money' I say, and explain about the chance meeting – 'Listen, a met that Joe McGrath. Fuckin nuts! Aye! Shopliftin! An then this cunt's ready tae batter the two ey us! Aye a fuckin bear! A noa wit yer sayin but this is the last time' I say – 'Nae mer ex-cons. Anyway Friday okay fur that message? Magic!'

I ask about his family – 'How's yer missus? Oh, that's good, aye. Right. Friday okay. Right then. Witsat?'

He asks about the book – 'Wit? Aye, nearly finished. *Autobiography ey a Murderur*. A canny call it anythin else kinna? A sensa wit? Aye right! Listen get coffee oan an al take a walk up fur a blether' I say – 'Na, nae pints, jist a coffee. Av jist powdered ma nose so a need an ear tae bend. Okay?'

Five minutes later I'm on the couch, having tea and biscuits with him. Tam enjoys my visits, whispering snippets of gossip, who's shot who, who's stabbed who.

This is his favourite topic. The head nodding and winking whenever his wife looks in for something. Tam making it obvious he's switching the subject – 'Aw Shugs! Wit a goal!' Football? Tam has never been to a game in twenty years! She just looks at the two of us knowingly, then he's back to the whispering, the nodding – 'Av heard thur's been a lotta truble throo in Glesga. You jist watch wit yer daen mate' he winks.

His wife lectures me as always – 'They bampots'll get ye the jail Shugs! Am tellin ye! Chase thum! Wid they dae anythin fur you! Aye so they wid! Yer daft so ye ur coz a bampot lik that kin cost you years! How's Caroline? Finished yer book yet? Oh wait tae ye see um Tam! The nose'll be up in the air wi aw es new posh friends! Coffee? Two sugars ey? Biscuits? See! Widid a tell ye Tam! Be fuckin high tea next!'

Maureen's beautiful. How Tam nipped her is beyond me – 'Aye McGrath eh? Honest! A fuckin shat masel Tam! Ye wantae a seen this fuckin guy tae! Muscles oan tappey muscles' I'm laughing – 'Am gaun like that – "How the fuck dae a get ootey this wan then?" Joe? Oh he's chalk white, fuckin nearly collapsin, haudin oan tae the railins an stutterin like a fuckin bampot. The guy'd a wiped the street wi us. The blade? Aw naw, ye kiddin? Joe hud the blade. A widnae go near a blade Tam. Yer nerves start gaun' I say – 'Then afore ye know it ye've stabbed some cunt. Na fuck that wee man. Al take a doin furst. Am finished wi aw that gangster stuff, s'aw bollocks.'

Tam agrees – 'Aye a ken. Anyway, how's Barry? Ye's gaun oot the night?' he asks.

I nod – 'Naw, noa the night, wur baby sittin. Caroline's sister's wee boy. Aw es a wee darlin. A seen um jist efter ey wis born. Wee Finlay' I say – 'Aye. Staunin er in that hospital wunderin wit aw the fuss is aboot. Weans? They aw look like wee monkeys, dint they?' I laugh – 'Wee Finlay, that's es name. Aw a wee darlin, geez me cuddles an calls me Uncle. Aye, Uncle Hugh! Caroline's es favourite. Well, am noa sure, but ey must be aboot a year, a think. Am hopeless wi dates, a don't even noa wit day it is the day never mind when ey wis boarn!'

Wee Scanlous. Steal the eyes from your head, but I'm fond of him for some reason, fond of his family. Sure he's earning off me, but that's life. No, the family have been good to me, accepted me as one of their own – 'Right, better get doon the road afore thur's a search party oot fur me! Ca? Na, she's bran new! She knows am noa fuckin aboot wi headcases ur up tae any tricks. McGrath? Ach, he'll noa last long. Aye we go oot noo an again, but she's very private, an a mean private. Wur baby sittin later the night so a better get movin. Wee Finlay, ye shood see um, cuddles me. Es Uncle Shooey! Okay, see ye later. Right Maureen! See ye later pal!' I shout, leaving.

Caroline is down in her studio, and in tears – 'Wit's wrang? Ca? Is there sumthin up wi ye?' I ask. Caroline isn't the type to get hysterical. I feel that paranoia worming into my questions – McGrath? I put my arm around her shoulder, take her hands into my own – 'C'mon wit is it?'

I'll kill that fucker if he's been down here. Fucking kill him – 'Ca wit's happened? Eh wit's the matter? C'mon noo, tell me. Wit ye greetin fur?' I plead.

She looks up at me – 'Hugh. Andy has a brain tumour, it's malignant.'

Death, life; that process is occurring through every moment of our existence, while we sleep even, and yet we never actualise it in our daily lives, realise it, that at any given moment it may come upon us, unexpectedly at any time, at night or day. I have been protected by prison from the harshness, guarded from the immediate impact of such a sudden occurrence, from the shattering effects of it, the shocking cruelty of it.

Andy is but thirty years old.

– 'Jesus Christ' I reply.

Wee Finlay's in my arms, looking out the window. I feel his tiny hand, down the back of my jumper, his arm around my neck – 'How's Lorraine Ca?' I ask – 'Takin it bad?' Caroline's pulling books out of her bag, kids' books found in old second hand shops, secret bookstores she's discovered – 'Ohh eh' she sighs – 'Well . . .'

Finlay goes to her – 'Look Feetie! New books! Aunt Ca'll read ye a story. Uncle Hugh needs to go outside. Yeeeees! Uncle Hugh is a naughty boy! Tell Ca. What's that up there in the sky! Up there, look! What's that? A Star! Yeeeees! Didje hear um there Ca?' I laugh – 'A Stah! And Mr Dark. Aye that's wit ey calls night time. Ey Feetie. Mr Dark! Here'

I say, handing him over – 'Al go an huv a fag oan the stair, ye goat um? Whoooof, wit a heavy boy eh Aunt Ca?'

Lorraine is devastated, but hanging onto any and every thread of hope possible that her husband might live, might live that bit longer than predicted by doctors, or by that thing called fate. While they are being cheated we can only watch, witness suffering, endurance, and pain.

Andy's life force burns like fire, like flames behind his eyes, defying those poisonous tentacles tightening their grip, spreading pain throughout his fragile brain, but these fights are rarely won. A personality disintegrating, being broken by disappointment, by the failures, brings more agony with each operation, as each effort to preserve his young life is maliciously thwarted.

While this light is being slowly extinguished, others are glowing, shining through this darkness, bringing the brightness of millions of suns, like the explosion of supernovas caught in space, in stars of newly born lives, stars in the form of Finlay and Roseanne. Who are these tiny people – Roseanne and Finlay?

Graham and Louise's daughter's pretty little face doesn't understand why people are crying. Why Aunt Lorraine is so upset. Roseanne has no knowledge of death. She is but a year from the place she was before she was born, but an angel has no memory of such a place, she can only wonder what's wrong around her . . . *learn* of such things. Death, the interloper, flitting in and out of our lives, is beyond her knowledge.

Wee Finlay. I feel his trust, his touching, the tiny hand down my back, that small arm around my neck, occasional gestures of warmth, reaching unexplainable, unexpected melting points – 'Aunt Ca! Uncle Hew!'

I *am* his Uncle Hugh.

This little personality forming, developing his experiences into memory, into likes and dislikes, shaping guidelines, protective barriers, for the future, for his lifetime. I feel part of him, feel myself being influenced, forced to think about my own life, and how this affects his life – they do make you think about life, these tiny children, about what you say, what you do, how you behave.

How can anyone deliberately harm children in any way? Surely there can be nothing more important in life than raising a child of your own? My parents; I've always taken them off the hook, but looking at this small boy I have to ask – Did they abandon me? They didn't parent me, they took no responsibility, nor did they explain anything, and yet guilt seems to rest with me somehow?

I've never blamed them for anything that happened but, if not for themselves, then at least for their child – why did I have to become a casualty?

Caroline and Finlay are now my life. Prison and ex prisoners are becoming but loose fragments, lost in those previous pasts, vague memories, alive only in ink – in words.

The telephone's ringing just as we get home from baby sitting – 'Hugh, the phone! I'm in the loo!' shouts Caroline.

I run through to the kitchen – 'Fucksake! This thing never stop? It'll be fur you tae!' I shout back.

I put the telephone voice on – 'Hullo?'

– 'You an yer fuckin book' sneers my Ma – 'Ye think yer a fuckin gangster. Bummin yersel up wi lies' the voice mocks.

I'm not taking any more of this from her – 'Listen Ma. Am noa takin eny ey these daft lectures. Yer noa sherrickin me every time ye phone. Naw ye won't. Am forty years of age, noa some daft wee boy! Lies? Dae ye want the fuckin truth?' I ask – 'You an that urra cunt coodny face the truth. Yer noa fuckin talkin tae me like this! Am tellin ye!'

She spits down the line – 'Am your fuckin *Muther*! Al say witever the fuck a want tae you!'

Bill Buford had published my short story 'Hard Man' in *Granta's Book of the Family*. I had taken the full responsibility for my violence. I hadn't blamed anyone in the short story so why is she so angry?

The timing's perfect – 'Anywiy. Yer Muther's got cancer. Am in the hospital, Stobhill' she says.

My head drops – 'Aw Jesus Christ. Cancer? Ur ye sure Maw? Aye, we'll be through the morra mornin. In the stomach? Jesus Christ. Aye okay Ma, al see ye the morra' I say – 'Right then, night.'

Fuck. Why does life have to be like this, in never ending fucking conflict? I'm hitting those sides, bouncing off the walls – 'Ca, where's the tems?' I ask.

All the physical beatings from life hurt, punished the flesh alone, leaving many scars, and other marks for anyone to see. But beneath the visceral substance, the spirit, the soul, or whatever, something still rages on, almost magnificently, with an invincibility. But she knows how to dig below, penetrate the deepest part, and inflict severe injury, wounding me there in my weakest, withering spot.

Caroline comes with me the following day, to visit her in hospital. We take a wagon to Stobhill. I say a wagon, because that's what it is, a stagecoach without any horses, rumbling along the ground, winding its way through Possilpark.

At Saracen Cross I can see myself dressed in an Indian outfit, with a big chief's head feathers – 'Ca, see this scar?' I ask, showing her the palm of my hand – 'Injuns! A fell there at the zebra crossin wi a ginger bottle! Dressed up like an Injun an screamin the place doon!' I laugh – 'A musta been aboot four, but a wean anyway. Ma Aunty Mary lives alang there. Lived here, maist ey ur life. Ma Granda, Granny Norrie, lived o'er there aw thur lives. Auld Bob died in that hoose. Mary an Betty ended up neighbours up in Auckland Street' I say, pointing to a group of buildings – 'Aw years ago. Aye it husny changed much. A canny remember that much fae they days, it's sorta jumbled up in ma head. Aye, Geronimo eh! Wounded wi a bottla IRN BRU!'

Stobhill. I was born here I think. I hate these places, reeking of decay and disinfectant – 'There she's in there. Ye awright Ma?' I ask – 'Wit've they said?'

Caroline places the flowers onto the pile on the bedside locker – 'Hi Betty. What have they been doing to you? Have the doctors said anything?' she asks.

She's sitting up in the bed – 'Hi Caroline. Naw thur noa sure yet. Ma ain doctor says it's cancer but this mob won't tell ye anythin at aw' she says, smiling cynically – 'Oh Linda McNee's here, wurkin. She's been in tae make sure am bein well looked efter. Linda's Hughie's pal fae the Unit' she explains – 'Aw a really nice lassie, she's been good tae Hughie. Jim, ur man's a nice guy, an luvly weans tae, int they Hughie.'

I nod my head – 'Aye Ma. Caroline's met ur. Linda an Jim bring the weans through noo an again. Linda's been through the whole lot, the Unit an aw the kerry oan when a wis in there' I say, more to fill the possibility of empty space – 'Linda's always been a good pal, an guided me through aw the wee moves in that place, otherwise a widda ended up like Larry Winters. Fuck me Ma, these rooms are worse than the jail, it's the same coloura paint tae! Ma Da been up?' I ask.

She pushes herself up, giggling – 'Oh Christ naw. He wis in that ward the other day there, visitin somebody fae Possil. God a nearly died when a seen um!' she laughs –

– 'Oh es lookin well, the doctor's diet an aw that. Aye! ey hud a wee attack, thought it wis a heart attack, ye know wit es like, a fuckin headcase! He'll ootlive the lottey us! You better keep in wi um son' she smiles – 'Aye! Es fuckin loaded wi money an sum big insurance policy! Och don't be daft, ye know wit es like Hughie. Oh aye, here's wanney these fuckin quacks cumin tae see me. Right, yous get yerselves hame. Thur operatin oan me the morra so if ye kin get through al let ye know wits happenin' she says.

I ask if she needs anything – 'Ye needin fags ur that?'

She raises her eyebrows – 'Fags? A canny, av goat tae sneak tae the toilet fur a fag! Wit a fuckin kerry oan eh!' she chuckles – 'Okay hen, al see ye's the morra ur al gie ye a phone, right cheerio then Hughie, ta ta Caroline!'

This *is* my Ma, my real mother.

Why do we always have to be in those terrible conflicts all the time? Alec and all the stupid remarks whenever we get together. That hostility is just part of their lives, their everyday living together. Their fury evaporates into words, but I have to personalise everything, to the point of violence, hanging onto the wounds, remarks, clinging onto my grudges, when they have probably already forgotten what was said.

– '*Now Hugh. You may be institutionalised.*'

Friday. Tam delivers the tems on the dot. I prepare the bath, and lie soaking up that heat into my old bones. I feel the tem kicking in, easing all my aching muscles from a training session earlier that day. Bang! Bang! Bang! Two left jabs and an upper cut! I love punching the bag, drenched in sweat, pushing myself. C'mon! That's it! Bang! Bang! and here it comes folks, that uppercut straight on the button – Bang! Then that burst with the ropes, clicking the floor – Click! Click! Click!

I love the fast training, but the slow motion action of Tai Chi, torturing those sinews of muscle, filling them with oxygen, layering them with protective padding, layering the muscle with more muscle, without all that steroid poison.

I stand up in the bath facing the mirror. I left jail physically fit, became fat from pints, but the tems helped, let me focus on getting into shape again – 'Noa bad auld yin, noa bad.'

Barry's at the door – 'Ca! I'm still in the bath. Will ye get the door, it's the big yin. Oh yes dear, the boys' night out, remember?'

Barry's still full of jail patter – 'Here! Check the size ey that wee thing! Caroline listen, if ye ever need a real man jist . . .' he laughs – 'The wee man right enuff eh?'

He dodges the flick of the towel – 'Fuck you! Ya big real yin! Here, Scanlous squared me up, ye owe um a cenny so dig in! A cenny? Aye, that's wit they call a ton, hunner quid through here. Didye no know that ya radge cunt ye?' I laugh – 'Aye eh, a radge. V'ye ever heard talk like that in yer life? A radge. Aw es gettin worse, but es a good laugh – "Ehm. How's Paul?" Aye! How's Paul! A coodny believe it that day! Fuckin headcase, but es got the tems big man so . . . Oh, aye! The Wee Godfather!' I continue – 'Es goat a fuckin neck eh? Ye wantae a heard um last week aboot the tems – 'Here Shugs! That geezer's gaun es holidays, wants rid ey the whole lot, five cenny fur this batch. Ken noo, that'll be the last fur a cuppla munths.' Barry dae a look lik a fuckin daftie?' I ask – 'A wee fuckin chancer int ey? Five cenny?'

Barry's Caroline's favourite lifer – 'How are things with you Barry? Your family, are they all right, coping with you being out?' she asks.

Barry smiles warmly, his handsome face softening – 'Och aye Caroline. Thur aw bran new. Glesga's heavy but ma pals make sure am noa involved in anythin. Rab looks efter me. Shug's met him. Rab's bran new eh Shug?' he smiles.

I smile knowingly – 'Rab? Aye, es brand new Caroline. Glesga's a different world fae this place. Ad huv lasted aboot five minutes through there, shot ur jailed. Nah, Rab's a good guy. A like when they come through here. Thur polite an at, but ye see cunts lookin at aw the Mars bars, takin second sights – 'Who's that mob?' Na, Rab's looked efter the big yin in the jail' I explain – 'Right. That's me. R'ye ready tae go big yin? Ca al be in aboot twelvish, s'that okay? Wull jist be doon at EH1. Wee kiss . . . ? See ye later.'

Barry kisses her on the cheek – 'See ye later Caroline! Al get real a kiss when es noa there!' he laughs.

He's looking good, tall, handsome and those sensitive eyes. He's one of the few guys I know who looks at you while you're talking. He's listening, not merely waiting to get an opportunity to get talking back first. People rarely listen outside, interrupting every minute someone pauses for breath. I had found it so difficult to cope with during that period in the gallery – 'Will you shut the fuck up tae av finished talkin?' I'd roar.

Barry though, I had long conversations with him in the jail, uninterrupted talks lasting hours, thoroughly discussed over days. Topics, cleaned to the bone, straight through without tangents – 'Didye hear aboot Andy?' I ask.

Barry's genuinely shocked – 'Wit? That lassie Lorraine's Andy? Aw Shug fur fucksake man. S'that the guy we went tae the openin wi?' he asks – 'Es only a young guy. A liked him tae, patter wis brilliant. That him? Fucksake man. Wit a liberty. How's she takin it, bad? Aw Jesus, wit a shame. Caroline seemed quiet there. Shug man widje no tell me fur? Am gaun oan aboot a loada fuckin shite tae. Tell Caroline am really sorry. Och a know but fur fucksake man' he says – 'She must be shattered as well eh? Wit a shame, a young guy like that. Fucksake, look at the things we've dun tae, an then a young guy like that, never hermed anybody in es life. Right. Naw al noa say enythin in here. A know wit ye mean. Lorraine's faimly know yet? Jesus, how they copin?' he asks – 'Aye, right, nae bother.'

Chapter Thirteen

EH1 IS HEAVING, good atmosphere, and music – 'There's Alan an Norrie o'er er, check. How ye daen wee man? Champagne? Aye al huv wan. Awright er Norrie? Place's fuckin heavin innit? Right Alan, hanks. There's a table o'er there, they're aw leavin. C'mon al grab the seats. Shug, get ma gless?' Brian shouts, securing the table – 'Aye fuck that staunin at the bar, cunts spillin drink aw o'er the place. Some pitch this innit? You've knocked it right aff auld yin. Ye don't get this in Glesga. Naw, this is brilliant Shug. These ur aw good people, an ye kin tell that they aw like you tae. Here, who's that? A know that face . . . fae the jail' he asks.

McGrath! Fuck I don't believe it. I try to slide under the table as he swans it through to the end of the bar – 'Aw fuck! He's seen me' I whisper. Alan doesn't know where he is – 'Eh? Who? Er, who, what?' he splutters.

The gleaming forehead's heading back down the bar. He must have seen me, surely?

– 'Barry, look, this bampot's heavy going, don't say anything, he'll probably leave in a minit' I say.

Oh he's seen me all right, but pretending he hasn't for some reason. That linen – '*olive green*' suit, glides back towards the door. He's probably feeling snubbed that no one has acknowledged his presence.

What film are we about to enter into here, I wonder?

What's he been watching on video – *Scarface*? *Mean Streets*?

A gangsterish scenario is about to unfold. I can '*smell*' it through his pores. He'll be full of something, full of 'game' pills, heavy dude tablets – 'Jo . . .' I try to say, but that linen jacket's deliberately flipped back, by accident, revealing the butt of a handgun, jammed into his olive green waistband. An eye tooth is exposed, as slitted eyes pull off a sneering grin, in my direction – 'Jesus . . . De Niro' I think aloud amid the din. The fingers pointed at the temple, pulling the invisible trigger – 'Blluch! Blluch! Blluch!' clinches it.

Taxi Driver! Fuck Joe, I've seen the film, done the same thing in a mirror – 'You lookin at me? You lookin at me?' Surely you can do better than this?

Barry knees me under the table – 'S'that aw aboot?' he asks, unimpressed.

– 'Och, he's jist oot. A better take a walk up an see um. Naw, naw, al be okay on ma own.' I say – 'Naw, es jist daft, bein dangerous, tryin tae dae a John McVicar. Al noa be long. Aye, keep ma seat, five minutes okay?'

He's leaning against a car outside the Oyster Bar. Aldo and Tony's fish and chip shop is just across from my front close. Caroline's in the house alone. Joe, you're pushing your luck. Honestly, Caroline would knock you clean out with one punch. Caroline's no fucking mug – 'Joe?' I peep over the newspaper he's reading – 'Joe ye okay?' I ask – 'Ye okay?' The hi fi phones plugged into his ears are sending other messages, other sounds, into the vacant space between them – 'Joe? Kin ye hear me noo? Oh, that's better. Saves us shoutin tae each other eh?' The touch of humour transforms the sneer into grinning knowingness, that 'you don't fool me' sort of look. I'm inches from him, from the butt – 'Wit's this aw aboot? Ye aff yer heid? Joe this is the Royal Mile, noa Dodge City! Look a don't know wit yer problem is but . . .' The forehead now speaketh – 'That Boyle bastart took back that muney, an goat me sacked fae wurking wi the *Big Issue*.

Well, forced me tae resign, embarrassed me in frontey every cunt in the place. He's blocked you fae daen eny articles wi thum tae. A wisnae tae crack a light aboot that. Collie. Did you tell him a wis dealin wi smack? Right a noa aw that but that's wit a heard, that you'd grassed me tae Jimmy Boyle.'

That film of sweat signals that he is building up for a real confrontation – 'That wit the gun's fur?' I ask. 'Listen Joe. A jist tried tae help ye but . . .'

The pitch of his voice is becoming louder, harsher, trying to find the rage, to pull the gun – 'DIDJU GRASS ME TAE BOYLE? THAT'S AW A WANTY KNOW.'

I've been here before with this guy. He'll be calling a special meeting in a minute to be defused, be made less dangerous, be made not yet that killer, the killer he wants so much to be – 'Look Joe. We kin shout at each uther aw night. You're the wan wi the message doon yer juke. Och Joe, c'mon hauf the pub seen the fuckin hing. Look Joe . . .'

– 'Here! Shugs! S'the fuckin story man?' a voice shouts from nowhere.

A lanky boy's head lurches forward, the face from a house, hash den I've been to in a daze some night – 'Iss radge cunt gettin wide wi ye Shugs?' The pit bull terrier's is a face anyone would remember, stoned or straight – 'He's noa been fed yet . . .' I assure him there's no problem – 'Naw Ryan, everythin's cool. Seen Marina? Tell hur tae gie me a phone. Na, Joe's . . . Wur auld pals. Right Ryan, take the dug away. Aye, al take a walk doon the morra okay pal. Okay see ye later.'

Joe's face has turned olive green now – 'Joe, yer welcome tae join the company, but, get shot ey that thing, is it loaded? Ye've dun yer fuckin nut. Anyway, think ur dae it, am easy either way. Al see ye aboot okay?'

Barry thinks I'm kidding – 'Wit? Where is the cunt? Is ey still up there? Al knock um oot the prick.' I pick up the warm champagne glass – 'Right! C'mon who tajjered up ma drink?

Cumon! You big yin! Nah, your tajjer isnae big enough! Is that right? A bet ye. Wit's that Alan? Aw here turn it up! Av fuckin seen yours in the gym. Aye nae danjur *wee* man!' I laugh—

Barry's keen for a walk – 'Aye Shug. C'mon, a hate these places, fuckin pubs man. Ye said ye wid show me the night lights in Edinbra. Am serious! Honest, ad rather huv a wee walk thegither, fuck this boozin lark.'

Alan and Norrie had left earlier, they had probably had enough – 'Right Barry. C'mon, fuck it. Look o'er at the castle. Look at that moon. Brilliant eh? A luv Edinbra.' These long walks become a regular feature during the initial months of his release. I look forward to them, but he's a grafter and works hard. Barry wants to start his own painting and decorating business – 'Al come through every two weeks Shug. Av goat loadsa homers tae dae, it's cash in haun tae. Wee Jake's wurkin wi me. Aye, he's a good grafter. Wit aboot yer book? Fuckinhell, it's nearly finished? Wit happened tae that guy fae *Granta*, Bill?' he asks.

Bill Buford had been head hunted by an American magazine, the *New Yorker*. They'd made him an offer he couldn't refuse. This had left me in the lurch for a time, but our friendship had remained intact, and the writing continued.

Barry's fascinated – 'The *New Yorker*? They offer um mer muney? Canny blame the fuckin guy kin ye? That's good that he stays in touch wi ye eh. So who's publishin it noo?' he asks.

I try to explain – 'Well, *Granta*'s different noo. Bill *wis Granta*. Am tryin tae terminate the contract. Canongate huv shown an interest. A young guy called Jamie Byng. He wants the book, but wull see. A lawyer's dealin wi the contract first, an then a kin go wi anurra publisher. He knows an agent, a guy called Giles Gordon.'

The Honourable Jamie Byng. He had been showing an

interest in an idea for another book I'd had about the faces of soldiers and murderers, but he had continually come back to *Autobiography of a Murderer*.

Barry's enthusiastic – 'Ye've dun well auld yin, made a lotta friends. People like ye. A kin see it fae ootside if ye know wit a mean. Naw that's good. A kin see change in ye ye know. Naw Shug, yer noa the same guy a knew in the jail. Still an auld fuckin bam but there's definately changes in ye. Auld Freddy Kruger eh' he laughs.

I laugh too – 'Aye, Bill's a good guy. Invited us tae es farewell party doon in London. Caroline an me. Bill introduced me tae that Salman Rushdie. Barry, honest es ded wee' I laugh – 'The telly makes um look aboot six feet, but es a dwarf! A looked at um at furst. Salman Rushdie? Naw, he's a big guy. Then a tippled! Fuck it *is* him! Seemed okay wi me, but aw that shite aboot the *fatwa*? A wis gonny say tae um that thur wis two guys ootside lookin fur um, two Arabs. Aye, they put a contract oan um. Och, slagged thur religion ur somethin like that' I explain – 'Aw the big names wur there, writers an that. Me tae, para rippin ootey me. Murderer stamped aw o'er the foreheid! They wur aw bran new wi me. Caroline luved it, chattin away tae aw the writers. She knows her stuff so she dis, literature an that. The tems propped me up, yappin ootey the side ey ma face – "Eh Salman, that book ey yours . . ." Aw ye kin imagine eh' I laugh – 'They musta been sayin – "Check the nutcase." Bill wis brilliant, intoducin us tae people. Na he's a good guy. Auld Billy the Kid.'

Barry takes the opportunity to pull me – 'Honest, the tems ur brilliant fur a walk an at but they're a bam's drug Shug. Na, don't be daft. A dae know wit ye mean, but guys through there frown oan tems. Thur fur bampots, junkies, dafties.'

He's heard the protests before – 'A liked thum tae. Shug a dae agree wi ye but honest mate. Thur fur bams oot here. So yer definately cumin aff ey thum? Good. Wan noo an again's awright but noa a mad habit' he says.

We're on our third trip round the castle, Princes Street, and the Royal Mile. He loves these walks. Those big fitbaw legs, like huge trees, striding along, and me there, two steps at a time to keep pace – 'Here fuckin slow doon! Fuck me man! Tems? Fuckin line a speed a need wi you big yin!'

He slows down – 'Aye Barry, yer right. The tems are fur bams. Ma life is changin tae. Caroline's been through a lot wi me. They first cuppla years wur really heavy. A hud tae get away fae drink. Ad a dun sum poor cunt in. A wis aff ma fuckin heid when a got oot, fulla frustrations, fulla hate. A wid blow fuses fur nae reason. Jist freak right oot. Aw, honest, fuckin bonkers man. Too long in there. The tems helped me tae get away fae drink, and the odd bits a powder, but a know wit ye mean' I admit.

We drift into that jail perspective of the world – 'Barry, am bumpin intae lifers aw the time through here, heids up thur arses. Fuck, look at McGrath. Twenty odd years in the jail, an ey still wants tae be a gangster? *Wants* tae be a killer?'

Barry's laughing at my antics – 'Och a know big yin eh' I say – 'Nae wunder ma heid's fuckin nippin! Between Scanlous an aw these fuckin headcases – "Do I know Paul Ferri . . ."' I laugh – 'A mean, we're up tae wur necks wi an overdraft, tryin tae keep the flat, they fuckin telephone bills, framin bills, buyin material, a studio an aw the other things like the food and fags. And then that nutcase – "DIDJU GRASS ME TAE BOYLE?"'

The Royal Mile from the top is amazing, looks straight down onto the docks. We're at the end of another marathon walk. Barry wants to go back to the flat to have a coffee before he heads back to Glasgow – 'So wit aboot the sculpture an at? The art things noa make ye a few quid?' he asks.

I look at him – 'Art? Are ye fuckin jokin? Thur's nae money in art, honest, but it is a world, a different world Barry. Ach, sumtimes a get pissed aff bein skint aw the time, bumpin intae arseholes dealin, pure pricks, loaded tae, but fuck that kerry oan. Sellin smack? Na, fuck that. Thur aw grasses anyway. It's jist that, a mean, ye feel like jist takin thur fuckin money aff ey thum' I say – 'Stick a fuckin message at thur heids, an take it aff them – "Here you Hectur." Plug thum an walk away, but ach. Av lost a lotta things big yin, but av goat Caroline, wee Finlay, Caroline's parents, lotsa friends tae. Na, am noa gaun back tae jail. A hate tae think aboot that fuckin place, an yet this fuckin book drags me back there' I continue – 'Honest Barry, it's fuckin murder. A hate this writin, it's a fuckin nightmare, sittin up aw night, an frozen tae the bone. McGrath's writin a book as well. Aye, gen up! Thur aw at it. Aye, aw the jails, writin books, mad bastards! Here, it's gettin chilly big man eh. Aw Jesus these fuckin stairs noo. Al be gaun fur a bed doon the morra eh! Wind Caroline right up – "Here boss, put me doon fur the doactur"' I mimic.

Barry's pissing himself at the front close – 'Here c'mon! Calm doon auld yin! Yer still good wi they wan liners, al say that fur ye ya fuckin headcase. Jimmy Boyle catches you yer in trouble! Anyway so dae ye think the book's nearly finished then? How dae ye noa when tae stoap? Dae ye noa wit a mean? Where dae ye say that's it? Dae ye jist thingmy?' he asks.

Thingmy? – 'Who knows, Barry? Al *know* when it's finished. A lotta cunts'll hate me. It'll be remorseless tae them. Ye noa wit a mean. Aw that – "Am sorry" stuff. A mean, Jesus, these stairs. Why bother wi aw that other crap ye read aboot gangs, jail, an the SAS.'

I'm relieved to be back in the flat. Caroline's out, probably up at Lorraine's, or visiting Andy. Barry heads straight for the kettle. I sort the cups, and start rolling a joint over at the kitchen table – 'Am describin the feelins ye experience, they real experiences, noa aw that "am sorry", the born-again bollocks. Aiym a new man an awrat. Na, fuck thum, ye noa wit a mean big yin?' I ask – 'Am apologisin tae nae cunt oot here.'

Barry's laughing at me – 'Right get the biscuits oot auld yin. Where huv ye goat thum planked?' he laughs – 'Cumonnnnn, it's me. Get them oot. Aye, a noa. A noa wit ye mean Shug. A see thum tae, bampots. Ye goat the auld rebel heid oan there? Wan joint ey, an yer fuckin steamin. Look it the state ey ye Tam.'

Tam? Barry Tammed me up in jail. Everytime he caught me stoned he'd pretend the screws were watching me – 'Here! Tam! That mob's clockin you man!' I'll get him for that one before he goes home I promise myself – 'Oh here, fancy a spliff fur the bus afore ye go hame? Ya big fuckin real yin ye eh! Just say No! Nah, am beginning tae forget wit it's like tae feel things, dae ye know wit a mean?' I ask – 'The tems block stress a suppose, but a wantae tae feel clean, be completely straight. Ach, al always smoke a wee joint fur bed. But tae feel sensations withoot drugs, tae feel the cauld, that fucking cauld blast fae the North.'

His eyes smile at me – 'Yer serious eh, aboot the tems? Good. Where's the wee yin the night by the way? Ma Wee Caralina?' he asks.

I take a drag – 'Caroline'll be up at Lorraine's wi Andy. Naw a canny face it Barry. A canny look at Andy. Look at us two eh, two fuckin murderers eh, it's crazy innit? Eh. R'you makin a coffee ur wit daftie?' I ask, laughing – 'How's Auld Bill? S'ey daen aw right? Yer maw? She's a good wumin Barry. Na, they canny understaun it, these life sentences, they fuck every relationship ye ever had, ye canny explain it tae people.' I continue, dragging on the joint – 'Sojurs must go through the same thing, efter years in the army tae, noa able tae communicate wi thur relatives, wi friends, it must be a nightmare fur sojurs. S'good hash this, noa like the shite ye get through here' I say, filling my lungs – 'Aw this mob through here shove it intae the micros, jist tae double thur profits, fuckin bampots, wastin a good smoke.'

Barry asks how my family are getting on – 'Ma maw? Eh, aye she's bran new. Right! You're daen the coffees big yin, an al roll a wee joint! Ma legs man! That wis a few miles there ye know, three times full circle roon the Castle. Too auld? Issat right big yin?' I ask, changing the subject – 'C'mon! Auld Shug'll teach ye a few lessons. Nah, yer too fast ya big cunt. A mind you tried tae set me up when we first met. Aye, tryin tae get me in sparrin wi ye, mind? A sneaked back doon the stairs, an watched ye oan the bag, gonny knock fuck ootey me eh?' I laugh, teasing him – 'A wis too fast then, didnae wantae take a liberty wi ye mate. Hauuuw!' I roar as he gets up to scud me – 'Al tell wee Caroline! Wit's that? Ma accent? Wit ye talkin aboot?' I ask – 'A don't talk posh. Naw honest, it's wi bein wi Caroline. Don't fuckin start big yin, listen you better get movin by the way afore that missus ey yours sends a possey through here tae get ye hame.'

Barry's falling around with the giggles – 'Fuckin auld bam. Right in there like a fuckin parana – "A dont talk fuckin posh!" Right' he says, getting to his feet – 'Here listen a better get movin. Check the fuckin nick ey man. That ma jaikit there? Ma legs ur deid wi walkin man.'

I take his arm as he lurches forward – 'Ye okay? Edinbra big yin! YER IN EDIN-BRA!' I roar.

Barry laughs, brushing aside my arm – 'Fuck you ya'n auld cunt ye. Okay, al gie ye a phone later in the week. Am the same, jist wurkin aw the time. Right. See ye.'

I hang in the door frame – 'Aye, nae bother, jist geez a phone. Here wit aboot Celtic? Wi-it? Away ye go ya big fuckin hun ye! Aye right! Okay Barry, see ye, night. Watch they coppers an at . . . might be watchin ye eh. Oh here, listen. Naw seriously. Kin you pick us up at the station the morra? Aye, ma wee maw's in Stobhill.'

Barry doesn't hesitate about the lift – 'Aye, nae problem. Yer maw in the hospital? Ye never mentioned. Wit's up?' he asks – 'Right, okay. I'll be across fae the station, hauf six? Okay, Caroline cummin throo as well? Right half six then, see ye later.'

Chapter Fourteen

CAROLINE ARRIVES HOME later that night. She's been at the hospital, but says nothing to me. I leave her alone with her thoughts, but make conversation about anything other than Andy – 'Ca, Barry says he'll pick us up if ye want tae come through tomorrow an see Betty. That okay?' I ask.

She's reading, but nods in affirmation – 'Yes, yes. You stoned? Ohh, what happened to the big night out with the boys then?' she asks.

I give her a run down, but miss out the scenario with McGrath – 'Och Barry, ye know. Hates pubs, wanted tae go fur a walk. Three times. Fuckin legs are like lead. We'd a good blether, takin the piss, ye know wit he's like. Anyway, the morra? Ye cummin through wi me? Right then, am gonny get an early night issat okay?'

Caroline's tired too, drained emotionally – 'Yeah Hugh, lets get to bed. I'm exhausted too' she replies.

Barry's there the folowing night, and drives us straight to the hospital – 'Possil eh. Ye live here long Shug?' he asks as we drive through towards Stobhill Hospital. I barely recognise the place. It was such a long time ago, during my childhood – 'Naw Barry, I went tae stay wi ma granny up the Garngad, Royston Road. Aye, Shamrock Land! Albert an at mob still stay there, been there aw thur lives.'

Barry laughs – 'The Shamrock eh. They wur heavy. Right! Here we ur. Wit ward she in Shug?' he asks – 'Right, nae bother. Fuckin parkin man, murder. Al jist wait here okay an drive ye's back tae the station. Aye, am wurkin the morra, up early an that' he says – 'Naw, al take ye tae the station.'

Betty's sitting up in bed at the hospital – 'A chink in the intestines. Aye, that's wit the surgeon said' she says – 'Well, the doctor thoat it wis cancer ey the bowels. Oh, fur fucksake ma sides ur sore an that anaesthetic. A thoat a wis fuckin dyin, could hardly breathe, but, that's the fags. But Jesus, a feel knackered Hughie. Aye, Alec's been up every visitin hoor, ye know wit es like Hughie.'

Alec eh, I see the pride in her eyes – 'Ach es a good boay Ma. Am noa the easiest ey people tae get oan wi, an av never hud a chance tae really get tae know um, no as a wee brother' I say – 'Caroline gets oan wi um. Ey phones ur noo an again. Es Da?' I sneer – 'Ach, that cunt. A never liked Ferrie. Anyway when ur they lettin ye hame? We'll come o'er an see ye, but it's the money Ma. Wit? Ye kiddin! We're up through the stratisfere wi debt, but ach, fuck thum' I laugh – 'Gaun straight? Fuckin joke, av never been sa skint in ma fuckin life.'

She's smiling as we leave – 'Better watch a don't bump intae ma auld man when wur leavin, fuckin nutcase' I grin – 'Naw Ma am never gaun o'er there efter that last time when a wis jist gettin oot. Speed? A wis runnin the fuckin jail an he's accusin me a stealin a gram ootey es pocket?' I say – 'Ma, honest, ey widnae look at me that day. Naw, he never visited me fur nine year an en aw that shite aboot a bitta speed? Naw am tellin ye, a won't even go tae es funeral' I swear – 'Here, mind that day a phoned um fae the jail? That's wit a shouted doon the phone at um! Aye! Then he shouted – "Good! Ya fuckin rat ye!" Ach a know' I laugh – 'That ten year an aw they doins, but fur fucksake Ma! Anyway, ye'd better get some rest. S'Jim up the night? Ach, he's okay Ma. Right, next week okay? Take care, an cut doon wi the fags. Listen tae me eh, sixty a day. Aye, right, okay. Geez a wee kiss an al see ye next week. Caroline's goat a paintin fur ye, a cracker.'

Caroline hugs her too – 'Yes Betty, you too. Bye then' she smiles.

I hate leaving. Looking back, I hope to never see her so vulnerable again. I believe the fire is more her style, more her way of expression, her only means of caring.

Why the fuck couldn't things have been different?

Possilpark, I hate the fucking place, hate the things it does to people, fucking up their lives. All that sentimental shite about being able to leave your front door open in the auld days. Leave your door open? There was fuck all to steal. Now we have the dish in the sky on almost every rooftop, those knickers, bloomers in every window, videos recording and re-recording the alternative worlds, the fantasy lives of Al Pacino, Robert De Niro, and Jimmy Corkhill – some junkie in your living room brandishing needles to take all that away from you, and take you into your *Reservoir Dogs* and *Mean Streets*.

'Glasgow's Smiles Better'

I glance at the huge billboard as we travel past the gasworks at Blackhill on our way back home, to Edinburgh – 'Caroline. Check that fuckin thing eh. *Brookside* oan the night? Great. Big Jimmy's brilliant, think he'll get the teachin joab? Na, nae danjur, it's another tester for him. That Jackie's a right cow, never geez um a break.'

I love getting home to the flat, especially after a trip down memory lane through the badlands of Glasgow – 'Ca, there's a letter there. Will ye see who it's fae? An al put the kettle on' I shout from the kitchen.

Caroline's reading the letter – 'It's the statue. De Marco must have sold the Blackfriars Street Church. They want you to move it' she says.

I slump on the couch – 'Aw fur fucksake man. It's jist wan thing efter the other. Read the letter oot again. De Marco, I thought ey owned the building?' I ask – 'So, es sold it, an disnae say a fuckin word, or gie us any warnin? Wit the fuck did a ever dae that daft fuckin statue fur?' I ask, frustrated by the news. – 'It's been a headache since day wan when the church commissioned me tae dae it. Ach Caroline, am fed up tryin tae go straight. Thur's always sum fuckin problem tae deal wi. Naw, honest, it's noa your fault. Don't be daft' I say assuringly. – 'A jist wish we could get some kinda break. A fortnight. That how long av got tae move the thing? Wish ad carved a statue a Satan ur sumthin.'

I hold my head in my hands, trying to keep down the frustration – 'Wit dae a dae noo? Jist let them smash it up?' I sigh – 'Might be for the best, it's been a pain in the arse, and noo this? A fortnight? Ach, fuck it.'

The Christ statue is about to be evicted from its temporary home. Blackfriars Church has been taken over by the Italian Institute. The letter states that the statue will have to be moved as soon as possible or be destroyed. I throw the letter in the bin, furious at the whole wide world – 'That Spalding bastard! We widnae be in this position if he'd bought it Caroline. Aw that shite aboot trouble with the neck?' I spit out – 'Wring that prick's neck if a see um.'

Julian Spalding *had* been planning to buy the statue. I had told him that there were a number of flaws in the work. What he did, though, was send his deputy to make the final assessment.

Spalding's deputy had rejected the possibility of the sale, stating there had been trouble with the neck, but later told people the true reason – 'We won't buy that murderer's work – ever!'

Andrew had told me one night after an opening – 'Hugh, I'm sorry . . . You've just been caught in the middle. What did

I tell you? He's completely mad.' I'd taken the news fairly well at the time. I didn't kill, have them slashed, harmed in any way, but now? I roll a joint for bed – 'Wit am a supposed tae dae? We canny afford the transport an haulage, an where kin a get it stored? Wit a kerry oan eh Ca?' I moan – 'A shood've hud they two cunts battered. Naw, they'd probably've got turned on – "*Oh harder, harder.*" The paira fuckin real yins eh. Well, McNairn a suppose a wee shag's oot the question the night ey?' I laugh.

Caroline puts her arm around my shoulders – 'Oh Hugh, I'm so sorry. I feel I dragged you into all this. You could have had a better life with someone else. I know that. I'd hoped for better things for you, it's so unfair. I know you love me. I love you too.'

Wee McNairn eh. I've never fathomed her out – 'Listen Ca. A don't care aboot money or anything like that. Av got you' I say, cuddling her – 'A cood get money. The easy way, sellin drugs, daen protection for pubs, ur even shootin people. Av got you, an a good life. Am jist a bit tired, that's aw. So don't be daft. The Christ statue? Let them worry aboot it, smash it up, ur witever they want tae dae. Let's go tae bed, and get sum sleep eh. We kin think things through in the mornin' I suggest.

I lie looking into the dark, smoking a last joint.

Thank Caroline. Bless Andrew, because they alone gave a murderer an opportunity, a chance to walk away.

But – *I'm still walking.*

The tabloids discover the situation, but for once actually do more good than harm by highlighting the plight to find a home, although don't miss the killer tag opportunity—

KILLER TO DESTROY CHRIST STATUE!

KILLER'S STATUE NEEDS A HOME!

Jimmy Boyle's contribution is more of a criticism than anything else – 'What are you doing involved with these people anyway? This Mickey Mouse mob?' he'd asked. Julian Spalding is the Director of Scottish Museums. As much as I disagreed with his decision on the statue, I actually got on well with him. His decision irritated at times, but he himself was honest with me – 'Hugh! I'm not prepared to take the flak about buying the statue. There would be a public outcry. Caroline and you still coming to our Festival party? Hugh, show me some new work.' All in one breath – 'Aye Julian, we'll be there. Think al get you mugged by the way' I reply, winking.

The Edinburgh University Settlement come to the rescue in the end. John McNeil, an ex prison governor, and his partner Nick Flavin, handled the transport and haulage of the statue. John I found a nice man. How could he be a jail governor? He's too nice a guy. Nick? Nick's Irish and likes a whisky, an ex priest – 'We'll store the statue and try to find a more permanent home, but don't worry about havin access, the store's in Bread Street. Andy, Hugh Collins! Hugh, Andy Meric! Andy's our press officer.' Meric. Meric? – 'Dae a know you? Edinburgh Zoo ur sumthin?' I'd asked him.

The pupils leering back show recognition – 'You've met my sister. Her man's a brickie. Remember? The Ross Harper thing? The Big Slipper an prostitutes? That wis us! She'd said she met you just the day before it happened. Aye, we set that up! Hugh' he whispers – 'Can we speak confidentially? Yeah? What aboot your story? I can get you ten grand. The *Sunday Mail*. Aw c'mon, your story interests the public. I can get you ten grand right now. Well, look, take my card. Naw, jist gimme a call and we can have a drink, nae problem.'

Caroline is relieved to be going home – 'What a little creep. Ross Harper? Did he say they set him up?' she asks.

I nod – 'Aye. Mind the time ey wis to be promoted or something. Well, his sister wis wan ey the birds involved. Och, ey wis spankin them an things. Meric, though, that's who tipped aff the tabloids. Harper was a brilliant lawyer. Aye a liked um. That mob set um right up' I explain – 'Nearly ruined es career, ballsed up any chances ey um becomin involved in politics. That Meric's fulley it' I say. 'Ten grand for ma story? They never gie up dae they, dirty fuckin tabloid bastards.'

Caroline wants to do some browsing, bookshops, secondhand shops – 'You can tidy up the flat. Get on with the writing. I'll look in on Lorraine and Andy. Oh don't be so silly Hugh' she sighs – 'No one's thinking those kind of things.'

Andy and Lorraine. I can't look at them. I don't deserve to be here. I've taken a life and here's this young guy fighting for his – 'Nah, al head up tae the flat. Tell thum . . . Ach, al see ye later, geeza kiss. Al get this book finished. A think it's there, jist wee odds an ends tae tidy up an it's finito, a think! Okay, see ye later, mind an bring fags back, ta ta!'

I'll have a half of tem, try to cut down. This book's driving me mad. Writing? I mean, it's a shape, a formula – life is definitely not. Autobiographical? Where are the lines, the boundaries? Do I try to find a balance? A balance in itself is false, almost a fake. I find the process impossible, providing pretty pictures or exposing the ugliness of it all. It just can't be done. Life, people's lives, can't be fitted into two pieces of board, with so many words, a certain number of pages, and evaluated as a book, a truth. To tackle this like stone carving, as sculpture, scraping the layers away until that block is left, the three-dimensional lump, there to be observed, walked around, assessed, read, or whatever. This is my only means of completion.

Fuck it. I'll do that other half tem. Shit. Who's this this time? Telephones aggravate me – 'Hughie! Alec! Ma granny's deid!' he's shouting – 'That Mary Norrie! They left ur oan ur ain. Wit? Naw! Listen Hughie! Am tellin ye! Wit? Naw! They better noa be at the fuckin funeral! Wit? She gets cremated oan Wednesday!'

Cremated? My granda, a socialist, gets a *Christian* burial? My granny, a devout holy water carrying Catholic, she gets cremated? Families eh – 'Right, al be there. How is ma Maw?' I ask. 'Right, okay al meet ye at the crematorium. Ma Da gonny be there? How? Ey didnae even know the wumin. Says anythin tae me al knock um oot. Calm doon, fur fucksake, am only kiddin. Oh you es pal noo?' I sneer – 'Books? Aw a see, gets ye books. Noa gie up will ey? Still fancies yer Maw. Ach, a know. Here wait tae ey reads ma book!' I laugh – 'Probably put a contract oan me. Aye, a fiver ur sumthin eh? Aye, it's oot in February. Al hiv tae leave the country! Wait tae ye see um by the way, ey'll be dun up like Marlon Brando. Don Corleone eh! The Family! This'll be es chance tae wear the black cashmere coats. Auld Norrie eh' I sigh – 'Ach she wis never the same efter yer granda died. A know, he wis ur whole life, poor auld cunt so she wis. Right Alec, al see ye there okay.'

Who is this man, my father? Wullie Collins the Hard Man. That short story I wrote for *Granta* magazine. The Hard Man – that really got to him. What does he see? How is he still so steeped in that world? The Robin Hood figure from my childhood. Did they do that, or was it my own imagination? Did I want him to be hard? He's been battered by that lifestyle. Why didn't he walk away from it? There were no Special Units then, but after ten years in jail, wasn't that in itself a lesson? He's intelligent, well read, but chose to continue down that murky path, littered with scars and marks, those wounds no one can see. Why? Was that world more important than his son, a child?

Finlay? Could I walk away from him?

The truth is that I don't know this man, my father.

Those previous lives, pasts, divide our relationship, like barbed fences, keep us apart forever. How can I blame him? I have invented a figure, so many father figures, and each collapsing in on themselves, time after time, until the disillusionment became a hatred, a loathing, a shotgun in his face – 'Al fuckin blow you away Da!'

Who are they? The woman waiting for me outside the gates of prison, he not waiting anywhere. I've built parental figures from monthly visits, day paroles, during sixteen years of jail. Sixteen years. That's one hundred and ninety two hour visits: eleven thousand, five hundred and twenty minutes. Six hundred and ninety one thousand, and two hundred seconds.

Time? Memory? Is this a relationship?

Life, moments, moving in a state of annihilation, each crushing the next. Are these moments one singular thing? Or are my shifting moments my own? Separated from theirs? And yet each pulling us towards unity in that final moment of death? Is death itself the relationship, while memory divides us in life? This fucking book. Why can't I *not* remember, leave those accumulated experiences, those previous lives, or pasts, leave them behind?

Can't I *not* remember? Look with fresh eyes?

My granny Norrie's thoughts are dead. Had I not answered the telephone would that relationship still have been alive, memoryless? Now I'm remembering fragments of the previous surfacing, bringing with them nostalgia, grieving, sadness. Had I left the telephone these feelings wouldn't be occupying my mind right now – she would be in my subconscious, alive and still there.

Memory, time, whatever. I'm trapped there, trapped, trying to catch up with the – now. Now is already moving into what we call future. That future hurtling forward, towards the past. The previous, I mean where does that go or end, but in death.

Tick tock. By the time that can be written, a billion, billion, trillion motions will have aready shifted in one singular flash. Letting go takes me there instantly, but writing? Writing then is a trap, a cage, of nothing more than memory, recollection in operation, remembering fragments of the previous, piecing together the pieces, blurred by the detail, by these tellings, by the teller doing the telling, but trapped there always, never actually in the present, is the teller ever there?

My brain feels dilapidated, hollow, empty. The tem is beginning to hit in, rousing the teller, the telling, fragmented pieces, continues . . .

Chapter Fifteen

FUNERALS. I NEVER know what you're supposed to do. My Aunty Mary is on one side, my mother on the other, all seemingly praying, but probably wondering about rents and bills. My father I can hear behind me singing quietly. I glimpse black cashmere from the corner of my eye. Dunky White's standing next to him. He winks at me. The cross-scarred face crumples into a million creases as he smiles at me. Angie Jack, my Ma's pal, had done him with two tumblers one night, left him with a cross covering his face like a saltire flag. I'd have buried her there and then had she done that to me, woman or not. Dunky looked fierce but was just a bit of a blowhard, looked the part but what a face. My Da'd turned his back on me at the front entrance, but I hadn't realised that it was him until my Ma said – 'Och, jist ignore him Hughie. A don't know wit es daen here anyway. Here, dae ye mind yer Uncle Robert?'

– 'How ye daen auld yin?' he says.

Uncle Robert? Betty and Aunty Mary's brother. He doesn't look like the figure from my childhood: the dashing dark curly haired hero. The man before me was bespectacled, balding, and much smaller than my memory allowed. He'd worn black blazer jackets, and white open collared shirts, in my mind, but now wears the inevitable middle aged anorak jacket. He too is much smaller, like that wee sparrow lying in the coffin. Are my family all shrinking?

I tower over him – 'How ye daen, Uncle Robert?' Shame aboot ma granny eh.'

He smiles – 'Aye big man. We aw huv tae go someday. That yer faither o'er there?' he asks.

I don't look round – 'Aye. Wur noa talkin. Aw he's aff es heid. Ye know wit it's like . . . Av noa tae talk tae ma Aunty Mary. They've noa tae talk tae ma Maw. N'ma Da's noa talkin tae me . . . Sum kerry oan innit . . . A don't know who av tae talk tae. N'd'ye think ma granny'd be talkin tae any ey thum?' I remark.

Cars are still arriving. God, I've no idea who any of these people are, but they're like most of the family, strangers no doubt. There's my younger cousin, Hughie Tannock! My Aunty Mary's boy. I haven't seen him since the day of the murder. Wullie Mooney had tried to demand money from him and his pals, professional pickpockets, thieves, earners – 'The cuzz! Shug! How ye doin man? Where's Ma Aunty Betty? Here! Nae geezer here's tellin me who a kin talk tae!' he claims.

Thank God – sanity!

I pull him aside – 'Listen Hughie, let's fuck off efter the service. How ye daen anyway young yin?' I ask – 'Aye, a goat aw yer letters. Ye still graftin? Aye? Must be worth a few quid eh? Naw, honest, am leadin a quiet life these days. Aye, come through an meet Caroline' I say, noticing people going inside for the service – 'Righto, wi better get inside. Ma Da? Naw, talk tae um. A grass?' I laugh – 'He called ye a grass? Och Hughie, fuck um, he's dun es nut. Right c'moan we better get in.'

Dunky's face creases when I wink back at him – 'Awright Dunky' I whisper, glancing, frowning at my Da.

Dunky looks towards the heavens, slightly shaking his head – 'Oh. A know son, a know wit es like, but ey is yer Da, Hughie.'

I acknowledge this unspoken gesture. I turn back to hear the end of the sermon and the beginning of the hymns. A familiar voice bellows out the first few lines at the top of his voice. A few unfamiliar heads turn discreetly to see who it is, but, there is only one man with such a powerful voice, only one such chanter – Wullie Collins.

Aviieee! Aviieee! Aviieee Mariaaaa!
Aviieee! Aviieee! Aviieee Mariaaaa!

Jesus! Thank God it's not 'Faith of Our Fathers'. That would be right up his street. I feel the presence of my Ma, swaying slightly, gently singing, almost in harmony with this . . . this ex-con, ex-husband, ex-father, ex-family. My Aunty Mary touches my hand as the sign of peace is made. I give her a wink, which she understands immediately – 'See ye efter the service son' she whispers. Betty isn't making a move to shake her hand. I nudge her – 'Ma, c'moan noo.' She reaches across but the look is cold in her eye, a gesture filled with accusations. I'm tempted to turn around and give it the – 'Hi Dad!'

Aviieee! Aviieee! Aviieee Mariaaaa!
Aviieee! Aviieee! Aviieee Mariaaaa!

He's getting louder with each verse. This for my benefit? One of his snide wind-ups? I hate looking at him. I do turn though. God, there's something horrible inside him. I don't want to be twisted like him, or even look like him physically. I sometimes catch myself wondering – Does he do this? Things that I do naturally. I find myself catching the movement, asking – Why did I do that? Is it genetic? *Am* I like him? Am I the . . .

Aviieee! Aviieee! Aviieee . . .

– 'Aw fuck off!' I snap viciously like a puppy.
I think he heard me. I don't look, but the singing abruptly

stops. Dunky'll be looking to the heavens – 'Ey *is* yer faither Hughie.' Singing, that's all he ever did. Singing in the end room, singing at wine parties, now singing at funerals. He sounded better in that drunken end room. He drinks no longer, twenty years now. Stopped when I went to the Special Unit, probably didn't want to embarrass Jimmy Boyle. Stopped, he said, because his boy was going to the Special Unit. I kill a man, and what? He stops being a drunk, a dosser?

My Aunty Mary hugs me at the reception – 'Look son. A know thur aw blamin me fur yer granny dyin. A know wit *she's* telt ye son but it wisnae like that. A tried ma best but a hud tae go in fur an operation . . .' she explains.

I hug her, my favourite aunt – 'Och Mary, c'moan. She wis like an auld bitta leather. When ma granda died that wis hur finished. Listen, al come o'er an see ye when this is aw finished okay? Where's the bold boy, Hughie Tannock?' I ask.

We spot him with a female distant, distant cousin – 'Oh Hughie, look at um, es chattin up a burd. She's es cousin tae. Christ, es goat weans aw o'er the place. Es an awful boay int ey son? Stone mad, an still thievin. A klepta maniac so ey is.'

Hughie Tannock. Stone mad right enough. He'd taken my Ma on a guided tour of his house in London – 'Aye, Aunty Betty. A stole that ootey a big kane, rich cunt's. A goat this ootey anurra pitch, an see that paintin? That's worth a right few quid, but a like a cuppley the paintins, thur better than your Shooey's!'

Betty loved her nephew, a real rogue. He was always my favourite too. Talking half Scottish and half Cockney – 'Ea cuzz! Wot you fink ey this little kettle en?'

The gold wristwatch dangling on his arm had to be worth a few grand but, no doubt, stolen from some expensive shop; loved his gold chains and diamond rings, anything gleaming, expensive, attracted him like a magnet – 'Ea cuzz! Ea, you ave it. A kin do wiv anuva yin enywiy.'

– 'Why are ye talkin like that? Ye sound like fuckin Del Boy!' I say, mockingly. He's unfazable – 'Ye Wot? Ea! Wot you on abaat en cuzz?'

We leave our relatives to the not speaking to each other and getting pissed together. My Da had disappeared outside the church into a cab. I wonder, does he pay his taxi fares these days? I'd felt relieved to see the cashmere coat stagger into the cab. His leg is worse than before, yet another example of the batterings, paralysed from a stabbing, stabbed in the neck while he was drunk. I remember seeing him in hospital, shouting at me – 'Widdy you want, money?' I had been about . . . a wee boy. Why did he hate me so much? The Hard Man piece had merely given him the excuse to show his true feelings to his gangster pals without reserve – 'That fuckin rat!'

I'd fucked up a few times, sure, but the venom? Was it the ten year sentence? Maybe the Special Unit? That I'd done longer in jail? Stolen his thunder? Do fathers simply hate their sons? Has the hatred always been there?

Hughie Tannock's father too had been a bully, battering the family. He particularly put his son in terrible states. My Aunty Mary had bruises regularly. Hughie, though, tasted leather belts and knuckles. He'd terrorised him as a kid. Hughie later paid for all the expenses in burying his father. I'd watched his tears, uncontrollable emotions, as he threw dirt on the coffin – 'Oh Da! Daaa! Daaa!'

I'll *spit* on my father's coffin.

Glasgow bars. They never change. Hughie's in full flight, describing the latest turn, a snatch here, a burglary there – 'Ea, there's a few quid. Al square up me mum, but the rest a them caants kin go faack themselves.'

God, Cockney accents just don't work with Glaswegians – 'Talk normal ya cunt. Hauf the boozer's lookin at ye . . . fuckin lunatic' I whisper.

– 'Wot?'

I smile – 'Here. Didje hear ma auld man singin in the chapel Hughie?'

– 'Wot? Woz at im? A fot it wuz sum geezer wiffa sore froat or sumfink!'

Jesus. What a boy – 'Right listen, here's ma phone number Hughie. Am headin back tae Edinbra. You gaun back doon south? Aye, don't hing aboot Possil . . . That cunt'll throw ye tae the wolves. Show es pals how straight ey is, fuckin arsehole. The Don a Possilpark' I sneer – 'The Cosa Nostra an aw that eh. Right okay pal, an stay oot the nick . . . Stay in touch Hughie! An listen, don't listen tae aw the mixin, yer Maw's bran new. Alec? Och Hughie, es jist a boay, es noa wide tae things, don't take it personal wi um. Al rip ye ya wee cunt if ye go near him, mind noo es ma brother. Okay, al see ye at the next funeral.'

I enjoy the train journey home. The landscape whizzing past, people reading mags or newspapers or just staring vacantly in your face. God. Those train journeys from jail to Glasgow. They seemed endless, and all the staring faces, feeding my paranoia, my anxieties – 'Relax! Look normal for fucksake! Look oot the windae or sumthin! Be cool! Fuck! Are we noa there yet?' Oh I remember all right, all that tension, trying to pull myself together, taking this drug for that, taking that drug for this. Jim doing that ridiculous daddy act – 'Hughie are ye oan heroin?' Alec huffing and puffing because his space is being occupied – 'Oh, s'the big hard man hame?' My Al Pacino look, all the mad suits, terrified to bend my legs, in case it ruined the crease of the trousers. A Secretary of State took some chance letting me out. Rifkind it think it was – 'Malky, I owe you one.' Hopefully I won't let you down.

I look at the sky. Auld Norrie . . . I wonder where she is? With Auld Boab no doubt, up there in that living room in the holy water department, singing and blessing herself at every turn. Auld Boab, smiling, amused, reading Burns. Waverley blots the sky out as we enter the station. God, all these stairs to get home, no wonder they call it the High Street – 'Caroline? Ca? Ye in? Oh yer there, sorry a woke ye up. Aye, it was as expected' I smile – 'Ma Da there, naibidy talkin tae each other. Hughie Tannock wis there, ma cousin. Ma Aunty Mary's boy. Och, he's a loony tune but bran new, aye puttin oan this mad accent' I laugh – 'Cockney Jock, a fuckin nutcase. A think al jist stop goin through there. Well, aw that aggression an bickerin. Am tired ey it aw tae be honest. Alec smoulderin at people. Jim, that grinnin. Ma Maw wis bran new but, ach a don't know. Maybe it's jist me. How'r Andy an Lorraine?' I ask – 'Eh? Another operation? Fuckin hell. A thought they'd cut oot the tumour?'

Caroline tries to explain – 'They did, but the tumour has tentacles. They keep growing so it's not looking good at all. Lorraine's in a terrible state. Andy has begun to make decisions, plans for his funeral. He's decided to have his coffin made of cardboard . . .'

I think she's joking – 'Cardboard? You kiddin me on?' I ask – 'Cardboard?'

She's not – 'No, he wants his friends to design, paint it. I think this would remove all the morbid aspects. He wants to be cremated, his ashes scattered in a river in Fife' she says.

Poor Andy, having to make such decisions, but cardboard?

Caroline reminds me that tonight is the National Gallery Festival party – 'Oh don't get into a panic. Your suit and shirts are all back from the cleaner's. You have a bath first and leave the water in. I'll get in after you . . . yeees. I bought new razor blades too so calm down. Where are you with the manuscript?' she asks – 'Do you think so? That is good then. When are you going to the lawyers about getting out of your contract with *Granta*? Yes, I'll come with you. They mentioned an agent,

Giles Gordon. He's come back here to Scotland from London' she says – 'Prince Charles apparently is one of his clients. Yeah, I've heard he's very good so get down to the lawyer's and get them to terminate the contract, and then you can finalise a deal with the manuscript. A half decent advance would clear the overdraft, and maybe lend us a well deserved holiday. God, we could do with one. All we seem to do is work. When is the meeting with them?' she asks.

I'm at the mirror, where else? – 'Next week. Giles Gordon might take me on. Dis ey live up here noo? This tie look okay?' I ask.

Caroline assures me the tie's fine – 'Yeah it's nice. Yes, that would be great if he was your agent. What about Jamie Byng? What did he say about the manuscript?'

I'm almost ready – 'Well, he thinks the writing's great. Ey says ey'll make me an offer when es spoken wi es counterpart. Sumthin like that. Wull see wit this lawyer says first an then see how wi get on wi Giles Gordon. Ye nearly ready tae go?'

Caroline sprays the final touches to her hair – 'Yeah, that's me. How do I look? Right then. Timothy Clifford was in the news again about the trouble over the Three Graces. Well, he was honest enough to own up to making one or two mistakes with the Getty Foundation' she says. 'Yes, they almost pulled out of the deal as the result of a silly statement he'd had made. He sorted it out. He's an honest man. Yes, he pled guilty, took the flak. Right, you ready handsome?'

The National Gallery Festival party – God. I feel like a film star with all the journalists hanging around taking photographs. The public too line the perimeter, gawking – 'Aye it's me!' Timothy is there greeting the guests as they arrive – 'Good evening Caroline, Hugh.'

There's something about him, a rascal of sorts, a necessary

asset in the world of art – 'Timothy. *Never* plead guilty!' I smile.

He returns the gesture with an open hand – 'Oh, aren't they wonderful! Go on in, and enjoy them! Have champagne . . .'

Champagne? It's flowing! My glass seems to runneth over. The establishment are in party mood, the atmosphere is euphoric. The Three Graces is a beautiful piece of artwork. My blurry eyes try to focus, looking for the hand, for the marks of the chisel. A true masterpiece of a carving – 'Oh, hello' I smile – 'Duncan.'

Duncan Thomson, Director of the Scottish Portrait Gallery, is looking at the piece too – 'Hugh, how are you?' he asks.

I shrug my shoulders – 'Aw fine, an yersel?'

He smiles – 'Hugh, I wanted to ask. Are you familiar with Jimmy Boyle's works?'

I feel those old hackles rising ever so slightly – 'Well av seen a few. How? Why dae ye wantae know?'

Duncan frowns – 'Well, we've received a letter from him, suggesting we put his works in the main foyer of the Portrait Gallery.'

I put on the best deep frown – 'We-ll, Duncan. Those early carvings I thought were original. Some were fairly good, well, for an amateur. But I discovered that most of the later pieces were an accumulation of other people's works and reshaped into one piece, *his* piece. I'm not an authority' I smile – 'But Boyle has never developed as a sculptor. No to be frank, it's just crap. Did you read the article by Clare Henry?' I ask – 'No? Oh, she described his most recent exhibition of works as . . . Well she was brutal I suppose, but said he's not an artist at all. The works were grotesque. Popeye-esque, I think it was she said. No, I'm just a face in his past, but certainly not a friend. Sorry I couldn't be more helpful. Yes, you too Duncan. Fantastic party isn't it!'

Champagne I find leaves but the traces of a hangover, but

what a night, what a party. I awake the following morning, the trousers folded over a chair, jacket and shirt hung neatly in my wardrobe, and yes my shoes sitting there too, shining brightly. I must be immune to spillage, exude an exclusion zone when dressed for a party. Yes, I had a ball, but the headache? No. Shakes? No.

The telephone tone doesn't touch those terrible sensory spots even – 'Hullo? Oh Hiya Ma! Wit? A journalist? The *Sunday Mail*?' I exclaim – 'Ye must be jokin! A widnae talk tae eny ey they cunts. Thuv goat ma address? Fuck. How'd they get it? Ach, it disny matter, but tell thum naw, tell thum tae fuck off. Thur's nae story. Aye, we wur at the Festival party last night.' I laugh – 'Naw champagne. The National Gallery. Jist doon the road fae the flat. Caroline's oan the guest list so a get invited tae. Aw it wis a laugh Ma. Aw that establishment mob . . . Thur aw crazy. Naw we enjoyed wurselves an came back up the road when it finished. Naw, we're never oot at aw. Fuck, we've nae money tae go oot. Aye nae bother. Al gie ye a phone later okay Ma, ta ta.'

Caroline's looking at me – 'The *Sunday Mail*'s goat our address. Och, ma Maw gave thum it without thinkin. Naw al chase thum if they come near the door. Naw al phone the polis, that's wit al dae. Say thur harassin us. Naw don't worry, they won't get yer parents' address. Ye makin a wee coffee?' I ask

KILLER'S HOLLYWOOD MILLION DOLLAR FILM DEAL!

The *Sunday Mail* headlines us the following weekend with this. Wee Meric. The little shit. He'd been listening to a conversation in a bar. Unbeknown to me he had been a few feet away as I'd told someone that there had been an offer from a film production company in Hollywood – 'Aye Tam, they wanted to buy the option for a film when ma book's published. A knocked thum back. They'd turn it intae aw that hero shite. The book's aboot finished. Am dreadin the publicity. Al get slautured, it's noa apologetic enough' I'd been explaining.

Tam Dean Burn. Tam's from the background I've left behind. The London National Theatre provided the platform, the boards, to pursue things less murderous. He found his feet as an actor. A Steven Berkoff devotee, he became part of the cutting edge part of experimental theatre. A tall, fierce looking guy, head shaved and mean, you could easily imagine such a menacing character in a gang. Tam though had found a political perspective through the miners' strikes in the seventies. His Leninist Party of six members had changed a flat he was sharing with art students, including Caroline. He'd transformed it into a cafe, with little tables and chairs, ashtrays stolen from other cafes, without having told his stunned flatmates beforehand – 'Aye, it's jist tae raise muney fur the minurs' strike, ken!' he'd told them.

Caroline had introduced me to him not long after my release from jail, and although we had become friends, I rarely saw him, unless he was acting in and around Edinburgh.

He had based himself in London, living with his young son, Skye.

We're just having a beer together, but lurking that few feet away is that uninvited ear, listening for a snippet. Tam's unaware of our parasitical guest as he asks – 'Remorse Shugs. V'ye never thought aboot that? Might make things easier.'

I think aloud – 'Remorse? Aw c'mon. Jist say yer sorry an at's it? The public luv that crap. Tam ad luv tae be a mulliuner, but aw that goodies an baddies? Nah. Av goat personal reasons fur daen this book. Sixteen years a served. The guys that a wis tae meet that night wur plannin ey dae me in. Aye, full me up wi acid an sling me o'er a high flats. We wur supposed tae be squarin up the trouble we'd had, but they'd other plans fur me' I say.

Millionaire – The Ear has heard what he wanted – he's gone.

Big Tam's amazed with the gang scene – 'How did that guy get killed then?' he asks. I try to explain – 'Tam, Wullie Mooney shoodny even huv been there. He wis jist in the wrang place at the wrang time, wandered intae a bad scene kerryin a blade.'

I continue down that track, almost re-enacting those violent events of that night in my mind – 'A didnae want any trouble wi him, it wis this urra mob, aw ma so called pals. We'd fell oot an en started chibbin each other. A nearly shot ma auld man as well . . .' I see it so vividly – 'Mooney wis in the wrang place at the wrang time. He jist didnae deserve tae get it, didnae know wit wis happenin, the poor bastart, walked right intae it.'

Tam asks – 'But did he noa have a knife tae, this guy Mooney?'

– 'A blade? Aye, he'd a blade, but hauf the pub hud blades. They kerried blades tae impress burds. Mooney wis jist in showin face' I explain.

Glasgow eh, knives to impress women – 'He wisnae involved, wisnae ready. Na Tam, honest, he didnae know, didnae huv a clue. A took a fuckin liberty. He'd nae chance wi me. A knew that this other team wur plannin tae dae *me*, ye see, an a *wis* ready. A wis tooled right up, ready tae go ahead' I tell him – 'A mean am lookin fur trouble fae thaem, dae ye know wit a mean? Am watchin every move. The next thing *he's* headin fur *me*, the haun in es coat. The next thing, bang es deid. Ach it wis aw a right fuckin mess.'

Tam finds the story unbelievable – 'Wit aboot the cops? A pub fulla guys wi blades?' he asks – 'A mean, the cops ur supposed tae prevent these things fae happenin.'

The police? What? Do you think the lads in blue simply turn up in a boozer, giving it – 'Right lads, lets have the knives first'? Oh they knew what was going on all right. I have no doubts about that. They had just been sitting back watching, waiting, to see who killed who first before doing their big dragnet act for the inevitable newsflash. A Frankie Vaughan appeal for a witness – 'Someone hasn't handed in their knife. We're looking for a suspect carrying a weapon. He may have blood stains upon his clothing or person.'

Tam's looking at me – 'The coppers? They'da dun thur usual – We're lookin intae the incident . . . end a story. They don't give a fuck Tam' I say.

Caroline told me of his political bouts with police, and the other clashes with political authority, but the placards could have been blades – 'Aye Tam, the seventies. That's when it aw happened.'

Tam asks about writing a play – 'A play? The Hard Man thing that I did for *Granta*. I'd written a chunk aboot solitary confinement at the same time. But it's written in ma ain language. Frenetic, that wit ye call it?' I ask – 'It's me gaun insane doon in a hole in the grun, a genuine dungeon, but ye kin huv a look, see wit ye think.'

He's interested, but I remind him that it was more than simple solitary, and a cowboy book – 'A wis cuvered in insects, mind, so ye'll huv tae get cuvered in chocolate an aw that!' I laugh.

Tam, I remember, is a method actor. This is right up his acting street – 'Naw Shugs. Ad dae the full wurks, ken. Make people think aboot prison. Wit thur daen. Wit purpose they serve' he states.

He's amazed that I've seen him acting for television – 'Oh, *Brotherly Love*? Did ye see that film? It wis a short wi Channel Four. Aye, it wis a good laugh. Did ye like the bit a threw um intae the water? Aye, Russell's ma wee brother! Ye wur greetin? Shugs, aw c'mon noo . . . So yer definately noa daen a film then?' he asks.

That million dollar deal eh – 'Na Tam, honest. Ad luv tae huv mullions. Who widnae?

But naw, noa a film, especially wi Hollywood' I reply.

We both laugh – 'Kin ye imajin? Stallone cuvered in shite? It wid huv tae be designer shite. Big Sly dolled up like an Apache Indian. Here Tam, didye see that Hayman in *Sensa Freedom*?' I ask – 'C'mon! Wee streaks here an there? Yer caked in the fuckin stuff, it faws intae yer grub!'

I take him through the downside of a dirty protest – 'Honest, ye huv tae haud yer heid back tae eat, ur flakes ey hard shite faw intae the bowl! Aye, gen up! Ye kin go right aff yer fuckin heid wi hunger!'

He's the one guy who could do it though – 'A don't know Tam. It might make noa a bad play fur you tae dae. You read it first okay?'

We then drift into other books, films and plays – '*Trainspottin*'s took right aff eh? Dae ye know that guy Welsh?' I ask. 'Aye? Wits ey like? A thoat it wis brilliant. Naw, av noa seen the film. Ach, films. They need tae huv an end, if ye know wit a mean, that wee happy picture.'

A film that hit me between the eyes comes to mind – 'Ye seen *Nil By Mouth*? A fuckin brilliant film Tam! Gary Oldman made it, an left it the way it aw began, aw sittin in a hoose, laughin at the boay bein back in the jail. That's *real* life. That's wit they shood be like, films. Aw that hero shite. A hate that fuckin stuff.'

Tam can't get a word in edgeways – 'Aye, *Trainspottin*'s a good book. Andy left it wi me in the gallery. A jist read it the urra night. That bit wi the boy shitin the bed! Aw man. A coodny stoap laffin' I say.

He knows what's been happening – 'Andy? Aye, liberty eh? Caroline goes up a lot tae see thum. A don't know wit tae say. A don't think ey'll last long. Jeez, poor Lorraine tae, it's a shame.'

Tam has a train to catch – 'Right then big yin. Okay, al send that stuff tae yer address in London. Aye Tam, you tae, wis good seein ye again. Regards tae wee Henderson an Jock Scott. Is Jock still daen the poetry readins? Aye, fuckin nuts ey. A read a lot ey es stuff, es a brilliant poet. Anyway ye better get movin. Me tae, av got a meeting wi an agent the morra, guy called Giles Gordon. The *Granta* contract's terminated so he's comin up tae meet me an Caroline.'

Meric caught the key word – millionaire. The headline secured a job for him with the *Sunday Mail.* Me? I've been living with it ever since – Murderer and Blood Money! I personally don't give a fuck what's written about me in newspapers. Tabloids sell for simple reasons – you can hold the paper up without effort on a bus, it doesn't tax that grey matter called brains. Personally I wouldn't wipe my arse with a tabloid paper . . . Caroline, her family, friends, though. They have to face the public, face the problems of association with a murderer, a cold blooded killer, taking blood money for a book. Bill Buford later called to say that they had offered a couple of grand to use extracts from 'The Hard Man' – 'Yeah Hugh, twelve hundred pounds. I'd take the money and run, they'll do it anyway. I have the faxes offering a cheque. Sure I'll send them to you.'

That *Sunday Mail*'s same editorial comment ranted and raved about murderers being paid for their stories – BLOOD MONEY!

Chapter Sixteen

CAROLINE IS FURIOUS – 'That little shit. I've a good mind to call him. What will this man's family think reading this? Yes, I'm going to call' she decides – 'Hullo? Andy Meric? Yes, Caroline McNairn. Hugh Collins' wife. What? Well, let's meet. Tuesday? Yes, that'll be fine. Yes, the Pancake Shop. The High Street, yes, ten o clock!' Slam! I stand back, watching – 'Little bastard!' she says, rearranging the telephone – 'Right. I'll prepare some snack things for Giles Gordon. You just relax and don't panic. I've heard he's nice. He's well known, gets writers good deals with publishers. Oh when have you to see that Jamie Byng?' she asks – 'Tonight? Great, hopefully he'll make an offer. The bank's talking about bankrupting us, well, unless there's something more concrete.'

I'm lightening things up – 'Aye. That wid be a good laugh. Tell the newspapers that they hud invested in ma rehabilitation eh? That the front door? Must be Giles. Right okay you dae aw the talkin, right Caroline?'

Caroline's reassuring – 'Yes, stop worrying. Go and put on the kettle. I'll get the door so calm down. You'll be fine.'

Giles Gordon is suddenly in our living room with my manuscript in his hand – 'What a view!' he exclaims. I'm stammering about hills and bridges, while all the time afraid to ask what he thinks about the writing. Please, please, please, don't destroy me. I'm terrified of what he might say, what he might be thinking – 'Stick to the stone carving' but no, he thinks the book is a page puller. His boyish charm is infectious. Caroline falls in love with him immediately, chatting away about writers, books, writers, books, and more books. I'm totally disarmed by his charm and wit, but he's here to discuss business – 'I almost didn't read it' he says – 'But I glanced at the first few pages and couldn't put it down. Have you had any offers from publishers Hugh?' he asks.

I describe the brief history of the book – 'A have a meeting tonight with Jamie Byng. A think thur interested. He'd offered fifteen grand for it the other night' I say – 'But av noa agreed tae anythin.'

Giles blurts out in astonishment – 'Fifteen thousand? He actually made a bid? What did you say, you haven't signed a contract have you?'

I'm puzzled – 'Na. A said a wid think it o'er' I say – 'Heard that es fae a rich family? Bought into Canongate? Well the story is that es there tae replace Stephanie Wolfe Murray. That's wit av heard, but naw, wuv arranged tae meet the night tae reconsider his offer. A don't think es keen on agents.'

Giles nods – 'Hmm. Did he mention me?' he asks – 'Doesn't like me.'

Caroline and I find him quite humorous, but there are more pressing matters. We are about to be bankrupted, the electricity about to be cut off. The Job Centre is looming on the horizon. I do have to do a deal – or sink.

Giles, though, breaks through those darkening clouds – 'Well, don't sign a thing until I get back to you, that is of course, if you want me to represent you as your agent?' My agent? Those twinkling eyes are smiling. My agent? I want to hug him, kiss him, thank him – 'You'll take me on?' I ask.

He's bemused – 'Of course I will! This is a bloody good book! Electricity? Oh go and buy candles or something. Tell Jamie Byng to contact me with his offer if he's still at all interested. That's amazing! A publisher who doesn't want agents? I send them a lot of new books all the time! Yes! Canongate!' he says, smiling.

What a charming man, almost reminds me of a heterosexual Andrew Brown.

Caroline and I collapse with relief when he leaves – 'Ca did ye hear um? Ma agent? Jesus! All we huv tae dae noo is wait. The bank? Al call thum noo, ask fur a coupla days.' I look to the ceiling – 'Oh please, please, jist wan break.'

The following days become a blur of activity. Canongate have us under siege with continual telephone calls, to reconsider.

Caroline has taken to answering every call. She lifts the reciever – 'Oh Hi Giles! Yes, fine thanks. Wh-at? Peter Straus? Macmillan's? Yes Giles, I'll tell Hugh. Oh he'll be delighted. Yes, you too, bye.'

The thumbs-up sign relieves the strain on my nerves – 'Guess what then?' she asks. I can't bear the suspense – 'Wit is it? Ten grand an aw the rights? Fifteen? Fifteen wi the rights? C'mon Caroline kin wi pay the fuckin bills?' I plead.

She smiles – 'Twenty five thousand Hugh! Plus all the rights, and also you're with an enormous publishing house – Macmillan's!'

I fall back in a chair – 'Thank fuck! Thank fuck! Twenty five grand! Call the bank Ca! Call thum right away to pay the electricity bill. Fuckin hell man! Wit a relief. Noo wi kin pay aw they bills, an maybe a wee holiday?' I gasp – 'Al be able tae answer aw the calls noo. God, wit a kerry oan eh. Jamie Byng won't be pleased, but he hud every chance tae get the book. Giles gave um every opportunity so ey canny complain. Aw Ca, wit a relief. A honestly thought we wur dun for there. Listen, am gonny get some sleep fur a coupla hoors. Honest, a feel shattered wi aw this.'

The relief in being able to pay all the bills, buy some decent food. I just want to rest a bit, and enjoy the luxury of having the money to clear my overdraft, pay the telephone bills, and buy some decent food. All I want is to try to earn a living out here like anyone else. I don't want to live off other people's taxes as a state free-loading pimp, or some thug in prison. I have the unemployable murderer tag. What am I to do? Lie down like a dog, whimper and wait for someone to scratch my head, or throw me a bone?

The following days relieve the bank manager's anxieties, electricity bills are paid, we are able to eat decent food, continue living our lives – three years down the line. I've never been out of jail this long, from ninety three to ninety six is the longest period. I arrange a meeting with the publishers to sign the contract and begin editing the book. *Autobiography of a Murderer* is to be published in February 1997.

Caroline, though, has other meetings – with Meric.

I don't believe this – 'You're hidin a tape recorder down yer brassiur? Naw, ye canny see it, but . . .'

She's still angry about the news article he wrote, those three page million dollar deal headlines. Still, the pressure's off now. I wind her up – 'Eh, Jamesh. Eh, Jamesh McNairn!'

I dodge the shoe thrown at me – 'Can you see it at all Hugh? I'll turn it on just before we meet. No, they can erase background noise. I'll speak quite loud. Well, wish me luck then.'

I give her a kiss – 'Okay. Al see ye in aboot an hoor.'

The mission is a success. She has him talking about victims' families – 'The families? So what?' he sniggers – 'A story's a story. Hugh? No, well, I didn't actually interview him. No he . . . I heard him talking. Have I been set up here?'

I can hear the panic in his voice over the background noise – 'He mentioned a million dollars. Well, I'm sure that's what he . . . I didn't actually interview him, no' he repeats – 'Yes, the two grand was for excerpts. The editorial? That's not my

. . . Of course. I . . . Yes, I landed the job with this story. A story's a story . . .'

Caroline suggests a break. The tabloid flak following on from the 'millionaire' stunt is wearing. The telephone calls, the doorstepping journos – 'Can we just have a word with him?' We fear leaving the flat: being followed, being chased, forces us into hiding – 'Hugh, let's go to my parents'. My sister's there. We can have time too with Finlay. God, I wonder how all this is affecting them?' she wonders – 'I do hope they are all right? Dad is almost eighty eight now. Mum will be worrying about us.' Caroline is often asked what it is like being married to a violent man. Are there any other kind? She is also often asked what it is like being married to a murderer. Well, this is what it's like being married to a murderer.

These people too are victims of a murderer.

My parents too are victims – of me.

Caroline's father is waiting to pick us up when we arrive at the end of the bus journey from Edinburgh – 'Hi Ca, Hugh. Well, how are you?' he asks.

They'd heard about the headlines, and other reports in newspapers, but chose to just ignore the matter. Caroline and I try to explain, apologise for the embarrassment, but he simply nods – 'Best forgotten. Finlay's excited about you coming down. Oh, he's been painting, and helping around the garden' he chuckles. – 'He's been having lots of fun with grandmother.'

I spot the tiny figure waiting as we drive up the stretch of road to the house. He's shy for a few moments until he spots his Aunt Ca – 'Ca! Ca! Ca! Ca! Ca!' he calls.

Wee Finlay. Aw he's beautiful. The wee face looking up, the hands behind his back, just like his grandfather, a chip off the old block, and so much too like Caroline. I see the genetic similarities running through the family – 'Hello Finlay! So, how are you?' I ask. Caroline has him in her arms already – 'Oh Finlay, hhmmm' she smiles.

Caroline's mum kisses my cheek – 'Hugh, lovely to see you. Come on in, and get warmed up!' she says warmly.

Finlay's cuddling everyone – 'My Gwanma' he says lovingly.

The warmth of him is infectious; everyone's picking up on this wee boy's generosity.

I feel myself melting in his presence – 'Uncle Hew!' he says, giving me my cuddle. I find myself just following him around the garden, but he loves being with his Aunt Ca. She's been reading him little short bedtime stories since he was born. Aunt Ca's his favourite – 'My wead a book Aunt Ca?' he says, dragging her straight to his favourite story book – *Pingu*.

No one mentions the press, but I feel terrible, bad that I have brought so much of that past into these people's lives. Little Finlay there, entertaining everyone with humour and love. I look at him, wondering, What will he think of me when he grows up? He is the first child I have watched growing up, the first child I have developed a genuine relationship with in a real sense, and yet this innocence will be shattered someday by the terrible things I've done to other people.

After a bit I hang out at the old mill, chain smoking cigarettes, hiding in the darkness, trying to avoid everyone inside, ashamed somehow – 'Hu-gh? Hu-gh? Tea's ready!'

Caroline's mum knows – 'It's cold! C'mon you can't stay out *all* night!' she calls.

Her hand rubbing my back feels warm, reassuring, commanding – 'C'mon. Let's have tea now! Yes, you can cut some logs tomorrow.'

Finlay has been painting – 'My dwaw Aunt Ca, Uncle Hew! Now sit down! Aunt Ca is sweeping! Ca! Ca! Ca! Ca! Ca . . . !' He likes the sound of his own voice. What a boy. I lift him up – 'Oh what is this? You've been painting? Yeeees! Fantastic!

Is this your Aunt Ca an Uncle Hugh? Oh I see. Oh this is me. The house? Where is the house? I think we should have the house, here! Yeeees! Aunt Ca! Look! Feetie's painted you a picture! Isn't that fantastic?'

Caroline's beginning to relax – 'What? Fantastic!' She looks to me – 'These are really amazing aren't they? Look, he has everything in perspective. Look at the tuft of hair! That must be you. Uncle Hugh? Finlay. Is this Uncle Hugh?' she asks.

He's lost interest in the painting now – 'My sitting down. Aunt Ca sits hea. Mummy hea. No, Daddy, you sit hea. Aunt Ca . . .' And so it goes.

Finlay dominates the table with manners of an adult, mimicking everyone around him, nodding and conversing when appropriate – 'My like bwown bwead.'

His grandfather has two addictions – brown bread and painting. The paintings are utterly beautiful. His grandmother too is an artist, but paints in her own style, not influenced in any way by her husband's.

Their house is filled with the most beautiful paintings, dating back to great, great, and great grandfather's earliest paintings.

Finlay, it would appear, will continue the long traditional history of painters within the family of the McNairns.

I feel privileged to be here. My previous lives disappear here, disappear down those thick woods, those living trees down by the garden stream, the beautiful flowers, and massive vegetable garden. Yes, I think I'm ready to hug that tree after all. Freedom I feel is beyond all that, all those previous lives, all those pasts, all that burning hatred. God. What book am I in tonight? What year is it now of my freedom, my third? How quickly it all passes. What – 'Feetie! Hiya pal. Oh Mr Dark, Feetie look, look up. See the stars?' I say, pointing to the dark sky.

Finlay huddles up in my arms – 'My was a sta befow my was bown Uncle Hew.'

A star before he was born? God. Who is this wee boy in my arms? He is three years old. A star before he was born? I hug him – 'A know ye wur pal. A know . . . Ohh Aunt Ca! Yes, time for bed! Say goodnight. Goodnight Mr Dark! That's it! Yeeees, you're a clever boy. Right c'mon en. Daddy an Mummy are upstairs. Yes, Aunt Ca an Uncle Hew are tired. You're an awful blether Feetie!'

He frowns – 'My not a bwevva. Feetie a good boy.'

Edinburgh is a nice city to come into by bus, car, or train. The views are all magical. The tabloid bloodhounds seemed to have gone. The rest has been good for us, but it is Festival time. There's five weeks' solid celebration, with tourists, drums, didgeridoos, bagpipers – morning, noon, and night. Edinburgh has flair like no other city, partying round the clock. We awake each morning to the sound of sand pipers, pleasant for a day or two, but after five weeks? The Scottish bagpipes, though, take the biscuit – that wailing is an assault on one's sensory system, grating on every thread of the nervous system, with national anthems at three in the morning and every hour, on the hour. Those windows being thrown open in the middle of the night brings momentary relief, some reassurance that we alone are not going insane – 'SHUT THE FUCK UP!'

That fresh pint of milk in the morning becomes a battle to cross the street. Wading in amongst Italians, Brazilians, French, and Japanese – ''Scuse me. 'Scuse me. 'Scuse me.' Japanese have no concept of queueing. Waiting, the fashion of lining in orderly manner to obtain an item. No, they simply walk to the counter – 'A fiwm woll prease, yes, yes, fow camewa.' Italians, though, they halt suddenly, half the population piling behind them, talking louder, louder, and louder. Absolutely beautiful though, they're stunning in every sense. Alessandro Del Piero, Michelangelo, what more can you say? But the pint of milk? Caroline and I take turns to . . . No, Caroline takes the brunt of that morning adventure across the High Street. The truth, and nothing but the ... *She* is the backbone, the provider, the go-er. Me? The suits have gone but – 'A canny go oot like this! Am noa shaved ur nuthin! Look at ma hair fur fucksake! Naw Ca, please you go an al dae the hooverin an aw that?' My male vanity is unfathomable. My dishevelled hair? A face layered with scars ... but – 'Aw Ca, c'mon. Look at ma hair. A canny go ... pleeease?'

Men eh.

DRINGGGG! DRINGGGGG! DRINGGGGG!

Oh no, the telephone. Alec? No, Betty's out of hospital, out of danger, no, it can't be him. I'm trying to ignore it. I'm watching the national news. There's a guy, a serial killer, he's being deported from Australia to Britain – 'Mad Dog'. The media are like a pack of wolves, all over him like flies, breaking through police barriers – 'Archie! Mad Dog! Arch ... How do ... What do ...' Jesus, this feeding frenzy has to be terrifying for the poor bastard, but he's doing the head down, looking cool, straight walking ... fuck you. DRING! DRING! DRING! DRING! DRING!

Whoever this is is determined. It's one of those – 'I know you're in!' DRING DRINGS.

Jesus. I have to give in – 'Yes? Hullo?'

– 'Hi, could I speak to Hugh Collins?' asks a voice.

– 'Yes, this is Hugh Collins' I reply.

– 'Hi, my name's Mick O'Donnell. I'm from Australian Channel Seven network ... I've just read your book and it's ... The *Granta* – "Hard Man". Oh, the book isn't out yet?'

I'm puzzled at first – 'Mick O'Donnell did you say? Yes, *Autobiography of a Murderer*. Eh February' I say.

– 'Yeah? I'm sorry, is this a convenient time? I could call back later.'

– 'No, it's okay, it's fine. Mick O'Donnell? Is that right? Right fine, okay. What can I do for you then?' I ask.

– 'Well, it's about your book. Would you . . . I wonder, would you be interested in doing an interview?'

– 'An interview? What kind of . . .'

– 'Well, firstly, I should explain. Are you aware of the guy that's being deported from Australia, back to Scotland?' he asks.

– 'Yes, I'm actually watching him right now on national news – Mad Dog?'

– 'Yeah. We're filming him for *Witness*. Your *Panorama* programme's very similar to our programme. Well, we were wondering if it would be possible to film you talking together. You and Archie?'

I'm getting the picture – 'Archie? That his real name?' I ask.

– 'Yeah, Archie McCafferty. We feel you are someone he could trust. At the moment we have him hidden in a hotel in Glasgow. There's been a lynch mob waiting for him there. He's lost contact with the authorities, and the media are all over him, so it's all a bit hairy. No one wants to know to be honest. He's a bit shaken by the reception in Glasgow. The authorities have, well, vanished.'

I look at the television – 'Well, I can imagine, but I don't want to complicate my own life. I've been out four years' I explain – 'My circumstances are now entirely different. I'd have to think about other people first, my wife, family, do you know what I mean?' I ask.

– 'Hugh I do realise the sensitivity of your situation. We were thinking along the lines of an interview about your book, possibly you explaining the difficulties that could be lying ahead for Archie and Amanda.'

– 'Amanda?' I ask.

– 'Yeah, Amanda's his wife' he explains.

– 'Oh. I see, how long'd he do in jail?'

– 'Twenty four years' he says.

– 'He must be in some state. Eh, listen, I'll have to think this over first. Can I call you back?'

– 'Great. I understand. He needs support but, sure, we can appreciate your concerns in all this. Anyway thanks for sparing your time. Oh, and, by the way, I meant what I said about your writing. It's a very powerful story.'

– 'Yes, fine. Okay then, bye.'

– 'Bye Hugh.'

Mad Dog? God. How will he survive? His chances are zero. He'll have no money, no relatives, no home in Scotland. What do I do? I can't just turn my back on the guy. I couldn't do that to an ex-con. My concerns are the tabloids. Hopefully they won't find out about my involvement – they'll slaughter me. I look at the worst scenario. What is my concern, my image? To hell with it.

KILLER MEETS SERIAL KILLER!

–'Hullo? Can I speak to Mick O'Donnell?'

– 'Hugh? You'll do it? Great!' he exclaims.

– 'Listen Mick. What's the strength of this guy? What's he like?'

– 'The Aussies see him as a sort of Charles Manson' he says, laughing.

– 'What? Are you kidding? Jesus. Right I'll see you tomorrow then at the studio. Oh just one thing. Definately no press okay? Right then, okay, bye.'

Charles Manson? God. What am I getting into here? This isn't exactly just another ex lifer needing support. He's being described as a psychotic serial killer. This guy killed three people – killed a fourth in prison. He might be suffering from a mental disorder. Might? Who am I kidding? After twenty four years in prison he'll be insane, really off his trolley. The media haven't helped matters with the carry on at the airport. The pressure may just freak him out, put him over the edge. Glasgow public, according to the tabloids, have made their feelings clear to the couple. I'm always amazed that the tabloid journos speak for almost a million people, some who don't even read tabloid toilet paper. What a voice though . . .

WE DON'T WANT MAD DOG!

Why did I pick up that bloody telephone?

Mick O'Donnell, Archie, Amanda, the film crew are waiting at the studio the following day. Caroline is at the hospital with Lorraine – 'Things don't look good for Andy' she says before leaving – 'I'll come wi ye the morra Caroline' I promised before going to meet these people.

Chapter Seventeen

ARCHIE'S DIMINUTIVE BUT wiry, with leathery, tanned skin, slightly resembling the film character, Crocodile Dundee. He looks fit, but battered, head hanging down, staring at the ground.

– 'Hello Archie. Am Hugh Collins. How d'ye feel?' I ask.

He looks up – pale blue eyes search mine. The handsome face breaks into a broadish smile as we shake hands.

– 'Hi Hugh. Good ta see a friendly face. Them blaady reporters ave been chasing us all over the place. I don't know what this fuss is all abaat. Baggars almost ripped off me blaady ear at the airport. Them cops had to carry me out bodily to get away from em silly baggars! D'you get this when you got out of prison? I didn't want to come to this blaady caantry in the first place.'

He seems to relax in my company. Well, he would wouldn't he, being with an ex-lifer.

– 'You're safe here so just take it easy' I say, nudging his shoulder.

Archie and Amanda watch while the film crew set up their gear. She has a lovely pleasant fresh face with a nice smile, an outdoor woman, a strong type of build. She's bewildered too by the media frenzy at the airport. Archie though does all the talking.

– 'They've kicked me out of the caantry with a hundred dollars. I can't carry money in me pockets and them blaady telephones. I hear voices when I pick em up. I just can't use em blaady things.' he complains.

I smile – 'Well, the voices usually indicate someone's on the other end Archie.'

– 'Na mate. Voices in here. In the centre of me head!' he says, pointing a finger at his temple.

My first priority is to re-introduce him to the appropriate authorities – including police – to allay any concerns of his whereabouts. I'm sure they'll want to know where he is in the unlikely event of any dead bodies, unaccounted for, surfacing in the city. The probationary services are conspicuously absent. It would appear that no one wants to take responsibility for this man, but he can't just be left to wander the streets. My most immediate concern though is his mental state.

– 'Wit aboot medication Archie?' I ask.

– 'Yeah, I'm on modicate, but I feel more alert withaat it ta be honest.'

Modicate? I'd had my share of prison drugs to control my behaviour, but I had never heard of modicate. I decide to call Linda McNee. Linda had been a tutor in psychiatry when we had first met in the Special Unit. She would know, having had so much experience in treating people with problems. She tells me bluntly – 'This is an extremely powerful drug. It's for psychotics Hugh.' She can't believe her ears when I explain my reason for asking – 'What? How on earth? Where are the social services, or his medical records?' she asks – 'You're joking! They've just dumped him? Get him to the doctor's right away, and registered. Why have you been landed with him?' she asks.

– 'Oh. It's a long story Linda. Yes, Caroline's fine and agrees with you. Anyway see you soon okay. How's Jim? Great. Anyway love tae the weans' I say.

I make an appointment with a doctor for the next day. Cameras begin whirring away as we walk up and down –

it's the jailyard scene from a film. Our conversation *is* the interview.

– 'Archie. Four people are deid. N'you killed thum. Wit're your feelings aboot the victims, and thur families?' I ask.

There is no flinching from my directness. The answer is clear, articulate, almost like a well rehearsed deliverance – probably answered a million times, in his head, for the psychiatrists in prison. Has he looked at his crimes? *Can* he look at his crimes?

– 'Yes. I do have regrets' he says – 'I was out of touch with reality in em days. My son had died. I was also doing a lot of Angel Dust. Sa-aam American mates from the army had laid a load of the shit on me. Me son spoke to me one night, appeared like an apparition, saying I'd to kill seven people to bring him back to life. Seven featured in every aspect of me life' he explains – 'I was put in a cell, number seven. Me prison number was – seven. If I combed me hair, it had to be seven times, even scratching meself, it would be seven times. We just want normality now, me and Mands.'

I nod, asking – 'Archie, av spent long periods a time in prison. Sixteen years wis the longest. A spent a very long period in an underground dungeon, in total blackness. A preferred tae be doon there, felt a deserved to be punished, huvin killed a man' I say – 'Wit aboot you? Dae you feel confused in any way, confused aboot being freed on parole?' I ask.

– 'Well, I'm not in prison, but I'm by no means free. When Australia kicked me out of their caantry the parole conditions became defunct – I'm not under any parole licence of any kind. Britain has no power over me. I can come an go as I please in Scotland. Australia feared I'd become a hit man for crims. I didn't want to come to this blaady caantry at all. People are hounding me because of them newspaper blokes. Mandy, an me, we just want left alone. We want some normality in our lives.'

I'm curious – 'Mad Dog? Where did you get this tag, in prison?' I ask.

– 'I've never been called that in me life. Them newspapers called me that. There are five other lifers all being deported to Britain. All from Glasgow. Now, these guys are real crazies' he explains.

– 'Ye killed three vagrants. Who wis the fourth person?' I ask.

– 'I'd been convicted of that murder in prison, but didn't do it. A killing that I did do, I got off with. The Star Chamber was everything – sanctioned killings, bashings, drugs, even prostitution. We were a death squad. See this scar?' he asks – 'This was our tattoo, but they had us all taken to hospital to have em removed. It was a death head, a skull. We'd sanction everything. The "Drop Kicks" or screws as you call em in your system. They were brutal, corrupt bastards. We ad one killed. Peter Schnidas, a lifer, killed im. But that is all in the past. I just want normality in me life, normality for me an Mands.'

I push it a bit – 'Did ye ever contemplate suicide in there, or ever greet at aw?'

– 'No, tough guys don't cry' he says, smiling – 'I'm a tough guy.'

During the following days, I find friends willing to let them have a flat, while I contact the authorities. I'm being slaughtered by the tabloids as expected, but how did they find out so quickly? My home is under siege, friends are followed, families too. They are distressed by the usual headlines. I discover the press are on to me walking down the street, splashed across a tabloid billboard . . .

MAD DOG ON OUR DOORSTEP – AND LOOK WHO HE'S WITH!

How are the press finding out about my involvement? How

do they keep finding out where we are? Waiting when I took him to register at the social security? Waiting at the doctor's surgery? Who can be tipping them off? Archie is unperturbed by the car chases. Does he think it's me? He doesn't seem at all surprised by the relentless bid to corner him for his story. Fortunately the social services relieve my position, letting me get on with my own irony, for a while at least.

Andy's dying – has days to live.

Caroline, Lorraine, and both families, have been living more or less up at the hospital. Me? I feel more aware of my past than ever before. I try to disappear, avoiding signs of anger. Lorraine has every right to feel anger at the world. Philosophical sentiment like 'Only the good die young.' They don't wash when your man is being stolen away from you, stolen by an invisible stranger, someone no one can see, or understand. A force slipping in, snatching, cutting you down, taking people's hearts, their life's love, their beliefs, their hopes, their dream of a life together – forever.

Andy looks so vulnerable as we sit around. Chic and Flora, Lorraine's parents, are all present. Andy, I feel, is saying goodbye to everyone. The wink he gives me is a final farewell. The look in his eye says it all. I want to hold him one moment to thank him for the brief friendship, for the lecture, for the laughs, for the advice he gave – 'Write the way ye talk. And Hugh, stop barin yer arse tae the world!'

Chic looks me in the eye – 'Time to let the women deal with things son.' I look back one more time. Lorraine's fragility, her beauty, her man – it's so sad.

Caroline is concealing her emotions. I feel her body shuddering at night, crying in the dark. I can only hold her, hang on to every moment we share, hoping to pass first from this life together. I couldn't face this loss, this grief, such a wound – 'Ca? Ca? That's the telephone ringin' I say.

I know before she says anything – 'Oh Lorraine. I'll be there as soon as possible. Yes I'll be there in ten minutes. Oh Lorrai . . .'

I make coffee while she dresses – 'Naw Ca. Lorraine an you go the gether. Al wait here but call fae the hospital when, sure okay then, al wait up at Lorraine's.'

I have a fag outside the house when they leave. The dark blue night sky, shining with glittering stars – '*My was a sta befow my was bown Uncle Hew.*'

I look up, wondering . . . has he gone yet?

Yes, he's there now.

Archie McCafferty's profile seems to appear in almost every newspaper in the caantry over the next few weeks. Every other day there's a new and even more sensationalist headline.

I STABBED TWO HUNDRED MEN – BASHED FIVE HUNDRED MORE!

CRIME KINGS MEET MAD DOG!

MAD DOG PLEDGES – I WONT MUSCLE IN ON UNDERWORLD!

Stabbed two hundred men? Bashed five hundred more? That's a lot of people. Must have been busy during that period. The Underworld? Crocodile Dundee meets Robert De Niro? Al Pacino? Reservoir Dogs meet Mad Dog? The tabloids are having a field day. I discover that he had been the one tipping them off all along. I must be getting old – 'Who's a naughty boy then Arch?'

A preview of the documentary reveals that he'd also been working on a *five year* pre-release programme in Australia.

Caant use blaady telephones? Caant handle blaady maaney? What's all the blaady fuss?

I've been taken for a ride, suckered. What did I expect

though? Mother Teresa? He's an ex-con. He's trying to survive with the only equipment he has – jail cunning. I find the irony appropriate. I mean, there I was, doing my social worker scene, thinking I'm doing something constructive for once, and, well, these things appen cobber.

A few weeks later who should reappear?

– 'Hi Hugh! Long time no see! How are you doin then braather? Em blaady papers . . . they won't leave us alone! What's all the blaady fuss? I don't understand it all meself. All we want is left alone. Whenna we gonna do a birra fishen en me old mate? Youv got saam good caantry over 'ere. We should get out there an do a birra haantin, saam shootin an skinnin. I aardly see you araul mate these days!'

It's Old Croc himself – 'How ye daen Archie?' I ask.

Twenty four years of jail just swaggered into my local. EH1 is the trendiest bar on the Royal Mile. He's dressed for walkabout. I half expect to find a boomerang jammed in the new expensive snake skin belt. But seriously – two murderers, together, in a bar doesn't quite come off – it's just *too* heavy. Mr Dog? He doesn't seem to mind all the attention. No, he appears to be enjoying the eyes upon us, the side glances, the open mouthed gawking.

He sips his coffee – 'I like this place Hugh. Yeah, I like it. Mands an me ave bought a car. Alan gave us a bit of cash' he explains – 'We appreciate what you've done for us. He's a good bloke. Hugh, he really an advocate? D'ya like another coffee? Yeah, I like this place, eh Mands?'

Mandy looks fine but strained. She'll be dealing with absolutely everything. That old institutionalised bit, the habitual long term absense of responsibility, induces a sense of inability, becomes an excuse for total laziness. Prison's brilliant for that – 'You go in. I'm not used to shops, buses, telephones, people, but I can roll a good joint!'

I'm not really in the mood but what do you say – 'Alan? Aye, he's okay. Any news ey a job ur a hoose?' I ask – 'A think ye shood try a stint wi SACRO. Sum good people wurk there, sum ex cons as well Archie. Wit's the shades aw aboot?' I ask – 'The rain's pissin doon.'

Don't tell me – tough guys don't get wet? – 'Here's Alan now' I add.

– 'Hi Alan! The sunglasses? D'ya like em? A young kid asked me where he could buy a pair the other day, called em the MD shades! Yeah, a nice kid he was too. Em people from SACRO?' he asks, turning back to me – 'Na Hugh, em welfare blokes is always asking questions. Mands an me. We don't tra-ast any of em. We just want to live aat in the bush. Yeah, could easily do that, eh Mands? Em journalists too, they all want a piece of me. I don't know what all the fuss is abaat.'

Please, please, don't say it – 'Mands an me just want left alo . . .'

Alan doesn't look comfortable – 'Okay Alan? How's things?' I ask.

– 'Oh fine thanks Hugh. Coffee?' he asks walking to the bar.

– 'Na, av wan there' I reply, following him, to stretch my legs.

Arch and Mands' grins are wearing me out. Their nudging and pushing doesn't go unnoticed – 'Wit's happenin then? Ye wurkin on any cases Alan?' I ask.

Alan I know will be close mouthed. Almost four years now we've known each other, and not one snippet of gossip – 'Just the bail appeals' he replies – 'How long those two been here Hugh?'

Those two? Something is wrong here – 'Ach, five minutes ur so. You gie thum sum cash?' I ask.

Alan floors me – 'Well, ehm. He said he was depressed. Said he was going to rob a bank. How much? Well. Eh two grand.'

Two grand? Rob a bank? I look at him – 'Alan. Wit? Two fuckin grand? Ur ye aff yer fuckin heid?' I exclaim – 'How's he plannin tae pay it back? Two grand? Wit if every ex-con ye meet threatens tae rob a fuckin bank? Are ye gonny fork oot anurra two grand?'

I'm embarrassed. I introduced them to him in the first place – 'Hu-uugh, please, don't say anything' he pleads – 'I can write it off but that's the last.'

I go to the toilet, more to defuse all the anger welling up inside – 'Okay Alan, but nae fuckin mer. Tell me if they try that on wi ye again, right?'

Alan's sitting back at the table with them when I come back. Mad Dog barks – 'Yeah, I've been paintin, Hugh.'

– 'Zat right?' I ask in amazement.

The fidgeting is a dead giveaway. He knows, I know, the stroke pulled – 'Yeah, can't sleep, up all night. Was it like that with you mate?' he asks.

– 'Naw' I reply.

Photographs appear from nowhere, stuck under my nose, down under material – 'I'm a white fella but gubba art's me thing. I've been commissioned to do a few for people we met, saam fella in a paab. We wanna open an art craft shop, an make some cash, sellin me paintins' he states.

I can't help myself at times – 'Easier than robbin banks eh?'

He doesn't go for the bone – 'Naah, dem welfare blokes. Told em I can do demolition work, dynamite's me thing you know. Yeah, when a wos a kid, we used dynamite taa rob banks. Yeah, dynamite an machine gans. Robbed seventeen banks we did. Hugh that one of em journo blokes? There with the camera?' he whispers – 'Mands don't let em see you.'

This Rolf Harris act isn't coming off – 'Japanese tourists rarely kerry anythin else dae they?' I sneer.

He's squirming around on his tail – 'Well mate, we gotta go.

Meetin one of em journo blokes, es from the *Guardian*. Wants to look at me paintins. There's anaather, wants to buy me book, *Seven Shall Die*! A publisher said it was too powerful. What does he mean by that, too powerful?'

Oh give me a break – 'Aye see ye later. Coffee Alan?' I ask.

I don't look round to see them leave, only another longer faced Alan – 'Jesus, Hugh. I don't believe it. He borrowed some more while you were in the toilet. Pay for the tax disc and insurance. No look, it'll be worth it in the long term. Now they won't come back.'

I look at him – 'Alan. Am gonny rob a bank. Kin ye lend me . . .'

– 'Fuck you Mr Collins' he delivers flatly.

We both laugh – 'A suppose yer right' I say – 'What aboot aw that sub machine guns an dynamite? The bush? Poor Mandy. She looks tense as hell. Wis a like that when a got out of jail?' I ask – 'Worse? Oh thanks, very good Mr Muir.'

Alan has to be back in court – 'I'll be back down later. Catch you here?' he asks.

I watch him leave. Poor Alan. Was I such an obvious arsehole? I tend to think these days that I'm becoming someone else, someone *nice*. I have to remember where this guy's coming from.

Who the fuck am I to judge a lifer? His circumstances may have changed. Well, *may* is an understatement. He's been torn from everything he knows: that jail power, that male reputation, a reformed lion, from a jungle of brutality and lunacy. Try his world for a bit, look through his eyes awhile, feel that kind of fear he holds dearly. I have to try to bear with him, keep his feet firmly planted – but remember the dangers.

Chapter Eighteen

LOOKING AT THE hand painted coffin I let the images flow through my head of the times with Andy. The Eyemouth fishing festival, those tents filled with the different types of fish. The fishing boats, wet wellington boots. Hearty laughing faces, that fish market atmosphere of smells and shells, strange scaly creatures. Andy himself catching the moment on camera – for us.

Caroline, Louise, and Liz have painted beautiful forms for him, mindscapes of every aspect of his life. Fife, Edinburgh, the Forth Bridges, flowers, fish . . . art. His cutting edge. His humour, you can't crystallise in imagery, in ephemeral ochres and blues. Andy's sporran on fire, him stoned, lent a whole new meaning to sparking up a joint.

The tongue-lacerating dryness: the beautiful expressions, the funny stories . . .

These things you can't catch in paint, only remember.

Bach playing throughout the church service.

He lived every moment of his life.

He was a good guy, an angel.

Lorraine, Louise, Caroline, and all of his friends, together scatter his ashes, as was his wish. I take to walking around on my own for a few days, walking around in the rain without any destination, without anything in my hand, without pretending. It's taken four years to be able to do this on my own, to walk slowly without the panics, without the pace getting faster and faster. No, I'm just walking, looking at buildings, looking into shop windows, looking at people's faces, looking at the dark clouds, feeling their drops on my face, feeling them reach into my bones, thinking about tomorrow, about the day after tomorrow, and the day after that day. What to get for my wife's birthday, what flowers to buy for her birthday? I'm thinking how the days become weeks, how the months become years, how time passes, learning to walk – how life goes on. I'd never have come this far without people like Andy, especially Andy – I'll never forget him as a friend.

Oh Jesus. Please, not today.

Those MD Shades. You can't miss them, especially in the rain. The leather jerkin's a new accessory. The Australian flag stitched on the arm is standing out a mile. Those 'expenses only' payments from them journo blokes must be going a long way. Mands too is looking more relaxed – 'Hi Archie. How's things?' 'Hi Mand, you're looking well these days. Am huvin ma coffee break. S'Caroline's birthday the day. She's upstairs wi ur family. A party, yeah. Am huvin a break. Saw ye in a news article.'

He switches on the tape – 'Hi Hugh. Yeah em tabloids. They wont leave us alo . . .'

I do like him though – 'Archie, listen' I say – 'Thur's a lot a good will towards you oot here. People want tae believe ye, believe ye've changed. But aw this daft publicity? People want ye tae get on in life, but ye huv tae help thum. Aw this publicity? It jist complicates things . . . it's aw bullshit.'

I'm wasting my time.

I keep trying – 'Archie. The press jist want a story. Thull turn on ye in the end, you'll look like a prick.'

Well I've tried.

– 'Whaat ya see is what ya get. I'm Aussie through an through. Hey! D'ya like this? S'me old huntin knife. So whenna we gonna do saam fishin then?' he asks.

The old hunting knife is a lockback blade, a weapon

favoured by criminals, concealed easily, and lethal in a fight. I believe having a knife lying around, it's just a matter of a scene and bad timing. They get used – it's an inevitable fact.

– 'Archie. What are you doing with that fucking thing?' I ask – 'Ye aff yer held?'

Jesus! A hunting knife? In a city like Edinburgh?

He looks at me – 'Ya know your traable mate? You've been aat too long. You've gone soft. Al av a coffee an en we're off haantin saam bear. Honest. Ya saand like an old woman mate!'

Oh please, please, no more.

Old Croc's blazed a publicity trail across the country over the weeks. Will he make it without too many knocks? I followed the coverage: there was interest in his painting.

Had I gone soft? Was I just an old woman?

I'd been about to concede to the idea when it happened – the publicity bubble exploded! The white fella was dismantled by critics with more serious interest in art. Gubba art was not *his* thing – it was an *aboriginal* thing. The stories had become more warped and more disturbing.

MAD DOG – I'LL BLOW ANYONE AWAY
WHO HARMS MANDY!

MAD DOG – WE JUST WANT LEFT ALONE!

MAD DOG – I'M NOT A THREAT!

Jesus. Is he losing it? He's putting on a good front just now though – haantin bear? One broadsheet newspaper in particular depicted him in the photograph as the figure in Munch's *Scream.* The whole article reeked of madness. I'd be demented with all this stuff about my sanity, but what can I say? I tried to steer him, guide him, but what was the point? I mean, what if I was wrong? I mean, he has mental illness stapled to his forehead. No matter what direction I took, he was going to have this thrown back in his face, his jail persona, his protective shield – Mad Dog.

Who am I to ask him to abandon that?

I feel I fucked up somehow. Maybe I should have guided him towards that Underworld after all, let him loose in a jungle where he could have survived, honed all those deep instincts into perfection, where 'insanity' means something to regard with fear, regard, yes, *regard*, with the fear of having to face someone who has earned a rep in jail as Mad Dog.

Nobody would have taken this guy's bone away without a fight to the death.

You know, what if all this concern, all this stuff about rehabilitation . . . What if it's all off track, a waste of time, in other words a failure? Prisons today contain mental illness, drug addiction, every social fuck up case imaginable, and AIDS.

What if prisoners just said fuck it, rejected all efforts to rehabilitate them, rejected this very notion that they have to change.

So what do you do? Write a strong letter of your outrage to little Jack Straw? I have already tried that. I'm still trying to read through the pile of paper his secretary responded with about addressing this problem of the deportation of psychos from all the Commonwealth countries. Can a psychopath be rehabilitated?

That 'Good and Evil' concept is so simplistic an approach to such a complex matter it is almost laughable, were it not for the fact that it affects not only warders, governors, prison doctors, secretaries, clerks, cooks, civil servants, the judiciary, and of course a government itself, especially when it lands on your doorstep with a used needle screeching – 'Geez the fuckin video!'

Jobs preserved oddly enough for the big boys in the domain of *business*. We *are* talking industrial business here, privatised, or in the process of classification for cost and effective analysis by privatisation experts, *male* experts. Prison *is* big business, is big money, so who wants rehabilitation with no one coming back? I mean where would all these people be without these prisoners, these jobs?

Prisoners, the work force. Those generations who are in and out so often it could well be described as regular employment under the New Deal at the Job Centre. But no, it is called the recidivist rate, in other words – 'You back in again? Dae ye want yer auld joab back?'

Yes, these are the eight to five pegs of the Underworld, working stiffs doing their daily shifts for an average four quid a week. Their families can send them a tenner a month. That family is usually a single teenage mother with half the world's politicians screaming that they're having babies deliberately to get benefit – that giro. Odd they're all male screamers but the tenner has to be there every month on the dot, lying oddly enough in the prison's bank account, building interest. Crime eh? Tut tut . . . Ever seen a man having a baby? Screaming? Is it that fucking tenner he's screaming about? I don't think so.

Four quid a week eh? No, let's call it a round fiver, save any arguments about those standard minimum wages for those too, who have dared refuse to work and are then given a half ounce of tobacco in the punishment cells. What a cheek eh – refusing to work, and then having the audacity to expect tobacco, or a bar of Highland toffee just because they don't bloody smoke!

I know what I'd do with them!

So this is what I pay tax for?

Where's that bloody pen?

That Jack Straw!

So, what if?

You can be stabbed for a bar of soap in these places. Someone dipping into that fiver a week means you're being fucked, done over with no representative to look over the claim that you're being underpaid. This work force has no union leader, just a blade to protect that minimum wage. THE ONLY union in existence in here are members of the Prison Officers' Association. And, as pointed out earlier, all mostly male members. These days there exist the token females, a pair of tits basically, constantly watching their backs, indulging themselves in those hard-ons pointed in their direction, or dyke motivated purposes, but they don't belong, aren't wanted amid male members of the union.

But to get back to that question of what if.

What if . . .

The women . . . Yes, the women, the birds, the wives, ex-wives, potential wives, future possible birds. Now what if they were to strike? Refuse to take the responsibility for those pegs who are in a permanent–temporary state of release and re-arrest, release and re-arrest?

What if they sent back the procession of love letters that follow yet another short term jail sentence?

Those 'Give me just one more chance' letters, the poems, the scrolls, declaring their commitment to that next time they pass through the revolving door of prison.

Those promise-filled 'A luv only you an ma wee Jimmy' letters.

Wee Jimmy Nobody? – the next commodity for rehabilitation, and that tenner a month on the dot.

Continuing that whole process all over again, the procession of poems, letters, declarations, promises – 'Honest doll. A luv ye. A drew awra wee floo'ers masel. Aye, am good at daen drawins an sculpture. Don't forget that tenner mind.'

Now what if women revolted? Never thought about that one did you? What if the real people, the women who have to face the brunt of that male population's temporary 'in-out' frustrations and failures, simply said fuck it?

Those tenner a month single mothers eh?

Wee Jimmy Nobody might take the wrong turning and end up at Oxford. It's a fact it's actually cheaper to keep and educate someone at Oxford than to keep them in prison.

Wee Jimmy Nobody though, from Muirhouse, Niddrie, Possilpark, wherever. Is he too dumb for Oxford? Does his dialect bar him from the opportunity of a life beyond jail? Does his dislocated backdrop prevent his chances? Does he have *any* hope?

Jimmy Nobody Junior won't let down his Da, won't break with tradition, won't show that he's afraid of jail, of doing the time, not until his brain dies of thirst, of a dullness that induces sucker/victim syndrome – or he may just become a dealer.

Why not? That's how it is.

The poor, the uneducated, they sustain prison as a business with a stable population, with a growing interest rate on those tenners every month, and a blind anger brought about by ignorance.

Mark Leech's book *Product of the System* has been influenced by the same deadly syndrome, it's stamped all over it. This 'I'm a victim' line. An inability to accept any responsibility, even when circumstances might have proved otherwise, when chance might have shown what he really could do, but it all takes time, and other people. In his case I feel that his hatred, disappointments, have dulled his senses, dragged them down into levels of self pity, and yet he has a brain.

A brain that is functioning, razor sharp, observant – but blighted by emotional anger. He is the type of prisoner who could tell you how many teeth you're entitled to have on a standard issue plastic comb – and he's going bald.

What a waste of energy.

I've had the privilege of watching him tongue-lash a warder first thing in the morning when bears are stumbling along landings with piss pot overflowing, flying all over the place with each step, as they try to defy gravity, dragging them down the long drop to the ground floor head first, defying that urge to just get it over with, after a night filled with desolation, defeat, an expected letter held back possibly, maybe even due to the tenner not arriving on time – debts in jail can get you killed.

Who knows why people jump, but they sometimes do.

Those piss pots bouncing, surviving the sound of the dullish, flattening thud of bone, flesh and hair meeting cold, welcoming concrete – 'Anyone for an extra sausage?' Mark Leech though, functioning, frustrated, fighting within a homophobic population who refused to back him because he was homosexual.

Cons? Cons are their own worst enemy.

I had a brilliant evening recently, watching him at work in a live debate on television. Mark Leech in one corner, facing what appeared to be his favourite opponent, the ex Tory Home Secretary, Michael Howard. The topic inevitably was – Does prison work? Michael Howard was dismantled, dissected, discredited, proved wrong time and again by a youngish, gay man, employing logic, intelligence, and instinct in wrecking every single argument thrown up by the Prince of Darkness.

A guy who was defeated in prison by that terrible homophobia, that 'Fuck him. He's a poof!'

A poof?

Oh, but they'll listen to the incorruptible black uniform standing on a landing with his bits of paper, paper clips, his frown, and concern. I'm forever amazed by people who believe that a uniform makes someone trustworthy, guarantees integrity and honesty. Anyone with half a brain knows that the police are racist, many are absolutely corrupt. Prison warders are usually failed coppers – never made the height, or maybe ex army. These jobs attract the worst kind – the upper working classes – the real enemy.

All this first name terms with each other nonsense. The breaking down the barriers of us and them, but they won't support a prisoner because he's homosexual? Are there no homosexual warders? Do they ever ask themselves this when they're begging for something – 'You want to borrow a pen? I'll let you use my own Biro. Could cost me my job, but yer a good lad Jimmy. Listen. I'm putting in a good report for you, and if you can't find an officer to take you out on your home leave, just see me. I'd be more than happy to meet the wife and wee Jimmy.'

Then there's the mixing – 'Now Jimmy a word to the wise. That Leech. He's trouble, makes trouble for other prisoners who want to get on with their time. A shirt lifter you know. Yes, a trouble maker that one.'

Wake up Jimmy. Forget the 'Thanks boss' routine. That frowned look 'fuck' gets a day off to take you home, gets paid to meet your wife and kids, gets paid while eating your wife's bought food. He's letting you get that fly quickie in the bedroom, like two animals in a pen, having a wee clock around your house to look for the potential little Jimmy Nobody Junior.

Wake up! have a long lie in bed, take the day off work, and listen to people like Mark Leech. He's a poof, a faggot, a queer, bent shot or whatever . . . so fucking what? That black uniformed incorruptible fuck is jammed up your whole family, eating your wife's provisions from her giro!

He's having the day out!

Look at it. Who's paying for all this? Who's entertaining who? The wife, or the bird, that's who.

So what if? The women, the wives. What if they 'just say no'? They alone face that rehabilitation, the reform, the you must change. Who supports them? Who organises that parcel of dope every month, that parcel to get you enough currency to afford that extra phone card, the tea bags, the little bit to get you a kip at night, the stamp for you to write about that undying love?

The fucking women do, they do it all.

Who will support her if she's searched, caught with a half quarter, the diffs, the tems? Or as in today's drug testing climate, that bit of brown powder?

Who looks after her? There are no voices in Corntonvale Prison. No Mark Leeches out there fighting for her so wake up.

Wake up Jimmy Nobody!

She might just revolt.

Mad Dog, much as I empathise with his plight, is about to see the other side of my own little Mary Poppins. Caroline has handled and supported seven lifers. Seven killers, who are now all resettled after a period of reminiscing about the good old bad days through a few joints, jail paranoia and the odd tems in our kitchen. They're gone, have gone, gone home – rehabilitated? They haven't murdered anyone else. Gone soft? Archie I was due home an hour ago. Caroline's family are waiting for me to get back up to the flat to celebrate her birthday. You're not invited – it's family. Serial killers, killers together as I said before just don't go together. I'm only out for cigarettes, and a wee quick break from party tension.

Hunting? Lockbacks? Gone soft?

When Mandy does revolt, you will begin to understand.

Flat surfaces, hard floors, tough guys don't cry? It will come to an end believe me. Oh shit. Here she comes now. Here comes that first taste of rehabilitation.

– 'Hi Carline. Mands has a birthday present for ya!' he beams – 'Appy birthday!' The fake crystal glass vase is ignored – 'HUGH! Where have you been!' she roars. – 'I met Arch . . .' I stammer.

The hands are on the hips. I've been here before with her, but there are no bars, no windows, no Sellotape, no knives. I'm for it.

– 'The one night I fucking need you! My family . . . WHAAAT?' she screeches.

Archie. No, no, no-ooo. Don't try it. The Crocodile Dundee act won't work. She's on full steam, ready for a battle. Your serial killer number is transparent. She'll eat you alive – she's a woman in revolt.

He tries again – 'Carline. Mands an me. We . . .'

She rounds on him – 'YOU! You shut the fuck up! This has nothing to do with you!' Mad Dog's jaw's still hanging open as I'm marched up the stairs – 'YOU Hugh Collins! Up the fucking stairs! NOW!'

I don't see him so often these days. Last time we spoke the future didn't look good at all. The press had disappeared, the film crews have gone, friends have been stung. I think people have become bored, tired, worn out with it all.

– 'Hi Hugh. Yeah, I'm pissed off. I don't wanna be aat here ya know. I preferred jails ta this. I blaady hate being out. I hate this blaady caantry. We saw a load of cash the aather day. I almost took it. We just wanna be left alo . . .'

No, don't say it . . .

Guess that's the end of that birra fishin an haantin then Arch. Well amigo, I've meant you no harm in any sense. You fucked me over. I've fucked people over – we're both ex lifers, it's no big deal.

Maybe in another life, another bush, another outback, but that walkabout is no longer a possibility. I'll see you around, and you'll find reasons to hate me, as a braather, as a man, as an ex-con.

The women are here.

It's finished.

Now you too must choose a path, find a reason to change, still rage on, but never kill. No, I'm afraid your rehabilitation is about to begin for real. She'll tolerate so much, so much institutionalised spiel, and then she'll fight you, tackle you physically. The Mad Dog days are over – this is real life.

Chapter Nineteen

THESE DAYS I use an answering machine to avoid speaking to anyone. I've become an unshaven recluse in my nest in the sky. The telephone answering machine does all the talking, granting me the privilege of having minimum contact with people, with an old enemy at that – the family hostility.

Autobiography of a Murderer has filtered out into newspapers. Snippets of slash and stabbings from the past creep into the present. The publicity has provided my family with the final excuse to stop talking to me altogether, but I feel that deafening silence coming in from the west coast, feel it cutting deeper than any knife could dig. I listen to the crackling mechanical message – 'We're sorry we can't take your call right now. Please leave your name and number after the tone, and we'll try to get back to you . . . Thank you for calling . . . Beep! Beep! Beep!'

– 'HUGHIE! PICK UP THE PHONE!' It's Alec. That voice, filled with the usual hostile fury, like some emotional volcano, waiting to explode. We haven't spoken for almost a year now.

The *Scotland on Sunday* serialisation of my book had been unflattering to those who felt that they should have been flattered.

Am I about to be scorched?

Part of the trouble with autobiographical books are the people who exist within the jacket cover – people who have an image of themselves. They take umbrage to the slightest diversion from the truth – *their* truth.

Autobiography of a Murderer isn't going down too well with my father – he's trying for an injunction to prevent its publication in February. Those who do feel flattered have a different perspective – 'Fuckin brulliant Shug!' While others display blatant, purely mercenary, interests – 'Much ye made then ya cunt? Ye must be fuckin loaded then ya cunt!'

What wrath is about to be unleashed upon my head now?

He's determined to get my attention – 'PICK UP THE PHONE!'

He knows I'm home, everyone know's I'm home – 'A KNOW YER IN HUGHIE!'

The voice has taken on a more serious note of urgency – 'HUGHIE! IT'S SERIOUS!'

Is it ever anything but?

I had predicted a crisis would occur before communications would be re-opened with my family, apologies have never been part of their dialogue. Crisis provides a bridge for reconciliatory talks, where grievances are, for the moment, forgotten, a temporary burial until drink releases the demons lurking below.

I catch myself falling into those old habits: the justification, the defence, the 'He said. A said!'

Glaswegians have this way of relating an incident by addressing some sort of invisible person while talking to you. They avoid eye contact with the listener while launching into this diatribe – 'A jist said tae um . . . An he said . . . So a said . . . – so a did!'

Arms flailing all over the place, and pointing fingers at those invisible listeners – 'Aye! A jist said tae the cunt . . . Am tellin you! An en he said . . . So a jist said tae um!'

To the observer they would appear to be addressing an object, a door, sometimes the floor. I did this for a long time after jail until I noticed people looking over their shoulders to see who was there. I'm doing it now. The thought of talking to him has this effect – 'He says wan thing here . . . Al jist tell um so a wull!'

My living room door is tired of being stared at, pointed at during dinner parties, hearing these prior to telephone conversations – 'Al jist tell um so a wull!'

Alec's tone is beginning to irritate me already. What now? I ask myself, preparing to take the heat – 'Aye Alec. Wit's up?' I ask calmly.

The furnace door's open wide – 'FUCKSAKE! Av been tryin tae get you aw fuckin day! Ma maw's in hoaspital!' he roars – 'She's hud a brain haemorrhage! You better get o'er here right away! She's in the Southern General! INTENSIVE CARE!'

He blasts me. Slamming the receiver down – 'Mind an be there you!'

Jesus. I'm stunned, for a moment. The Southern General? Where is that? How do I get there? Where is it? This fucking family. I don't have his mobile number. I don't have *any* numbers.

YOUR FAULT – I feel it coming at me in waves, *guilty, guilty, guilty . . . arsehole*. The bewildered door flinches – 'Wait tae a see this fucker! Al jist fuckin tell him!'

I'm pulling trousers on, shirts, socks – 'Alan? That you? Listen, Hugh here. Eh, listen ma Maw's in the . . . Aye, a brain haemorrhage. Southern General. Could you run me through there? Naw. Al find the way tae the hospital wance we get tae Glasgow' I assure him – 'Al ask sum cunt.'

– 'Shall I pick you up at the High Street?' he asks.

I'm standing at the front close as he screeches to a halt – 'Hello Alan, thanks. A got a telephone call, ma brother. Thanks. Wit? Am noa sure. He . . . Well, a can ask. A taxi driver'll know where. Well, the Intensive Care wis aw ey said. Al find it.'

I wonder how she is? God. Only recently I told someone

that I wouldn't go to either of their funerals – hers or my father's. Said – 'I fucking *hate* them!'

I remain silent throughout the journey, mindlessly nodding as Alan tries to make light conversation, staring straight ahead into flashing headlights, and the unknown – the Southern General.

The hospital looms up from the drizzling darkness – 'It's ward sixty five Alan.'

I literally dread these places: that presence, hanging there thickly, suffocating you. A bare, broken skull packed elevator taking us to the wards picks up a few more people, people who have had the tops of their heads sawn open, thick black thread stapling a torn head, puckering the flesh, pulling tightly together with crude stitches – a wound. Has my mother's skull been sawn open? Has her head been stapled?

I'm pinned to the wall. I'm paralysed by fear as the elevator stops at the fourth, while my stomach continues the journey to the fifth floor and beyond. I don't want to be in this place. I want to turn and run, pretend nothing is happening, take a line of smack or something – hide somewhere else.

A friendly warm staff nurse guides me towards the room – 'Well, she's unconscious at the moment but that's what normally happens. We can't predict the outcome but feel there is a fifty fifty chance of recovery. A lot will depend on how strong she is. These first forty eight hours are the most worrying. We're draining fluid from her brain just now, and then we will see whether or not she is strong enough for . . .'

Alec literally birls me round by the shoulders, while the nurse explains the procedure to me – 'Where the fuck've you been? Av been phonin aw day fur fucksake!'

I can see her lying on her back over his shoulder: those tubes from her head must be the drain the nurse was describing, her face looks drawn, her translucent skin almost like silk – 'Aye Alec! Right! Right! Wit've the doctors said?' I ask.

He's glaring – 'She must've known sumthin wis up. Laura came hame and found two basins fulla vomit. The doactur took ur straight tae Stobhill. She's noa been takin the pills fur the high blood pressure. The Stobhill doacturs musta knew right away. They brung ur here.'

Jim's at the far end of the bed, pinned against a wall. He looks pale – stunned. They have been together for almost fifteen years – 'Jim, you sit here, beside ma Ma.'

I feel clumsy holding her hand. I adjust the oxygen mask covering her mouth to seem to be doing something. God, I don't. I can't hold my own mother, while she lies here seriously ill, possibly dying. What are you supposed to do in these situations?

Will this happen to me?

Will I go down like this?

She looks helpless. I've never seen her like this . . . so, so vulnerable. She had told me to kill her if anything like this ever happened – 'Ma? Ma? Kin ye hear me? It's me Ma, Hughie' I say.

I feel so ashamed. My fear is a shameful aspect of my life. I'm barely hiding my deep terror from the others in the room. Are they feeling the same way? Alec's been with her all his life. How does he feel seeing his mother in this condition? He's talking to her, whispering – 'Here missus. Ye've gave us aw a fright. Shooey's here. Am the urra son, the wan that visits ye *aw* the time' he snipes.

I almost leap over the bed, but manage to pull back from the remark. Linda touches my arm, smiling, knowingly. She's been through the family battles, appreciated how difficult it has been. Alec continues whispering, encouraging her to live – 'Aye Ma. A think ye've goat ma attention so ye'd better get better. Yer noa finished yet auld yin . . .'

Why do I hate him so much? Hate his patronising tone?

I feel relieved when a buzzer signals the end of visiting time. I kiss my mother on the forehead – 'Night Maw.'

What the fuck am I doing? I've never kissed her. Am I acting a role? I'm numb, cold to all this. All I feel is terror. Am I doing the oldest son act here?

Zoe and Laura, Jim's two daughters from a previous marriage, are waiting outside in a room for visitors. Alan's talking to them as we come out – 'How's Betty, Hughie?' Laura sees her as her mother – 'Ma Aunt Betty, Hughie, she all right?'

Alec's back in my face – 'Right, listen! A don't want Mary Norrie, ur any they cunts up here! Av left instructions wi the staff that thur noa allowed anywhere near ma Ma, so they better noa show thur fuckin faces! Wit's that?' he sneers.

I try to reason with him – 'Alec, look. This isnae the time fur family feuds. Yer Maw's seriously ill in there. She'll need peo . . .'

He's thundering, baying like a bull – 'NAW! A better noa see eny ey they bastards up here! Am fuckin tellin ye! A wis there when they left ma fuckin granny tae die! Ma Maw widnae want thum here so they better noa be up here fuckin gloatin!'

Jesus. Linda guides me out into the night. Alan has the car running – 'Linda, thanks. He's fuckin nuts eh? Wit was aw that aboot?' I ask.

Linda walks me outside – 'Don't worry. She'll be fine, but it will take a bit of time. I'll look in as often as I can when I'm over at the psychiatric wards. Anyway. Give me a phone, and don't worry. Love to Caroline. Bye then.'

Alan's in a hurry to get back to Edinburgh – 'How is she? Yeah, that's true. You never know what's lying ahead do you? Pardon? Oh, fine thanks. She's pleased that I have finally stopped drinking. Dad too, I don't think he knew the full extent of the drinking. You don't realise how much of a hold it's getting on you until . . .'

Alan continues to make idle chat, keeping my mind off things. I listen as he chatters a bit and realise once again how lucky I've been to find so many people willing to help me make it out here, particularly guys like Alan – 'Well Hugh, here we are. Listen I'm doing a case tomorrow but if you need a lift just say, don't hestitate okay? Right, well. Call tomorrow okay, night mate.'

I'll see if Norrie's in EH1. Elaine, the manageress, is behind the bar – 'Hi Elaine. Has Norrie been in?' I ask. She's a nice lassie, friendly – 'No Hugh. Keith's over there. A coffee? How is your Mum? Alan called earlier' she says.

The place is busy – 'Well. Who knows. The doctors don't tell ye anything really, but a don't know, it disnae look good, but who knows eh? Dis Keith huv a drink? It's busy the night eh?' I say.

Elaine just smiles – 'Yes, been like this all day. End of the month an all that. I'll bring your coffee over Hugh.'

Keith's an architect I'd become friends with through Norrie. He was going through his own problems. I liked a lot of these guys. They had never judged me, other than the usual questions about how I'd got into so much trouble – 'Hi there Hugh. How's your Mum? God, you never know the minute dae ye?'

– 'Ach who knows big yin. How's things with you?' I ask. Keith smiles, raising an eyebrow – 'Do you really want to hear? How's the book? Saw a huge article on you the other day. No it was all right, fairly positive. How dae ye deal with all that Hugh? The publicity. I mean, dae people recognise you on the streets? D'ye ever get headbangers trying to . . .'

Just then a head in a sky blue suit pokes me in the chest – 'Hope am noa interruptin ur at boays but eh . . .' it says.

Fuck me. Here we go – 'Naw mate. We're jist huvin a blether' I assure him.

Lager's splashing my face – 'Ma friends o'er er. We wur jist sayin. Listen! Al tell ye . . . Am gonny be your friend! Name's McLean. Good Proddy name. Know wit a mean?' he asks.

Oh, I know what you mean all right. Poke, poke, poke – 'McLean? Aye, nae bother' he persists.

Keith's picking up vibes – 'Hugh, fancy the Bank? Norrie's over there. Said he'd stay for a . . .'

Poke, poke poke – 'Aye! Am gonny be your friend!'

Sky blue's getting louder by the minute. People are looking over as a silence begins to descend into an atmosphere. These things happen in bars, but rarely if ever in this place. I try to ignore him without causing any offence – 'Aye, nae bother mate.'

Keith's tugging my sleeve – 'Hugh, let's go across . . .' but I'm pinned to the bar.

Poke, poke, poke – 'Tell ye wit! Am gonny be your friend! A run a bissness up at the Castle! Am gonny take you tae meet ma wife an weans! Aye! Me an you! Am gonny be your friend!' he shouts.

Big John Black, the bouncer, appears from nowhere – 'Hugh! How ye daen mate?' he warns Mr Sky Blue. The message isn't penetrating – 'Hullo John. Jist huvin a coffee, an up the road. Caroline's got the tea in the oven. Oh a know! A better noa push ma luck eh? How're the weans? Aye? That's good. Aye, fine. A problem? Nah, don't think so' I assure him.

John crushes my hand in a grip of reassurance – 'Okay Hugh. See ye before ye go up the road okay mate?'

John and Warren are two bouncers I *do* get on with, unfortunately for Mr Sky Blue. He has had a pleasant warning but paying no attention – 'Aye! Take ye tae meet the wife an weans! Yer welcome in ma hoose! Aw here! Haud oan a minute! Kin a trust you? A mean, ye won't molest ma weans wull ye?' he shouts again.

Molest his children?

Mr Sky Blue has just called me a monster. Now honestly. What would you do? There you are, bothering no one, and someone's calling you a child molester. Now tell me. What would you do? Call the bar staff, make a complaint? Call the police – have him removed? Throw a pint in his face. That's what you would do, isn't it, or wallop him? Me? I have very limited choices in these situations. A drink in the face would put me in jail for the rest of my life. I want to rip his fucking head off, but I can't, can I? I take him aside so no one can hear – 'Molest yer weans? Listen pal, kinna huv a wee word wi ye?' I ask.

Sky Blue becomes pale blue – '*Look* pal' I whisper. All Clint Eastwood like – 'A don't know who you are. A don't know wit yer tryin tae prove. So. Why don't ye jist fuck off eh. Ma heid's fuckin nippin so jist walk away. Ye'v dun yer gangster act okay. So jist fuckin beat it.'

I'm in the freeze frame. The point when all you see are someone's eyes staring back, giving those telltale signals, signs of fear erupting. This is familiar territory. I'm well experienced in this field, and can read him like a book. A mug who *has* recognised me from the newspapers, but read all the wrong signs – I don't look like a killer.

Now Mr Sky Blue sees only murder in my eyes – and that fear explodes in more spittle. He's turning white, shouting – 'AW HERE! A WIS OOTEY ORDER ER! A APOLAGISE MATE! NAE AFFENCE?'

My eyes alone have hate, but me? I just want to get home, get as far away as possible from this prick – 'Fine. Elaine! A lager fur the guy in the blue suit' I call.

I have fear too in my belly, the fear of what I might do to him if he keeps pushing. I've been through the fear he's experiencing, that sudden realisation of trouble that makes for flight. He's insulted me in front of a whole bar of people, people who believe that I have changed. The fear I deal with is what I can do to people like him. I don't like a prick in my face, calling me a beast, but I have no choice – I have to walk. All I'd been looking for was someone to talk to, someone who would listen before going home, an ear to absorb, defuse the past few hours of hospitals.

I finish the coffee – 'Keith I'm heading up the road okay. See ye later mate.'

I hear the rumblings as I leave – 'NOA SCARED EY THAT CUNT!'

John and Warren laugh – 'Send doon Caroline Hugh! She'll battur um! See ye at the weekend!'

Mr Pale Blue doesn't know how lucky he is. These two guys would've taken him apart just for the suit alone. I pretend to laugh too – 'Aye! Thanks! Night en. See ye later' I shout.

Caroline's waiting to hear of any news when I get upstairs to the flat – 'I read the note you'd left. How is she? Is it a haemorrhage right enough? Oh dear . . . What have the doctors said?' she asks.

I try to explain – 'Well, a don't really know Ca. She wis unconscious aw the time. Jim an Alec were there. Laura as well and Zoe. She's got these tubes in ur heid tae drain away fluid but . . . Wit's that? Well, am noa sure. The nurses said the first forty eight hoors ur the maist crucial.'

She asks how the family are coping with it all – 'Ach, Alec wis daen his usual. A don't think es copin wi it. Aye, sure, ye can cum through next time if ye want, but a think it would be better tae wait. It's really heavy wi Alec. Alan's gaun a bit weird jist noo' I say – 'Chucked drinkin so it must be heavy a suppose. Aye, talkin non stop.'

Chapter Twenty

THE SOUTHERN GENERAL seems like another part of the world. After four years living in Edinburgh I hardly know my way around Glasgow. Barry, though, insists on driving at a minute's notice, picking me up almost every night at the bus station and running me straight to the hospital – 'It's goat tae be at night Shug. Am workin durin the day, but nae problem man. Jist phone the day before okay, an al come straight fae work.' I just have to give him a call, and he's there – 'Barry? Aye, it's me. Fine, aye. Listen kin ye pick me up at the station tae go tae the hospital? Great. Right then, aboot six at the taxi rank? Catch ye there then.'

Big Barry, won't even take petrol money or anything – 'Wit? Ye fuckin kiddin! Knock ye oot ya fuckin aul' cunt! Petrol money? That'll be fuckin right!'

In the past I've always enjoyed the journeys from Edinburgh to Glasgow. You have to pass Barlinnie jail. I don't take delight in the idea of other less fortunate people in there, but passing the security camera pointed directly down to the yard of the Special Unit brings back memories of my time in there, in an old previous life. I'd looked up at that camera so often while in the yard working on the Christ statue. I'd felt that lens peering at my back as I hacked the stone, pushing my body beyond its physical limitations, bloodying knuckles, tearing muscle, to show them, to be hard, enduringly tough – to prove how tough we all were, the hard men of Scotland.

How naive. No wonder I did so long. Travelling past – in the warm interior of a travel coach – now that *is* sensible in getting to *them*.

Barlinnie. There it is. The depressing blackness of those huge halls. I wonder what's going on in there right now? All the heavy mob eh. They're sitting in there, sweating. Glasgow's top 'heavies' have all been rounded up after months, years of surveillance involving customs, Special Branch – almost every police force in Britain, Europe, and South America.

Had I taken those killing contracts when I had been released I would have been in an empty cell right now, a cell accompanied with high security measures and batons. It would have been the end for me – literally.

Thank God I walked away from it. Oh sure, there's lots of money, serious money, and all the glamour attached to that power. The lure of that world is almost irresistible, but thirty stretch in the henhouse? You can have a good run, but they will come for you in the end.

I'm glad I walked away.

Walking away *is* the success.

Politicians are the only types who can sell guns, drugs, and kill people – *and* get away with it. They *legalise* it. Walking away is the difficult part, but once you take that first step, there can be no turning back, no matter who's in your face.

I'll be poor but free from that life, from those police helicopters hovering above your home, and the armed response units ready to pop you – or the two bullets in the head from some rocket who needs to feed a mad heroin habit, some cowboy living his life through his video of *Scarface*.

– 'Barry! Barry! O'er here!' I shout.

Barry turns the car when he catches my waving from across the street – 'Didny see ye there auld yin. S'that grey wig yer wearin. So, how's yer wee Maw? Still that bad? A didny realise' he says – 'They'll look efter ur. These people know wit thur daen. They know how tae deal wi people who've hud a bad turn. Fuck, ye never expect it . . . That wee Maw ey mine as well. Wit a wumin, a wee diamond. Honest, heart a gold Shug.' Big Barry. It's always good to see him, it's reassuring – 'A know. Ma granny wis the same. Aye, Auld Cathy Collins' I agree.

I think back – 'S'funny, everythin changed efter she died. The whole family, they aw disappeared when a came oot fae borstal. There wis just nae family. That's when the trouble really began tae get oot a hand. Albert, Wee Joe, the Bear. We wur jist daft boys, but a bad combination, a violent combination' I explain – 'Albert n me, we wur like brothers. A daft crowd a boys, but it turned nasty – vicious.'

These talks, the car drives. They provide a necessary sounding board for us. Looking back, asking ourselves where things went wrong in our lives, how things happened. It lets us look to the future, how to prevent the anger within ourselves spilling into even more violence, appreciating the implications of murder and difficulties faced by both of our families as a result of long term imprisonment. Lifers can be recalled for being in contact, recalls involving more years in prison, and yet we need each other, having an understanding of the problems faced by any long termer. Neither of us wants to go back to jail but who else can we talk to? A welfare worker? Someone who has never been in prison, felt the frustrations, the deep fears – that sudden experience of being catapulted into total confusion on the street?

Barry exclaims – 'Aye, that's right. Your granny broat ye up eh. A mind you tellin me wan night we wur stoned. Ad furgoat aw aboot that. Ye don't get on wi yer Maw dae ye?' he asks – 'A know they stood by ye durin yer lifer. But it's never the same is it? They life sentences fuck the whole faimly up eh? This boy ey mine. Am tryin tae talk sense tae um . . . Witsat?'

I ask when his son was born – 'Wis it before ur efter the lifer?'

Barry explains – 'Aye, jist efter a goat the lifer. He wis jist a wean. Aye, it's hard fur them these days, an they want every fuckin thing tae! He's fourteen noo. Aye, so it's designer gear' he laughs – 'Shug, ye'v nae idea. Weans? Aw don't get me wrang. A dae luv ma boay, but he's trapped. That ex wife ey mine. Hur heid's nippin wi the wee man. He's been expelled fae a don't know how many schools. Shug he's in the middle ey it' he sighs – 'Ey dis es best, an en he's boxin wi sum urra boay. Then *his* Ma's held's nippin, an en she's screamin at me tae dae somethin wi um. Honest Shug! Intelligent? That's wit gets tae me. If a cood get um oot ey Pollok. School's a fuckin joke. Aw here, listen. Shug am sorry, nippin yer heid here like a fuckin bampot. Huv they said how she is, yer Maw?'

Barry's intelligent. I liked him in prison: that's where you see people, where you get a good insight. You see the strength of them, especially when it gets heavy. Some guys just can't cope, and end up suicidal, or have mental breakdowns, end up in Carstairs.

– 'Och she's . . . Fuck, a don't really know tae be honest Barry' I reply.

He listens as I continue – 'A don't know how it aw happened. She's likeable, an likes a laugh. It's just aw the kerry oan. Tryin tae control ye aw the time. They don't talk, the way we did, inside. They don't know wit happens tae ye in jail' I say – 'Things ur never the same efter a life sentence. Twelve, sixteen years. That's a long time Barry. Ye don't know these people, don't know yer ain faimily. Dae ye know wit a mean? A don't even know ma ain family.'

Prisoners *are* expected to simply come out as if they have just been on some sort of a vacation. Many families fail to understand that their sons or daughters have been in a completely different culture to theirs, a culture where all responsibilities have been taken away from them, an environment where they have become emotional cripples, unable to function without all that pent up aggression, without all that violence to get what they want.

Putting on those fronts for the visiting hour, pretending to be happy, or depending on what they've been expecting that day – the huff, for an hour. The new thing is *family* visits, with a screw pretending to know the prisoner intimately – 'Yes, thanks, I'll have a sandwich! Yum! Yum! Yum!'

Many too have never faced their crimes. Prisoners are never faced with the effects of their actions on victims' families or their own, and so become themselves the victim in most cases. After long term periods they become convinced they've done absolutely nothing wrong, or as in some cases can't come to terms with the crime, and invent an image of what happened, a picture they can live with for a time, but to come home is like meeting strangers for the first time, trying to live with them – *their* habits.

Barry had experienced difficulties too on his release, but had had a closer tie with his family – they'd been a family before he'd been sentenced. My situation had been very different. I had told him in prison to tell his son the truth about what had happened to prevent him thinking that violence was glamorous, a task easier said than done, but it would pay off in the long term, maybe save him from prison.

I try to describe the difficulty of my situation – 'Honest. A tried tae build up sum sorta relationship wi thum. The thing is. They don't know me. Auld Cathy wis ma real Maw. Dae ye know whit a mean?' I ask – 'A mean, a knew that fucking nutcase that wis next door tae me fur five years. A knew him better than ma brother. Then when a came oot? You knew me in there, ye knew wit a wis like. A'd still huv been in if a hudny fought they bastards. You know that Barry' I say – 'A had tae threaten ma way ootey that fuckin place fae day wan cos a stabbed they three screws. Ad nae choice. Ma family wid never a coped wi me when a first got oot. Honest. A wis aff ma fuckin heid. A jist wanted tae enjoy masel, aw the time. A hated people tryin tae control me, tryin tae run ma life.'

– 'Wis it that bad Shug?' he asks.

– 'Barry, they first two years wur heavy. That frustration? Sixteen years ey insanity?

A freaked right oot, smashin up studios' I explain – 'Caroline n Andrew. They took the brunt ey it. Ma Maw? They'd have freaked oot, nevera handled that kinda thing.' Barry's laughing, but, he *knows* – 'Barry, a wis off ma heid. Sometimes ad miss being in the jail, actually miss ma jail pals, greetin an aw that! Honest! A hated bein oot. A hated bein free' I say – 'Goin in wis easier than bein liberated. That wis a nightmare, fur me, and everybody else tae. Aye. Smashed up three studios, it wis fuckin crazy! S'aw rage spewin ootey me.'

Barry's puzzled by my anger – 'How dae ye let it get tae ye Shug? Yer foamin at the mooth man!'

I have to ackowledge his point – 'Ach. Ma Maw an aw that, know wit a mean.'

Barry's curious – 'How? widdae ye mean?' he asks.

I can't tell him what I know, can't tell anyone – 'Ach it disnae matter. They aw blanked me. Jim, Alec, the faimily. They think am loaded. Alec dis the brother act when he's efter money. Then when ey found oot a wis skint – nuthin, nae phone calls. It's only when es got bother wi es burd's ex man. Aye, wanted me tae batter the guy.'

Barry thinks I'm joking – 'Wit? He asked *you* tae chib a guy?'

I assure him it's the truth – 'Aye. An there's ma Maw lyin there tae – dyin. Am sorry big yin, ma heid's up ma arse. A don't know how tae deal wi this. Believe me, this'll be ma fault. Wait tae ye see this brother ey mine. A fuckin headcase man . . .'

Barry pulls into the hospital driveway – 'Wit ward is it Shug?' he asks. I apologise for the tirade – 'Sixty five. Sorry there, heid's jist dun in wi aw this.' Alec pulls me as we enter the room – 'Where the fuck've you been? Six fuckin times av phoned! Caraline noa tell ye? Wit's that?'

I can't take much more of this. He's towering over me, right in my face – 'Naw! She's still unconscious. Ye better get in an see her' he orders.

Zoe and Laura are sitting by the bed. Jim nods from the far wall – 'How is she?' I ask. Jim keeps staring. Laura lets me sit by the bed – 'She's been much the same Hughie. The sister said they might remove the drain tomorrow' she explains – 'She'd stopped taking her tablets for the high blood pressure' she says – 'That's what caused it.'

There's a huge scar above her temple, a hole. I rub the bed cover. She feels so frail underneath. Her hand too feels fragile, skeletal. How do these things happen? A few days ago she would have been doing her shopping, housework, or whatever. It just blasts you from nowhere. Why does the body give no warning? She must be all right, surely? We would be able to tell if she was going to die. You would see it, wouldn't you? She'll be out of it for a few days, and then be back to herself. Aye, she'll be fine. I'll be here the minute she opens her eyes. I'll make sure of it. Please don't wake up without me Ma – 'Witsat? Finished? Oh right, sorry, a minute' I tell the nurse.

Barry nods, he'll be outside – 'Right Barry, catch you out there' I reply.

Alec's hostility flows towards me. Searing hot waves of rage – 'Alec, listen. My Aunty Mary phoned last night. She's worrie . . .'

– 'WHIT? Who the fuck told they bastards?' he snarls.

Where's this coming from? – 'Look, Alec, people're bound tae fi . . .'

– 'AM fuckin tellin ye! They better no . . .'

Jesus Christ – 'Well, who've you told?' I interrupt.

– 'Uncle Robert. A told him, an yer Da. A contacted yer Da furst!'

My Da? Contacted him first? What does this have to do with him? Alec keeping him sweet? The huge insurance policy is it? Betty had been at me to keep in with him to make sure he had me in his will. She'd pushed me awhile back, before I was let out on parole. Fuck him and his money, I'd said at the time.

– 'Widye tell him furst fur? Ma Maw hated the cunt' I state.

The hostility makes sense now. It's thawed out, in fact cooled down into a speechless cold stare. There are things going on here, skeletons rattling – 'Ach, it disnae matter. The thing is, feuds wont help matters so . . .'

– 'NAW! Hughie am tellin ye! Ma Maw'll go mad if she wakes up wi that mob roonur bed! Av left instructions wi the staff so they wont be allowed in' he says smugly.

– 'Och, suit yerself Alec. See ye's later Jim' I say, leaving.

Barry has the car running – 'Ye okay Shug? He's fuckin heavy. Jesus Christ man. He is right aff es fuckin heid! A thought ye wur gonny battur um. Honest. How the fuck dae ye handle him? Is he really yer brother? Nae wunder yer heid wis nippin wi the visits in the jail. Is yer wee Maw any better? Nah? Wit a fuckin shame eh.'

I'm relieved to leave the hospital. Barry's determined to drive me back to Edinburgh. It's almost midnight – 'Naw Barry, fucksake man. Al get that last bus. It only takes an hoor. This rain'll be aff by the time wi get tae the station. Al get a taxi up the road. Ma Maw?' I say – 'Ach she's still unconscious. Aye that's the brother. He's jist a daft boay at times. Thinks Betty'll be proud that es angry. Ey'll calm doon again wance she's better. He's been wi her aw the time, never left the hoose tae ey wis aboot thirty so es takin it bad. Listen, that's wit aw ma home leaves wur like! Kin ye imagine?' I laugh – 'Nae wunder a took drugs!'

Barry asks why there was a fuss about my Ma's sister visiting – 'Wit wis that aw aboot Shug? He's fuckin potty.'

I try to explain – 'Aw, he blames hur fur ma granny dyin, but. Ma Aunty Mary, she's a diamond. Fuck. A tried tae shag ur when a wis jist a boay. Aye, gen up! Aw, she jist laughed, me climbin up the fuckin drainpipe. A wis oan a weekend fae ma borstal an said ad jist dun ten months! Wit a fuckin brass neck the next mornin, wakin up, an en rememberin wit ad dun! Dusty Springfield, that's who she looks like. God, the fuckin embarrassment. She wis always good tae me when a wis a wean, looked efter me . . . Aye, Mary Norrie, a real diamond.'

The journey back on the coach isn't so warm this time. The driver, probably trying to stay awake, has his window wide open. I'm seated directly behind him, chilled to the bone by the time I get back to Edinburgh. The walk home from the bus station gives me time to think. Why do I have this problem with Alec? The thought of having to go through to face him, trying to talk to him, is already doing my head in.

Caroline and I live a very quiet life together, always working all the time. Betty, Alec, and Jim. They don't understand. They think it's all a big party through here. The art world is just a big party to them. That's how they see things. They don't know a thing about my life, how much has changed in my life, or Caroline's.

They're trapped, steeped in that past, entrenched in that whole culture of sentimental self admiration, marvelling at their own sense of humour, respecting people like Paul Ferris

– 'That boy understauns the world he lives in. Ye huv tae respect um. He knows wit es daen.'

I'll bet he does. That humour too – 'Oh wit a laugh the other day! A siege in the high flats! Polis an helicopters aw o'er the place! These two boys, hingin ootey a windae shoutin the odds, they'd guns as well. The polis! Ye shooda seen thur faces! A mean ye canny help laughin.'

Is it me? Have I been taken too far? There was a time I didn't care, didn't give a fuck what happened. Now I just don't find these things funny. I hate gangsters. I hate that whole world. Where's the humour in gangsterism?

They're terrorising ordinary people, selling them drugs, killing them so what's the big joke? What's funny about that? What's to admire? I'd rather stay skint for the rest of my days than sell heroin.

Alec thinks I've got money, they all do – 'You must be minted fae yer book.' How do I deal with this? How do I get to the hospital every day? We have no income. Caroline sells an occasional painting, barely enough to survive.

Boyle, Kay Carmichael, they will all be waiting, waiting to point the finger. I can just hear them – 'Betty was there for him. Sixteen years the woman stood by him. Where is he now when she needs him?'

These people have flitted in and out of my family's lives. Lifted them whenever it has suited their purposes. I'll be the baddie again – oh well.

Caroline's waiting for me at the front door – 'God, you're wet. How'd it go? Is your Mum any better? Here, sit at the fire. I've made some nice soup. That's it. I'll hang these to dry. My parents called. They were asking about your Mum. Oh, they're fine but they worry about us. My Dad says he'll pay for that framing bill so we'll see . . . Anyway tell me about your Mum. What have the doctors said?'

I'm chittering with the cold, even with the coal fire – 'Think av caught the cauld. Barry hus it aw the time wi paintin an decoratin, snotturs trippin um fae the fumes' I say – 'We'd a good talk aboot things but the hospital. A hate they places. Alec's gettin oot ey order, growlin at people. Wit's wrang wi him Ca? How kin ey no be mer civil wi people?' I ask – 'That aggression aw the time. Nae wonder ma Maw became isolated fae sa many ey the family. Jim? Well, he's no been livin wi ur fur awhile apparently. Naw, it's serious' I say – 'Think es got a bird somewhere. She must've expected this, it wis bound tae happen. Thur wis too much ey an age gap between thum. She's fell oot wi everybody. People canny take that aggression aw the time. Witsat? Och Mary wis lookin efter ma granny fur a while, then when she died they wur aw blamin each urra. Ma Maw's heavy. You know that fae experience. Why ur they like that aw the time?' I ask.

Caroline's faced that same aggression, for no other reason than taking her son away, taking what she saw as control over me. Betty had treated her like dirt from the very beginning. Caroline, however, is no pushover – 'Well, Hugh, I know how difficult it all must have been for your Mum. Being left on her own with you when your father was sent to prison. She's an intelligent woman, but has had a battering throughout life. I mean, her anger would have sustained her in many ways. Alec too sounds as if he's taken it on, the mantle of anger . . . He's only doing what he thinks your Mum would've wanted' she explains – 'Try not to be too harsh on him. Oh, I know, I know, but try to understand, he has had a battering too. His Dad laughing in his face, he's terribly injured inside. Yes I know that but you *have* changed. Your circumstances are totally different now, you're not the same person, and they can't understand that. No, Hugh, they're proud of your achievement, but they're living in another world. What are you so afraid of anyway?'

Afraid? Am I afraid? Afraid of what? – 'Och, am too tired

Ca. Av caught this flu. Am shivery, an the back ey ma nose feels aw that snottery wi . . . Witsat? Oh, sorry . . . Am sorry.'

– 'God, thank you for sharing that with me, how the back of a nostril . . .'

Chapter Twenty-One

I'M FILLED WITH flu. My head feels like a crash helmet – 'Jethus. Caroline! Caroline! Caro . . .'

She's in the kitchen, listening to the radio, having her morning coffee. There's really something quite reassuring about these noises, and aromas – hot bubbling cafetiere, the barely audible radio, newspapers rustling, occasional chuckling. She loves these morning rituals, and reading. I've never met anyone who reads so much. She reads at every opportunity, chuckling away whenever she comes across something which is amusing, a warm infectious sort of chuckling which never fails to raise a rumble from me.

I feel her side of the bed to find it's still warm. She can't be up long – 'Caaaaaaaaa!' her blonde head pops round the door, smiling – 'Yee-sss? Oh dear. You won't be out of bed today. I'll make you a hot drink, and go to the chemist later. Coffee?' I try to blow off the crash helmet – 'Aw Jethuth Critht!' Caroline brings coffee and sits down on the bed – 'I'll have to phone the bank manager. Tell them the first payment is due so we can pay off some of the overdraft. No, I don't think they'll bankrupt us just yet . . . I'll call the hospital too. They won't let you in with flu so just stay in bed. Yeah, a flu could be fatal in a hospital. Did you get any sleep at all? Don't worry, I'll call Alec . . . I'll finish the papers first, then get moving.'

Shit. The flu. They'll think I'm just making excuses. I'll have to get up. I can't lie in bed all day. Oh Jesus, my bones – 'Caroline! Bring they tablets fur the arthritis. Feet are really thore. Am gonny tell that shtupit doactur! These fuckin things. Oh Fuck. Ya bathtard! Honetht Ca, thur really thore. Aw Jethuth. Did ye get ma fagth?'

Caroline's become accustomed to my morning rituals too, the farting, the coughing, a spluttering lung – 'Fuckthake! A canny get a draw fae . . .'

The bear with the sore head routine, waking up grumpy faced and in a bad mood – a bad mood, *every* morning? I didn't know I was doing this until it dawned on me one morning that the bad mood was just a habit from prison, a performance of acting out the role of Big Bad Shug. I had employed that tactic to keep pests at bay but, like all the other routines, it becomes habit forming, carried over into mindless behaviour. *May be institutionalised.*

This was genuine grumpiness, a mood which lasted two whole days – 'Fuckthake how long doeth thith fuckin flu latht Caroline?'

Angie, Aunty Mary's daughter, called later that night – 'Hughie? Aye, it's me! Oh fine. Well, she's jist the same, ye noa ma Maw! Hughie, listen. Alec wis up at her door. A heard aw the shoutin. Aye! Shoutin that she wisnae tae go near the hoaspital! Alec! Aye! Ma Maw goat a fright. Ye know wit es like. Ad a fuckin battured um if ad goat a haudey um, the cunt! Hughie, here . . . Ma Maw wants a wee word wi ye, speak tae ye soon pal, same tae yersel Hughie.'

– 'Hughie? Hiya son. Aye, told aw yer Ma's pals that av noa tae go near the hospital. Hughie, she wis up here a few weeks ago lookin fur me. Eh son? Aye, she wis up the road, up at Possilpark. A wis oot so she'd left a message. A think she wis lonely son. How is she? Aw wit a shame. A know son, a mean, am yer Ma's sister. Oh, that boay hus real problems. The things ey wis shoutin at me, aboot yer granny Norrie. Hughie a tried ma best son. Aye son, you gie me a phone an al go up wi you tae see Betty. A feel sa sorry fur ur, she's hud nae life at aw. Aye, wit a shame. Okay then son. Aye a know. Right al speak tae ye the morra then. Oh, ye know me son, Dusty Springfield!' she giggles.

Poor Mary. What's this bampot trying to prove? I'll have to speak to him. He can't be allowed to go on like this. I'm definitely going to pull him this time – 'Ma Aunty Mary. Aw she'th nithe Ca. Always dun up wi aw ur jewellery! A luv ma Aunty Mary. Alec? O the usual, up at her door. Fuckthake man! Mary widnae herm a fly.'

The 'He said. A said' scenarios keep me awake for the following two days in bed. I'm relieved to be back on my feet, to be heading on a travel coach to Glasgow – 'Wait tae a see this cunt. Al jist tell this bampot!'

Alec's bulk is dwarling my mother as I walk into the room. Laura and Zoe pick up the bad vibes as soon as I pull up a chair – 'She's conscious Hughie. She's had the drain taken out. She's better, but confused. They said her short memory might be slightly impaired' says Laura.

Alec's trying to talk while I hold my mother's hand – 'She's been sleepin maist ey the . . . The doacturs huv said . . . they're waitin tae see if . . . then they . . .'

I cut him dead with an ice cold glance. What the fuck am I doing? Why am I pouring all this energy into giving him a hard time?

A voice creeps into my head – *Fuck him! He's your brother – So fucking what? Oh are we becoming 'good' now? He ain't he-avy! He's my bro-theeer! Fuck him!*

Alec tries to explain her condition again – 'A heard ye the furst time.' I enjoy it as my remark rips right through his heart. Don't do this. He doesn't deserve this. Zoe flips into nervous chattering. I know full well that I'm putting them under real pressure but do nothing to relieve it. Truth is, I'm enjoying it – 'Jim been up?'

I knowingly smirk when they say he's working – 'Wurkin? Time dis ey fini . . .'

Betty's looking straight at me – 'Ye awright Ma? Hughie, it's me Ma.'

Her left eye has turned slightly inwards. The drugs, pressures would have caused this to happen – 'Yer a stranger' she barks.

What? I flinch from her remark. Please, please Ma. Don't blame me. I hold her hand tighter for my own reassurance – 'Av been here every day, Ma, hones . . .'

She's looking at me – 'Ye wurkin? Where? Pardon?'

The questions are barked at me – 'Jim? Is Jim here? Where is ey?'

Zoe sits on the bed with her – 'Betty? How ye feelin? Alec an Hughie are here . . .'

She knows where she is. She responds immediately – 'Terrible! Food's crap! Where is Jim? Jim here yet?' she repeats in that strange bark.

She seems back to normal – 'Naw Ma' I say – 'Es been here aw day, but hud tae go back tae wurk. Listen, there's nae paralysis ur anythin like that. Ye'll huv tae dae wit yer telt this time. Nae mer dancin ur blawin hash pipes, jist a good rest fur awhile, an ye'll be back oan yer feet. Witsat?' I ask – 'Aye Ma, Jim's at es wurk. Es been really shattered wi this aw happenin. Ye gave him a right fright. Naw, Jim'll be back later. Caroline's asking fur ye, an Anne Goring. Anne? Aye, she wis askin how ye . . . Witsat? Aye, Jim's cumin the night tae see ye' I continue – 'Ma Aunty Mary wants tae come an see ye, she's been really worried . . . is it awright tae bring ur in tae see ye Ma?'

Alec's head drops – 'Oh Mary, thur's nae time fur feuds . . . nae time fur anger. Oor Alec disnae mean anythin . . . thurs nae time . . . nae fightin . . . nae time . . . Pardon?' she asks.

I bow my head too. She's right. There is no time. No time

for anger. I've never heard her speaking like this. There's definitely something different about her. What is it? I try to think. What is it? What feels different?

God. All these years. I've been afraid of *her*. Afraid of her anger. Now, I don't feel it anymore. Betty's gone . . . the *old* Betty. The accumulated experiences, the memories, the very knowledge of 'Betty'. That's all gone, disintegrated. The woman speaking to me now is my real biological mother. She's beyond all that, free from that anger, the terrible hopes, the disappointments, the torments of her life – of being 'Betty'.

I lift her in my arms. There's no awkwardness this time, like in the past whenever I tried to touch her – 'Ye comfy noo Ma?' I ask.

She's smiling like a wee lassie – 'A feel tired son' she whispers.

I put pillows behind her head – 'Aye Ma. Well, ye'v taken a doin here.'

The buzzer signals the end of the visiting hours. I feel relieved, almost triumphant for some reason. I leave the room to call home and tell Caroline that I'll be catching the last bus home to Edinburgh.

Alec's trying to talk while I'm calling Caroline – 'You noa talkin, ur sumthin? Kin we noa talk aboot it? Wit? Ach suit yer fuckin self then' he snaps.

I blank him – *Fuck you – Brother!*

I feel robbed as he storms away. It wasn't supposed to work out like this. *He* was to be left feeling like a cunt, not me – 'Caroline, that you? Aye, much better. Al see ye, aboot twelvish. Naw, probably be later, the last bus an at. Wit? Naw, ad rather walk than take a lift fee *him*. Av got keys so don't wait up for me okay pal? Aye, fine then. See ye later, bye, kiss, kiss.'

The darkness of the coach is comforting. I close my eyes. My poor wee Ma. That fear has always been there, like a physical barrier, a barbed fence. Her confusion. I guess it's normal under the circumstances. Linda said she will need a lot of physiotherapy to fully recover. She'll be fine though. The confusion will clear up once she is home, back amongst more familiar surroundings, she's just tired. Poor Alec. Why did I have to put him through that bullshit? He's displaying that he cares more than anyone else, but so what. He's her boy too.

Poor Alec? Oh he's her boy too? Think he gives a fuck about you? FUCK UM!

Caroline's awake when I eventually get home – 'How is she? You must be tired. Yes, do you want toast?' she asks – 'I could make something to eat, oh well. That's good, it might not be so bad then. Alec's probably depressed, but she's recognised people around her? That's a good sign. Sounds as though there isn't brain damage. Yes, it is always a concern with these sort of things. The fact that she recognised you. That she was able to communicate, speak to you. Yeah, the short term memory can come back with time. Oh, I wouldn't worry. Alec'll calm down, but keep an open mind.'

I feel glad to be out of bed in the morning, after a night filled with nightmares. Anne's driving me through today so it will be less tiring. Anne Goring has been a lifelong friend since the Special Unit days, always willing to help people. She'd helped me in the past, through some terrible troubles. She's helped a number of men in and out of prison – 'Ca! Think that's the door. Kin you get it? Probably the postman . . . Witsat?'

I call – 'Who?'

Two detectives appear in my living room – 'Hugh Collins? We're here to take a sample from you – DNA.'

DNA? This is for sex offenders – 'DNA? Wit fur?' I ask.

They tell me that this is applicable to every lifer released within the past five years of a life sentence – 'Wit happens if a refuse?' I ask.

He becomes all menacing, glowering, heavy dude like – '*We've* the powers of arrest. I take you to the police station. Heavy team holds you down. *We'll* take a sample one way, or the *other* Mr Collins.'

The fingerprint kit and swabbing materials are on the table. I don't have time to go all moody, do my ex lifer tantrum demonstration – 'Am takin it, but against ma will. You threatened me. Av nae choice.'

Caroline's furious, boiling mad – 'Why has there been no notification? What? This is my home! Why haven't the authorities . . . This isn't a bloody police station! This is my home!'

They're giving her the 'just doing our jobs' line. I'm fingerprinted and swabbed – 'Ye want piss?' I ask. – 'Naw? Finished then? Right. Oot the fuckin door. Wuv got urra things tae dae. Right then, cheerio, ta ta.' ARSEHOLES!

Caroline's fury subsides – 'I don't believe this. Fingerprinted in your own home? The probation officer should have notified us. This doesn't ring true somehow . . . Anyway you better get going if you're meeting Anne. Love to Betty.'

Anne drives me through to the hospital – 'She's frail, but better than expected. Well a don't know. They're insertin a shunt into her head. This drains fluid. God a know, a thought that tae. A shunt. Sounds like . . . There! It's ward sixty five.'

There's something different this time, something not quite right. She's listening to me, but – 'Ma, listen, there's nae long term damage, but yer gonny need tae take yer time wi things. Jim's devastated, but es copin. Mary's cumin back in the morra tae see ye. Witsat?' I ask – 'Well yer eye's a bit bruised, but thur's nae paralysis. Aw yer faculties ur fine so ye kin recover fae this, but ye'v goat tae rest. Wit's that?'

She's been listening to me but her eyes – 'Who are you? Hughie? Ma Hughie's away tae school. Where's ma other son?

Alec? Naw, ma other son. Wullie Collins disnae know aboot this wan. A never meant tae hurt Wullie Collins.'

What's she talking about? Anne chirps in – 'Hi Betty Yes, it's Anne . . . Anne Goring . . . Oh fine. How are you feeling?' she asks cheerily.

What's happening? She's all over the place. This isn't just confusion, something is . . . something's not right. I recoil from her. Jesus, I can't face this. She's singing at the top of her voice, wailing and arms flailing – 'Anne let's go. Let's get the fuck away!' I snap at her – 'C'mon!'

That image of my mother is horrifying. I don't want to see her like this. I can't get it out of my mind. I lie back later, unable to shake it off. What is it? What's doing this to her? She was listening to me. I'd been telling her what had happened but it was that look in her eyes. Staring right through me. I'd felt shock when it dawned on me that she hadn't been listening, but trying to figure out where she was, and then crying out for her own mother – 'Oh Mammy Mammy!'

I try to distance myself, try to pretend to myself. She's fine! She's all right, there's no need to worry! Alec'll manage. Jim's there too. They don't need me. They'll manage without me. They'll know what to do – 'Oh Mammy Mammy!'

The terror in her voice, like a lost child.

Caroline was out when I got back. I had immediately rolled a joint to escape – escape from her face, her eyes, her voice.

God. Please, please take this away. Don't let this be happening. There are things to do, to say. Don't do this. Don't terrorise her. She doesn't deserve this.

Why not? The question explodes in my head. *Why fucking not?* NO! NO! NO! I don't want to hear this! I love my family! *Is that so? Why do you say you hate them then?* I don't hate them! I've never said that! *Yes you fucking did. You aren't going to any of their funerals are you?* I didn't fucking say that! *Oh I think you did.*

Am I going mad? *Shusshhh, there, there, there. Shusshhh, baby, don't you cry.*

I feel the pull of my own central gravity force, pulling me down from the visceral level of pain, downwards into the sublime, the non experience, mere space. My brain, heart and nervous system are in reprieve, free for the moment, free from pain, fear, whatever.

– '*Oh Mammy Mammy!*'

The disintegrated piece breaks from the main bulk of thought, free-floating downwards behind the lids covering the eyes, bringing with it all the association with pain, all the links with fear – it's unable, however, to touch down.

– '*Oh Mammy Mammy!*'

This piece, the voice. Is it my own? Is fear mimicking my mother's voice? The terror feels far off, in the distance – '*Nae time fur anger.*'

Did she call me son? I felt her fingertips say son, yes . . . *son.*

Son? Aw come onn! Betty? They abandoned you for fucksake. Get with it will you? This is the fucking nineties! Number one and all that! Numero Uno – get it? Oh, it's all getting too much for you then? Aw, the shame. Boo hoo, fuckin hoo! C'mon man let's have fun! They've had their lives. Fucked them up too. That's their doing. Think they'd be bothered if it was the other way round? We all have to go at some point. Oh get real Mr Collins . . . Whatever it is you call youself these days. All this previous lives shit. All this fucking metamorphosis. Let's have fucking fun! All this prodigal son . . . What a routine by the way. Oscar material. I like the spirituality stuff, the inner self or selves in your case, sorry, cases. The lost innocence, the poor childhood. Brilliantly done, beautifully expressed – Oh Mammy Mammy. Give me my Mammy! The Tai Chi, the yoga, super stuff, excellent – OMMM! OMMM! OMMM! OMMM!

The hard floor meets creaking bones on the way up. Jesus, I've fallen asleep. Numb, stiff, I flood back to life. What's that? The door buzzer. BZZZ! BZZZ! BZZZ! BZZZ! Caroline's downstairs – 'Hugh! Heavy bags! Heavy bags!' She's half way up – 'Your fags are at the top. Take this one, it's the heaviest. Any phone calls? Wooof! God!' I throw water on my face to waken myself out of the haze – 'Sorry. Musta fell asleep. She's much the same' I explain – 'Aye, still confused. Lorraine phoned. Thur's that openin the night at the National. Al go back through tae see ma Ma again the night. Naw a canny be bothered wi openins jist noo, but you go wi Lorraine. There'll be the usual crowd, and plentya nibbles. Anyway. Al have a quick bath, an en get movin fur Glesga.'

Chapter Twenty-Two

JIM'S STANDING OUTSIDE the ward when I get there – 'Aye, she's fine. A bit tired. Alec? Naw, he's wurkin late. Zoe and Laura are here. Eh? We-ell it depends on how strong yer Maw is Hughie. The sister said they might operate, but they'll wait a few days tae see how she is then.'

I can hear my Ma's voice, barking – 'Pardon?'

I sit by the bed, saying nothing really, agreeing with anything she's saying – 'Hughie Collins? Who's that? Listen, don't let thum furget, ye canny let thum furget.'

I feel her drawing circles on the back of my hand – 'Aye Ma okay. Al tell the nurses noa tae furget. You jist relax. Jim's here. Aye, he's here. Here ey is. Al see ye later pal.'

Jim's holding her hand, leaning over her, but, I can hear from the door – 'Jim? Jim? A need tae know sumthin, wull ye tell me the truth?' she's asking.

Zoe and Laura walk with me to the elevator – 'We'll catch yer Da ootside' I say.

Linda's waiting outside as we step into the rain – 'She all right? I looked in yesterday. How are you feeling?' she asks.

– 'Ach, fine Linda. She seems better, but wit's causin aw the confusion?'

Jim comes out as she's explaining – 'She'll need things around her that are familiar . . . A lot depends on the physiotherapy. Taking her to a cottage wouldn't really help with her needs. She needs family and friends around to help her recover.'

I agree – 'Ma Aunty Mary's comin up so that might help.'

Jim flinches at the mention of my Aunty Mary – 'Hughie, by the way. A tend tae agree wi Alec. Yer maw wisnae pleased wi Mary. Ye know they'd aw fell oot. Oh, Alec kin be arrogant but that's just him' he smiles.

Linda senses some unpleasant exchanges are about to occur – 'I'll get the car. Hugh I can drop you off at the bus station. Bye Jim.'

Jim's jaw drops – 'Jim, listen. Mary's visitin an that's final. Maybe if you hudnae tried tae fuck ur daughter ye mighta felt differently aboot aw this. Wit? Listen Jim. A don't gie a fuck. Ma Maw's health is ma only concern here. Wit you dae in yer spare time is your business. A don't care who ye shag, an as fur Alec? That's jist him? Naw Jim. That's noa good enough. Wit if ad taken that attitude? Slashin people an jist sayin – Aw that's jist me? Time he learned tae respect other people an live es ain life. Time ey stopped performin fur other people. A know es findin it hard. That disnae gie um the right tae abuse people' I say – 'You try an talk tae um. He makes me fuckin sick tae be honest. A think ey furgets am es fuckin bruthur. A hud tae explain tae a nurse that thur wur two sons. *Am* the next a kin. Noa you ur him – *me*!'

Jim hasn't smiled like that in a long time – 'Fair enough. Al try tae huv a wurd wi um, but you know he's noa the easiest a people Hughie. A know wit ye mean, but al try an talk tae um later' he concedes.

I sleep for the best part of the journey home. I feel better the air has been cleared but I hope he listens to Jim. How he hasn't been slashed already is beyond me. The chip on the shoulder will get him into trouble one day. He could end up with no family the way he's carrying on. I don't want to see that happening. He's been with his mother for too long. He'll have to grow up – fast.

I take the next couple of days off. There's nothing to do,

but wait. I'm sick of having to prove my undying love for my mother to other people. The telephone links me into the event of an emergency. Jim didn't look too happy that last time, but that smile. I have never been able to put my finger on it – there has always been something about the smile, about the ease of those flashing teeth, or is it the unsmiling eyes?

He has been too slick, never putting a foot wrong. Angie's dirt had been handy. I had thought for a moment he was going to deny it, but – that smile said it all.

Alec might not respond to him talking about his attitude. Jim had called him a waste of space on one occasion. Alec had taken it to heart. When he'd told me I'd laughed thinking – What does he say about me? Alec has never had any sense of humour. All that had been suffocated by books, the performances. Those bastards. Maybe I ought to call him myself? Telephone calls are impersonal, but maybe that's what's needed right now. I dial his number.

– 'Hullo, Alec? Aye it's me. Don't hang up. Listen, am sorry a blanked ye' I say – 'A wis oot ey order. Am no copin wi this either. Wit? A know aw that, but ye'll huv tae jist think aboot yer Ma. Mary's yer Ma's sister, an you know yursel if it wis the urra way aboot she'd be at hur bedside. Alec, a know that. You've been brought up wi yer Ma. A know this must be difficult fur ye' I continue – 'But ye canny go tae people's doors shoutin. Alec let's be honest here. Your noa exactly known fur yer diplomacy ur ye? A know. Am jist sayin thur's nae need tae display yer emotions fur people. Ma Aunty Mary hus ur fuck up's tae, wur noa perfect. She has feelins tae so. People react tae this kinda thing differently. Thull dae things they don't normally dae. Eh? Aye Alec, this is painful fur everybody, noa jist Alec and Shooey! Jim's hidin es feelins, but es jist as devastated. Wit? Alec, c'mon noo. Jim an yer Ma huv been thegither fur a long time. Back in the hoose? So what?' I ask – 'Ey kin shag . . . Alec! Listen! Yer Ma needs Jim! A don't care if es got anurra burd. So fucking what? She needs him right now an it's mer important that he's there. Yer an awful boy Alec. Al talk tae um tae make sure she's noa left oan ur ain in the hoose. That's right, we'll huv tae wurk the githir. That's right. We need tae communicate wi each urra, an en wull noa fur certain that she's okay.'

I take a deep breath – 'Listen, am really sorry aboot the urra night. Ach, am fuckin hopeless wi these kinna things. Alec, yer ma wee bruthur fur fucksake. It's difficult tae say things ye feel, dae ye know wit a mean?' I ask.

Alec asks if Jimmy Boyle has been to visit Betty.

– 'Who-o? Sarah phoned. Caroline spoke tae ur. They were off tae Australia. Him? Don't think so. He disnae speak tae me. Mr Wonderful eh. Anyway, listen, am glad wi hud a talk. A think this'll be a long haul. She might no recover so prepare fur the worst. Naw, a know that, but be prepared because ye never know. Anyway al see ye later okay.'

God. He believes she's going to just wake up – like Sleeping Beauty. I did too, but, I think – this is real life. I express as such to Caroline – 'Caroline, think al fire through the morra, spend sum time on ma ain wi ur.'

She asks about the call to Alec – 'Alec? He's fine. Naw, there wisnae any growlin. A think ey needed tae be taken aff the emotional hook. Wit a shame. Ey keeps sayin things. Things that indicate he disnae realise the full extent ey er condition. Dae ye remember ey said she would go mad? Aye, he said something – 'Ma Maw'll crack up if she wakens up an aw that mob are sittin roon the bed.' Ey thinks she'll *wake up* an be back tae urself.' I explain – 'Dae ye see wit a mean? Caroline, ye don't *wake up*. Brain damage is permanent. Ye don't wake up. Well, that's wit it seems like. Brain damage. When Anna took me through the urra day. A knew then. That body in the bed's wit's left a Betty Norrie.'

I hate getting up early in the morning, but this is different. I want to have a day on my own with my Ma, just sit with her for a few hours. Caroline's still asleep as I leave for the early coach to Glasgow. The Barlinnie-scape flashes past, but I don't bother to look this time. Glasgow. I hate the fucking place, with all its sentimental shit about itself.

A Belang tae Glasgow! Dear Auld Glesga Toon!

Fur Wit's The Matter Wi Glasgow!

It's Goin Roon an Roon!

Who wrote this fucking nonsense? They should have fucking strangled him at birth. The sister on the ward looks surprised – 'Morning. Oh, much the same. They're going to put in another shunt. It's much the same as the fluid drain, only it will be inside to help, and it will be permanent. We'll have to wait and see if she's strong enough.' I hear someone singing, someone in her room – a familiar voice – 'Who's that?' I ask. The nurse explains that he's been here all morning – 'A quiet, elderly gentleman, has a bad limp? Yes, he does have lots of scars on his face. Oh, your father? Well, he is here every morning.'

I almost go in, but decide to leave them alone, together. I hear him faintly singing to her as I pass the room. I see her tracing the back of his hand, her finger going round and round, smiling.

Funny how . . . . . . can change!
. . . . so inseparable!

Think this is the bit I came in at . . . The bit in *their* previous lives, the bit from flashback pasts, from *their* old memories. They're there now. In that place. Where I was *not*. A place where *I* was not yet in existence.

– '*My was a sta befow my was bown.*'

Five operations later I find my mother back home, frail, but rational – 'Och am fine. A canny remember much but . . . Naw, honest, a jist came ootey it wan mornin. Av tae get physiotherapy. Naw son, honest am fine.'

She is back but this is a different woman, determined to rediscover her old self, which is, I feel, gone forever. I keep expecting her to flip back into the confusion but no – 'Oh al be back tae normal. A jist feel there's somethin missin. Am fine, back daen aw the crosswords. How's Caroline?' I see the painting by Caroline above the fireplace – 'A think she's workin, but wants tae come o'er tae see ye as soon as.' I notice one of my pastels of a baby fresh out of the womb on another wall – 'Och Ma . . .' I hold her for a moment – 'Wull try tae get through mer often, it's the money, wur still skint.'

– 'Don't worry son. You better get yersel hame before ye miss that last bus.'

You know that feeling, when you think nothing else can go wrong? Well, that is all it is – a feeling. You can never turn that corner and say – 'That's it – Made it!'

Nature is cruel – relentlessly crushing down upon us, as we cling together, clinging to the idea of God, of an afterlife, but we are nothing but another species, living – dying – never knowing when our next cliché is about to be smashed into oblivion – destroyed by the darkness of disillusionment.

Alec's telephone call brings home that grim reaper lurking, waiting to catch you at the next bend – 'Hughie. Alec here. Yer Da's had a massive heart attack . . . Jackie Collins found him in the hoose. Disnae look too good brother' he eases over calmly. Not my father too. Is this some cosmic conspiracy? Let's do that Collins Mob? Is it? No, the truth is plain and simple – it's a fucking massive heart attack. God? Don't be so fucking stupid. That life has caught up with them. That battering has finally taken its toll on them. That Glasgow 'Hard but Friendly' lifestyle.

Glasgow how I fucking *hate* you.

Alec drives us to the hospital, but waits outside in the car. My Ma hangs onto my arm barely able to walk – 'Naw, he wis askin aboot ye son. Read oot aw yer wee poems . . . The wans fae the Special Unit. Eh? Aye, ey kept thum. Al tell him yer ootside waitin.' I don't want to trigger off any anger in case it kills him – 'Hughie. Yer Da wants tae see ye son. C'mon in. Wullie, here's Hughie.'

– 'Ye awright son?' he smiles.

I sit beside him on the bed – 'Fix yer hair Da.' I brush back his whitish hair, touch him for the first time in what seems a lifetime. The lump in my throat prevents me saying a great deal. What is there to say? He forces himself into a sitting position, determined to show he's not yet finished – 'Nurse! Nurse!' he shouts 'Watch wit ye say in front . . . Nurse! Thuv planked ma troosers so a canny sign masel oot. NUUUUUUUUUURSE!'

– 'Yes William?' A huge, stoutly built matron asks.

William? He's grinning away. She's like an old warder, and he's enjoying it. He is on familiar territory now – an institution.

– 'This is ma wife Betty, and this is ma boy Hughie!' he announces proudly.

The poor old cunt. Is this all he ever wanted to say? Now I begin to understand it all more.

Oh, here we go again. My poor family is it? Charmont? What did he do to you? This the angry young man part now? Oh sorry, we're what? Forty seven now eh. Ohh The angry old-ish man bit. The conscience and all that. Don't tell me. A Little House on the Prairie? This the next stage? Collie, oops, sorry. Shug, seriously.

Okay, Hugh . . . God! Oh I forgot, you don't believe in God do you? Why don't you just blow out your fucking brains? Nevermind all the bollocks. Let's see some real rage, some of all the old hatred C'mon, let's see you performing again. C'mon how hard are you? Honest you really deserve an Oscar.

FUCK YOU.

Ohhh. Sorrrryyyy. Touch a nerve there? Big depression now is it? Oh well, let's see now. Yeah, the bit of depression. No tablets this time? Oh this will be fun. Oh and by the way – FUCK YOU TOO.

Our financial situation makes it almost impossible to go over as often, but the phone provides a link. Barry had been there throughout my mother's illness, but I can't lean on him forever. He has his own life to live, so the telephone becomes my means of more regular contact with my family, a contact which is more often filled with crises than anything else.

I call my mother to find out what's been happening with my father, find out what his condition is – 'That you Ma? Hughie. How's things wi ma Da? Is he any better? Eh? Back in the hospital? Yer kiddin. A thoat ey wis stayin wi Billy Beattie?'

I'd last heard that he'd been released from hospital, but he's apparently fallen over in his house, and been taken back into hospital, having cut his head – 'Where is he?' I ask – 'Stobhill again? Dis ey fancy that auld nurse ur wit? Threw away the Zimmer? Aw fur fucksake Ma. Seven stitches? Where'd ey faw? In the hoose? Yer jokin. Ey chased the home help? Jesus Christ. WIT? Ey punched another patient? Wit fur?' I ask.

My Ma's laughing – 'Oh Hughie, ye know wit es like. Ey thinks thur aw screws an the patients ur aw cons. Some auld guy wis in yer Da's bed an said tae um – "C'mon in wi me darlin." Oh a don't need tae tell ye, yer Da walloped um oan the jaw!' Jesus Christ. He just won't lie down – 'A locked ward? Wit fur? Doped up? Ma it wis a fuckin heart attack! Thur's nuthin wrang wi ma Da's fuckin heid! Fuck this. Am noa wearin this. Al be o'er the morra. Ward wit? Forty five.'

My Ma panics – 'Hughie! Don't go, it's depressin. The Cuckoos' Nest. Naw honestly. You're yer da's next a kin. Get oan tae the authorities. A know ye want tae take um hame, but the best thing tae dae is get social wurkers oan tae it. Yer Da needs your help this time, noa yer emotions, use yer brains' she pleads.

I can't sleep all night. Images keep flitting through my brain. I'll take him in a load of pills, get it over with. That's what I'll do; he'd have done that for me. Take pills in . . . *Use yer brains son.*

I take that hour long twisting journey to find him slumped in a wheelchair, dribbling, filthy, and doped out of his mind. The hard-punching hand grips mine, his son – 'Get ma wife an ma boay' he mumbles.

I sit looking at him – an old man. I don't see any of the black cashmere coats or those scarred faces by the bed – only other old men, wandering around in a stupefied daze – it could be the jakey hall, the bottom flat of B Hall in Barlinnie.

That same smell of piss, and stale piss-soaked mattresses.

What has he proved? That he was loyal? That he never grassed? That he had certain principles? That he was a man of honour?

I look at him – battered by life, to prove something to his pals?

What pals? Where are they? The hard men? Are they too afraid of what they might see? What might be lying ahead for them – a locked ward? Does he deserve this? Death; the invisible dimension. We are terrified of its message. We see it, we feel it, but we don't know death. We theorise, pretend, devise beliefs, develop blind faiths in countless religious cults, we even pay homage in our churches, praying to the idea of what it might be, but it is only an idea, someone else's thoughts, someone else's fear of death.

We have invented time to measure the length of life, but life is immeasurable – death is the unknown, what we don't know, and when she delivers that final message to our doorstep, those primitive fears erupt amid the deep loss no matter how much chanting we do, but I guess we need that, we need to sing and beat our hearts, maybe the loss is what makes us human.

Caroline's tearful eyes brought the message that he was gone – 'Hugh, it's your Dad' she said quietly – 'Your Mum's on the phone.'

She'd liked him – 'He's a nice man, but he's been battered' she'd said after meeting him – 'I don't mean his face. You can see it in his eyes, the effects of that brutal lifestyle in Glasgow.'

I remembered the things you remember when someone dies; the things he did for me in life, he'd never laid a hand on me, never an angry word, so why had so much gone wrong? I don't think I cared anymore – 'Aye Caroline. Ma Da wis bran new.'

Chapter Twenty-Three

– '*HOW DO YOU feel?*' someone asks.

I'm standing outside the room where they have lain his body; the nurse holding open the door senses my hesitancy – 'A feel okay, s'awright nurse.'

Jack and Charlie Collins have been in to see him – 'Ye awright Hughie?' asks Charlie

– 'Ye want us tae go in wi ye?' asks Jack.

Jack had been with him right to the end – 'Yer Da wis a brave man Hughie. You think ey aw the things that happened tae um. Yer Da never complained. Ad phone um, an say how ye daen Wullie? 'All right, am all right' ey wid laugh. But when ye think aboot it Hughie. Aw they doins fae the polis, the big jail sentences, an huvin tae go through life wi es bad leg. Naw, Wullie never complained aboot anythin.'

I'd later stabbed the guy who had paralysed my Da way back when I was a boy but the revenge was meaningless; there he is now, lying there dead, my father – 'Auld Bullet's deid.'

I put my hand across his forehead; they say touch the dead and you won't have those haunting dreams – 'Da am sorry' is all I could say – 'Am sorry.'

I fix his hair before leaving – 'See ye later auld yin.'

Jack and Charlie take me round to his house; I hate dead houses, they feel burgled by the living – 'Jack, gie whoever's been merried aw the furniture. A jist want some odds an ends tae keep an any photies.'

Collie Beattie and my Da smile back from a celluloid strip;

I'd had this photograph on my cell wall for years – 'S'Big Collie sayin Jack?' I ask – 'Takin it bad?'

Jack looks at me – 'Aye Hughie. Wullie wis es best pal. Es no cummin tae the funeral by the way, says es gaun up the Highlands.'

Charlie looks at the photograph – 'Aye. The big yin eh, that wis taken a long time ago eh, yer Da n Big Collie. Wullie musta jist finished es ten year when that wis taken. In fact that's ma fuckin coat es wearin!' he laughs – 'That bastard eh, a wundered where that coat went tae.'

We're all laughing when he remembers the storm the night my father died – 'Oh here. Did ye hear that fuckin storm the urra night? Jesus! A wis lyin in ma bed gaun like at tae masel. The same thing happened in 1968. Mind, when ma Maw died, remember? Be Auld Cathy waitin fur yer Da' he laughed, but it was true. A huge storm had torn the roofs off buildings when my granny died, and the same thing had happened again the other night – 'A know, a wis lyin in bed shitin masel as well' I laughed – 'Aye, eh. Auld Cathy waitin fur ma Da.'

Jack and Charlie, I hadn't seen them since being transferred from the Special Unit in 1985. The traditional system limited the number of visits you can have and as a result we had lost contact until now, and yet somehow it seemed like only yesterday we had sat in my cell wondering what had happened, some relationships never die – 'N'wit's Alberto daen es days?' I asked – 'Stull trainin Jack?'

Jack smiled – 'Albert Faulds? Aye Hughie, es bran new, es always askin fur ye, askin how yer gettin on. Witsat? Albert? Naw Hughie, Albert's changed. Aw, don't get me wrang, es stull a handful, but es a different guy noo. Charlie'll tell ye. Charlie. Wit's Albert like?'

Charlie picks up his jacket – 'Wi gaun? Albert Faulds? Says es gonny fuckin kill you Hughie!' he laughs – 'Nah. Albert's like yersel Hughie. Ye's wur jist young boys that went aff the rails, cooda happened tae anybody. S'jist wanney these things that ye's fell oot but es never said a thing against you.'

Jack locks the door behind us – 'In fact. Al tell ye this. Albert Faulds said tae me. We wur at the boxin an ey said that it wis aw his fault. A didny know wit ey meant at furst an then ey said "Naw your Shooey. Wis me that got um intae aw that trouble. Hughie wisnae cut oot fur aw that, jist wantit tae play fitbaw an av got um oot screwin shops." That's gen up by the way, blames es self, but naw es a different guy.'

Albert, the last time I'd seen him he was chasing me with a butcher's cleaver; change? Had Albert changed? I still had apprehensions about bumping into him, and yet I had made no other friends like him, and missed that bond that had existed between us, it was like we were brothers – 'Honest Hughie. Ye coodny meet a nicer guy, canny dae enuff fur people, but at the same time, nae cunt'll mess aboot wi um, stull super fit, an playin fitbaw every Saturday n Sunday.'

Charlie agrees – 'Aye, Albert? Fit as fuck. Boxin three times a week. Takes us tae the boxin aw the time dint ey Jack?'

Jack's nodding – 'Aye, Hughie, listen, if your stull gonny catch that train, ye better get movin, next wan's in an hoor. Witsat? Aye, nae bother. Look, jist leave aw that. Me an Charlie'll sort aw that oot an see ye at the chapel. Aye, St Teresa's. Dae ye know where it is? Possil? Oh wis she? A didny know yer Granny Norrie wis deid. Fuck, it jist shows ye eh. Right, anyway, you head off an wull see ye at the funeral. Shug an aw the family'll be there. Shood get a good turn oot. Right okay. Tell Caroline a wis askin fur ur. Right Hughie see ye.'

Charlie waves – 'Right Collie! See ye!' he laughs. Collie, I hadn't been called that in years – 'Big Collie fae the Shamrock eh?' he's roaring as I jump the bus – 'Right! Aye Jack! See ye at the funeral! Right Charlie! Cheerio!' I call back – 'Cheerio!'

Caroline and my Ma are on either side of me as we make our way to the chapel a few days later – 'Hughie, there's Jackie Collins. You go o'er wi thaem n we'll see ye efter the service. Right Caroline, ye right then? Jesus, wit a turn oot' she laughs – 'Wullie Collins' pals, look at thum, a rogues' gallery eh' she chuckles – 'Ey'da been pleased. Aw es pals roon um.'

Kenny Kelly, Big Bobby Dempster; they're all there, all his pals, young and old – 'Aye Ma ey widda been pleased awright' I say, leaving the two of them to make their way into the front of the chapel – 'Ye awright Caroline? Some crowd eh? Right, al see ye efter the service.'

Caroline takes my mother's arm – 'Yes, yes, off you go.'

– '*How're ye doin?*' a familiar voice drawls.

Albert's looking at me as I turn around; that charming broad smile, the dark brownish eyes, impishly watching me – 'Albert. Fucksake man' I smile, taking his hand – 'Am bran new, listen. Albert, listen, am sorry aboot . . .'

That frown is so familiar to me, even now; thirty years almost, vanishes as that gravel voice expresses puzzlement concerning my apology, but I persevere, I've waited such a long time – 'Naw Albert, listen. It wis me that caused aw that kerry oan, it wis me, a caused aw that trouble. N'Mooney as well, it wis me that got um killed.'

He punches me on the shoulder – 'Och Shooey, furget aboot aw that, s'aw in the past. Al get a talk wi ye later, but listen. Tell aw yer family tae head up tae the Hibs Hall up the Garngad. Tina's laid everythin on, sandwiches an that so tell thum tae go straight up there when the service's finished. Al catch ye up there, ye better get in, there's yer brothers o'er there' he grins – 'Auld Shooey boy eh, s'good tae see ye, right al see ye later.'

A 'See you later' that bore no threat; he'd taken me off the hook when he could easily have turned my whole life into another nightmare. I felt more than relief, I felt nothing had changed between us, nothing really, only time, admittedly a passage littered with torn faces and a body, but I could do nothing about that. You can take responsibility but nothing can bring back the dead; the plasticity of human beings, living and dying, like little Plasticine forms, takes us all in that direction, and, if not now, then at least, one day – 'Okay Albert. S'good tae see ye.'

The priest looks across the coffin at the congregation – 'Well, Willie Collins. Our dear departed friend. What can we say about him?' he smiles – 'Cood tell ye quite a few things' whispers Charlie – 'Wit aboot ma coat?' he giggles – 'Aherm, aherm.'

Jack, Charlie, Shug, Alex, Margaret, and Cathy; the family lined the front pew. Jessie, the oldest sister, alone was missing – dead too. Behind us, their children, and in some cases, their children. I was no longer the wean in the family, and yet, this could have been a gathering at our old home, Tharsis Street. I looked across at the coffin; there he is, surrounded by family and friends, and yet in life he lived by the iron rules of the criminal world, a life that had isolated him from many of that same family, many who today wept tears, and others who used humour to hide them. I wondered if he knew just how much they had cared about him?

I look over my shoulder; the chapel is packed full with scarred faces and the battered souls of his world – 'And now, please stand' asks the priest as the service is brought to an end – 'Amen' murmur the congegration – 'Jesus, ma knees.' whispers Charlie – 'Trust Wullie eh' he smiles, wiping his eyes – 'Shame eh son.'

An Irish Republican song plays as we walk down the aisle – 'Yer Da luved that song' whispers Jack – 'Said ey wanted it played at es funeral.' I shuffle along with the rest of the pall bearers, my father's brothers; the coffin's hard edge biting into my shoulder helps hide the tears, but I'm relieved to be in the car and moving away from the huge crowd outside – 'Hughie. There's the Big Yin' says Charlie – 'Knew ed come.'

Collie Beattie is standing across the road from the chapel; the last time I saw him was at his house, the police had been waiting to arrest me for murder. Collie's flanked by Kenny Kelly and Peter Jordan – 'Aye so it is' I reply – 'That's good, am glad. Ma Da's hud a good turnoot.'

The Hibs Hall; Albert and I had never set foot in this place as boys, in fact none of our generation had and for that very reason, being boys, teenagers – 'Been tae mass son? Naw? Canny get in then, too young anyway, cheerio.'

Back in those days things had been different; men came and went as they pleased, did whatever they felt like doing; drinking, gambling the wages week after week, it made no difference so long as you were at mass on Sunday – 'Bless me father . . .'

The Irish side of our family has come to see him off; they're mostly uncles, fond of my father; I look along the length of the table's faces; their stories, memories of the more colourful events in my old man's life – 'S'a nawful man wint ey . . .'

The conversations begin and end up with them all roaring and laughing – 'D'ye mind the time . . .' Charlie's remembering now – 'Aye Wullie. D'ye mind the time wi aw the taxis oot in the street? Wullie's drunk, mind? S'noa payin the guy? Ma Maw's oot in the street! Aye, knocked the guy oot! Wallop! Poor taxi driver's lyin in the middle ey the street!'

Big Teresa and Billy Beattie; Janis, their daughter, had visited me, they'd been good to me as a boy, good to my old man too. Young William, a man now. There's so much of the past here – 'Teresa, how ye doin hen?' I ask – 'Ye'v noa changed.'

Big Teresa looks up at me with eyes weary – 'Oh Hughie Collins. Look at you, like yer Da staunin there. So ye ur, yer the doubla Wullie Collins. Shame eh. A liked yer Da. Ey wis straight' she smiles – 'Wullie Collins, gie ye es last so ey wid. Janis luved um so she did, always fightin, but yer Da really liked Janis. Oh, ey wis a pure pest when ey wis drunk, but a luved yer Da singin. Oh Wullie cood chant so ey cood, a great singer so ey wis. But him an that Wee Bennett? Bad wee bastard that so ey wis, but yer Da? Naw, a liked Wullie Collins.'

Colin Beattie, Collie's son, looks up; his father's double, he takes my hand – 'Hughie. I had hoped we could have met under more fortunate circumstances, but. Poor Wullie, it's an unfortunate life. Pardon? Oh, your mother? She's here? Well, hullo, Betty.'

Betty too is overwhelmed by faces, the past, people paying their last respects; they had been a handsome couple in their day – 'Hiya Colin. Oh, your yer faithur's double. Aye yer Da wis a big handsome man tae' she chuckles – 'The walkin wounded ur aw oot the day eh. Even the jakeys hud thur faces washed alang at Saracen Cross. Aye, wit a shame, aw staunin there as the coffin passed. Oh Wullie Collins wis well liked so ey wis.'

Caroline and Albert are sitting at a table – 'Shooey huv you met Tina?' he asks – 'Tina this is Shooey.' Tina's blonde fringe hides lovely brown eyes – 'Hi Hughie' she says quietly. Manchester; I recognise her accent immediately – 'Hullo Tina.'

We remain behind as people leave; there are a million things to go over but we have all the time in the world to dissect the past – 'How did ye find things when ey first got oot Caroline?'

Caroline smiles, rolling her eyes – 'Well, it was very difficult. What about you? Hugh said you served twelve years? Hugh's had a lot of problems. I think coming to terms with the past . . .'

Albert's philosophical about life – 'Aye, takes time efter a long sentence. Ye'v jist got tae accept the past Shooey' he says, turning to me – 'Wuv aw done things we regret, but ye'v got tae progress. Ye canny talk about a future tae ye'v dealt wi that. We wur jist daft boys runnin aboot the toon.'

I look across the table at him quietly sipping a juice; still doesn't drink or take drugs, never has done, a big blowout is a half pint of Guinness – 'Ye stull noa drink?' I ask. He grins – 'Nah, never bothered wi it. S'the first time av seen you drinkin. Wit aboot drugs? Heard ye wur takin heroin, s'at right Shooey?' he asks – 'See a lot ey young yins oan that stuff. Av been lucky, never bothered wi stuff like that. Oh oh, here she comes, Tina.'

I turn to find a beautiful teenage girl walking towards us – 'Who's that?' I ask – 'Jade, ma daughter Shooey' he replies – 'Daen ur nosey' he laughs – 'Jade, S'Caroline an Shooey.'

Caroline and I shake her hand – 'Jesus, yer daughter?'

Jade smiles; she's his double, but her mother's the stronger gene – 'Hiya, am pleased tae meet ye' she giggles – 'Da, al get the dug but al need money tae get hame.'

Albert laughs – 'See wit a mean Shooey? Night clubs an aw that, got ma heid nippin. Right then, al see ye later' he says, bunging her a few quid – 'You nae weans?'

Caroline laughs – 'One's enough don't you think?' she asks.

Tina's twinking eyes smile knowingly – 'Yeah Caroline, I do' she replies – 'We were the same when he first got out, it was very difficult, wasn't it Albert?'

Albert agrees – 'Aye. At furst a jist ran marathons an trained aw the time, but it scared people. A didny know, but gradually people saw that a wisny interestit. A mean don't get me wrang, people don't let ye furget, specially us two Shooey. Oh wait tae ye see yersel, some cunt always says sumthin 'Aye a mind ey you two.' But that's it, people always remember the bad things, but maist ey thum don't bother. Did you find that wi people Caroline? People diggin ye up aboot his past?'

Caroline nods – 'Yeah, well, goes with the territory, but you're always asked what you are attracted to when you marry a murderer' she smiles – 'I mean, I didn't know who he was or anything about his past. Pardon? No, I'd never been in a prison. We were in the gallery one day. Hugh was working there at the time, and I asked who he was. I was horrified when he told me everything.'

Albert's puzzled – 'A murderer? Shooey? Aw right a see noo, Mooney. Ach well, we wur aw involved in gangs, jist daft young boys. Mooney shood never huv been there that night, but a know wit ye mean. Think it wis you that hud committed a crime wint ye? Aye, ye'v got tae get oan wi it, jist let people get tae know ye an be yerself. Tina had tae go through the wars as well eh?'

Tina nods – 'Yeah, it takes time' she replies – 'But people do forget. The Garngad is a good place, good people.'

Albert looks at his watch; the only piece of jewellery, no gold chains, no flash. It's the way he is, quiet, reserved, easy to be with, and not contrived in any way – 'Shooey ye better watch the time.'

Caroline hugs him – 'Well Albert it's been nice meeting you' she says – 'Aye Tina wis nice meetin ye' I say, getting up – 'Right Albert, listen . . .'

He punches me on the shoulder – 'Right Shooey boy, jist geez a phone. Here, stick at in yer pocket' he says, pushing a bundle of banknotes into my pocket – 'Av got a few tickets fur the boxin next week. Jackie's gaun so fire through. Al pick ye up doon the toon an wull go fur a meal doon at Mannies.'

Caroline and I wave as we leave for Edinburgh – 'Right Albert! Next week! Right! Al definately be through! Okay! Cheerio! N'Albert, thanks! Thanks Tina!'

Glasgow looks, feels different somehow as we drive home; I look out the car window, remembering, wondering where the years have gone. Change? Blame? Be great to blame someone. Blame would make it all so much easier. It's funny – no one blames me – 'Caroline, huv a really changed dae ye think?'

Epilogue

FORGETTING THOUGH, THINKING I'm home, I turn to say something to my wife, then realise she's not there. Her absence becomes more obvious by the empty space on the steel bed across from mine. That feeling of being home disintegrates – 'Caroli . . .'

I have to be having a nightmare. Is this a nightmare?

Barry and I had been preparing for one of our walks – 'EH1, Shug. Fancy huvin a wee coffee there first? Then, dae a good long walk? Av parked the car doon at Leith. A know, the tourists are amazin. Reminds me ey the backpackin trip around Europe. A liked the different sounds ey thur voices. Wit a day. Honest Shug, it's brilliant tae get away for the day. That Pollok's heavy man. Thur's nuthin there fur people. Don't be complacent aboot wit ye've goat through here. Edinburgh's different class. Look at it man! People know ye, they like ye . . . Glesga's heavy.'

I do appreciate this city – 'Aye Barry. The flat's made a big difference. The tourists ur great but efter a few weeks? Honest, the traffic's stressful, tryin tae get tae the shops, the daily things, but sure. A know what yer sayin. Am noa dodgin bullets!'

Barry and his girlfriend have looked after the flat a few times, whenever we've had an opportunity to spend a weekend at Caroline's parents' – 'The flat? That last time. Shug honest man. We had a brilliant time. We had a meal somewhere, nice an quiet, then walked back tae the flat. We jist sat at the windae, lookin doon at aw the lights. That wis amazin.

A cuppla pipes an jist sittin there watchin sunsets aw night. Dae ye ever dae that? A wee joint an sit there?' he asks.

Do I? – 'C'mon big yin, it's me, Shug? I spend hauf ma life sittin lookin at sky lines wi a wee joint in ma face. Ye dae get used tae it, but we never get tired a lookin at the different landscapes. Even the winter's amazin tae watch. The colours, an they hills wi snow peaks. When it's crispy clear, wintery. That's when ye really get a view. Av drawn quite a few things lookin across tae the hills. Listen, dae ye fancy campin some time? Glencoe or sum place? Heard thur's a sad atmosphere up there?'

Barry drives out to these places as often as he can with his son – 'Glencoe? Serious? Freeze the baws aff ye! It's a sad place though. A take the wee man up north tae get um away fae Pollok. Campin? You got tents an that? Shug, look, ye need . . .'

I dig him in the ribs – 'Here big yin! Think am too auld? Listen! Av been campin fae a wis a wean. Aye, daen the berry pickin. Naw, naw. We slept in a tent. Honest, al show ye. Seriously Barry. We fantasised aboot daen it in the jail, remember? Well . . . How about it?' I ask – 'Caroline? She'll be gled tae get shot ey me! Naw, she won't mind. Naw Barry, Caroline trusts you. Jesus, dae ye remember when ye first got out? Turnin on the telly, the feet up. Thought ye wur still in a cell. Caroline used tae laugh when it first happened. Aye! A wis the opposite! Terrified tae move if we wur in sum hoose wi people she'd jist introduced me tae' I laugh – 'Honest Barry, a hated visitin ur friends, it wis a nightmare! Tryin tae be polite! Drappin cutlery everywhere! Och Barry man. Honest! Ma nerves were shattered when a came oot. Naw, the sentence wis too long. A knew that ad been fucked, ma heid wasted. Ach these days. Na a like the telly, watchin soaps an that. Honest! The auld *Brookside*? Big Jimmy Corkhill? Brilliant man!'

Barry thinks I'm joking – '*Brookside*? Nae danger! Na,

am jist windin ye up. Nah, me tae. A like comin hame fae work, huvin ma tea, daen a few pipes an watching things like documentaries, history programmes. History is the . . . The wit? *The X Files*?' He's looking at me – 'You at the wind up auld yin? *The X Files*?'

– 'Wit? Dae ye noa believe in aliens?' I ask.

– 'Och Fuck off!' he laughs.

Sarah and Elaine, the manageresses, come over – 'Hi Barry. You two out for your wee walk then? Oh fine. You still working Barry? That's good. Not like our *Mr Collins*!' they laugh.

Elaine's Betty's double – 'Al bring that photie doon fur ye. Ye dae look like ma Maw. Naw, when she wis your age. Honest! Your ur double! Here! We gettin they coffees ur wit? You two jist lookin the part?'

EH1 bar staff are all attractive, but these two lassies are stunners. They all know we're ex lifers. This place has been good to me. I do most of my writing here, have done a better part of the first book here, sitting all day at the tables, easing myself into one of those previous lives, into that earliest violent past: that terrible past, now itself, truly passed, gone, existent only in *Autobiography of a Murderer*. Yes, I have the first of those lives completed. The process of meeting the present may take a little longer.

– 'Two coffees Barry?' asks Elaine.

Barry smiles – 'Aye, thanks doll.'

He's a big charmer – 'Funny. We always seem tae get served quicker when you're in here. Me? Think am a fuckin daftie. Honest! Naw, thur bran new eh. Av knocked it off through here. Glesga?' I laugh – 'Makes me fuckin nervous aw the time. When a go o'er tae see ma Maw. Yer watchin aw the time. Caroline laughs but a never feel at ease.'

Barry asks about Albert – 'Albert Faulds? Naw, es bran new Barry. Does marathons fur weans an aw that. Dis a lot fur people. Albert grew up in real poverty, right up aff the flerboards. Es different class. Ey'd stull chib ey if ey thought ye wur gettin wide but es a crackin guy, alwis wis. Jack? Ma bruthur? Jack's bran new. Ad lost touch wi aw ma family. Honest thur bran new' I smile – 'See when ma granny died? Ad thought nae cunt cared aboot me. Aye, av told ye this before but a hudnae realised how it hud affected them, they wur aw devastated tae. N'see that day when ad got oot ey Borstal? Cunts hud told ma faimly the wrang date so nae cunt knew. Anyway me n Albert ur stull the besta pals. A go o'er tae see um aw the time, stull a keep fit fanatic tae, fit as fuck. But naw, Glesga disnae belang tae me big yin. An a don't belang tae dear auld Glesga Toon!'

Barry's laughing, tussles my hair – 'Auld Rabbie Burns there eh? The Bill Clinton hairdo looks good ye know.'

– 'Wit? Aye, that'll be right! Bill Clinton! Does it look like a wig? The grey . . . Wit? A badger's arse? You're headin fur a doin big yin. Am tellin ye!'

Barry likes having fun with me. That's the beauty of pals from prison. There are lots of decent guys in these places, men who have just made fuck ups. He's the only one I have remained friends with from that whole period. He's never been scared of me, so our relationship isn't sycophantic, or based upon fear. He gives me a hard time when he visits, challenges my views, and reminds me of my good fortune – 'Glesga's okay, in sum ways, but *you're* better aff through here. See Ferris is done again. Ach, who knows. How's Wee Scanlous? Wit's he up tae these days? *How's Paul?*' he mimics. We both laugh – 'Aye, *How's Paul?* Es gettin worse. Och, a like um, but the lies? A don't know where ey gets it aw fae. The stories ey cums away wi . . .' I laugh – 'Knows mer aboot things through there than a dae. Honest Barry! Phones me wi gossip, but it's a wee dig as well – 'Shugs? Tam here. Hear that pal ey yours is dun wi a shootin? Aye, thought ye mighta heard.' Barry, es stone mad. Oh aye, ey gave me fifty tems. Got thum this mornin.'

Barry pulls me about the Temgesics – 'Thought ye were chuckin thum? Och, av heard it aw afore Shug. C'mon. It's me yer talkin tae. A like thum tae, but thur a bam's drug. A know, but fine, make these the last then. Al be glad, tae be honest, because that wee prick up there's usin ye. Shug! Ye ran the whole jail fur fucksake! N'then, a cunt like him talkin oot ey the side ey es face. Chase um, the fuckin wee prick. *How's Paul?* A good fuckin doin he needs. He widnae last two minutes through there wi that mooth ey his. Naw, but dae ye know wit a mean? He'd be bin bagged an dumped up in the Campsie Hills. Anyway, fuck um. Puts ye on a downer talkin aboot um. Here, how's yer Maw?'

Poor Wee Scanlous – 'Och, who knows Barry. That's five operations. A canny face it. Fuckin kills me seein ma Maw like that. Aye, we fought aw the time, but she stood by me right through that lifer. Maws are aw the same, always gettin oan at ye. A took it too personal, the argyaments an fights wi Alec. Naw Barry, they *live* like that. In jails ye never heard an angry word exchanged wi people. Well, ye know wit a mean. Naw they've had a tough time wi me. Ma auld man? Ach well, ma auld Da.' I smile – 'Aw remember the kerry oan wi the speed? Dae ye remember that? When a came back fae the five day home leave? Well, apart fae then, we'd hardly spoken fur aboot fourteen years. A saw him afore ey died, up at the hospital, me an auld Betty. Aye, singing tae ur . . . shame eh. Naw, well av never really been wi the two ey them at the same time. When ey got that ten year, that wis it fucked. It's a liberty, they'd nae rehabilitation in they days. Ten years, an slung oot the door. Ma Maw? Aye, she's no bad.'

Barry finishes his coffee – 'C'mon wull dae a right good wee walk the day.'

– 'Aye. Check that weather oot there eh' I say – 'Brulliant innit.'

Barry's paying the bill – 'Here. D'ye hear aboot Wullie

Bennett? Twelve stretch? Aye he wis dun in Glesga. Smack. He'll huv tae dae the lifer recall tae. Aw fuck that, man. Kin ye imagine? Twelve stretch? How long did ey dae fae the lifer? Twenty? Jesus Christ! Are ye kiddin Shug? Twenty year in wan go? Fuckin hell man!'

– 'Och, The Thug wis a laugh. Thur wis two camps in the Unit, so we wur always at it wi each urra. Hated Boyle. Saw me as his pal fae the beginnin so. Naw Barry, ey hud brilliant patter. That wis the thing ye see. Ye'd be bammin um up, thinkin that ey wis a laugh, but the next thing ye'd be makin the tea, then daen messages. Afore ye know it, yer es tea boy. Read ye like a book Barry. Twenty years a pure jail, lookin at ye, sizin ye up. Aye, a knocked um oot, but it wis ootey fear' I continue – 'Naw, the cunt cood punch ye out wi wan dig but ey coodny fight. He banged me in . . . Aw listen tae me, pilin up the bodies. Here! Get a skip fur the deid bodies! But dae ye know wit a mean? The Thug *likes* the jail. Prison gies um an identity – Wullie the Thug!' I laugh – 'Looked like a sorta Jack Nicholson. Patter wis brilliant, great wi wan liners, irresistible wi bampots, but lethal. Pure poison. Put rumours oot aboot ye tae dae yer heid in. Ach, a don't know, ey *didnae want* tae change. Here, ye payin the bill ur wit? The lassie's waitin oan ye daftie' I say.

Barry's laughing – 'Daftie? Wait tae a get ye ootside ya fuckin auld bampot! Caroline canny pratect ye noo eh? C'mon let's go aul yin. Caroline doon in ur studio? Fancy takin a walk doon that way? Make a wee change eh. She paintin the noo? Bourne's Fine Art? Brilliant Shug! Another exhibition? Am a invited? Aw definately. She's an amazin wumin int she. Ye must admit, she's really looked after you eh.'

Looked after me? That would have to be the understatement of my whole life – 'Aye, Wee McNairn eh. Oh she tobered me right up. She's a real handful ey a wumin. Am lucky Barry. Guys come out wi nae future. Caroline's literally fought me tae get me in shape. She's tolerated everythin, drugs, drink, bampots like that wee arsehole wi the tems. Naw, listen. That's the reason a want aff ey thum. Don't get me wrang. Ey served a purpose, but the thing is that a don't need thum. It's pure habit. She's never got on my back aboot drugs, so maybe noo is the right time. Straight up. Your bang on aboot controlling me. A jist slipped intae an easy oasey thing. Ey is usin me, but a needed somethin Barry. Av used him as well, dae ye know wit a mean?' I ask – 'But McNairn. She's brilliant Barry. A really dae love ur ye know. Ach, we aw eye up the odd bird, but a wid never betray her. Mind in the jail tae, me telling guys never tae get merried an then bang! Right, look, let's go. C'mon, wull end up staunin here aw day yappin as usual. Wull head doon that way for a change, pass the studio, say hullo tae Caroline' I suggest.

– 'Aye, c'mon. Let's go. See ye's later Sarah!' shouts Barry.

Sarah and Elaine smile back – 'See ye's later boys!'

We hit the street – 'Here Shug. When's the book comin oot?' he asks.

I thought he was never going to ask – 'The morra! Published the morra!'

He's looking – 'Ye kiddin? Fuckin brilliant Shug!'

I'm being super, super cool – 'A know!'

The High Street – 'Barry look at that! Check that view. The Thug eh. He'll be headin for the dining hall abo . . . ooooommmmmpppppphhhhhhh!'

Four guys hit me, appearing from nowhere, from another dimension. My arms are up behind my back, being handcuffed. My head's being pulled back by the hair. A voice is screaming in my ear – 'DRUG SQUAD! DRUG SQUAD! DRUG SQUAD!'

Barry is pinned against a wall, arms cuffed behind his back – 'Wit the fuck's this?' he shouts.

The terrible, terrifying fear knots the pit of my stomach. My brain can't take in what is happening – 'DRUG SQUAD! DRUG SQUAD! DRUG SQUAD! DRUG SQUAD!'

No, please, don't let this be happening. Kill me. Do anything. Not this. Please don't do this to me.

I'm being dragged backwards – 'WHERE ARE THE GUNS? WHERE ARE THE GUNS?'

I'm bundled into a car – 'DON'T MOVE! DON'T MOVE! DON'T MOVE!'

Three faces are an inch from mine, staring, glaring, watching every move . . . Caroline. Oh fuck. What have I brought into her life? She's never dealt with anything like this in her life. Tears are burning behind my eyes. I've never felt like this before. I can't clear my brain. The voice screaming back at them is my own, barely recognisable but mine definitely – 'BASTARDS! BASTARDS! BASTARDS! BASTARDS! BASTARDS.'

Caroline. Poor Caroline. Her face fills my head. Caroline, I'm so sorry . . . so sorry . . . so. Something is crushing down on me. Pressing down, inches from my face. A blackish shape in the dark. A black shape that is vaguely familiar. That smell of sweat. Where am I? The silence is deafening, like an old acquaintance, from a previous life, former past – 'Caroli . . .'

A dark head protrudes from the shape above, looking down. The red tip of a cigarette flickers – 'Didje say sumthin there Shugs?' asks a stranger's whispering voice.

– 'Naw, a wis jist dreamin' I reply.

– *How do you feel?*